To my parents, for their unwavering love throughout the years

Table of Contents

List of Tables   vii

Acknowledgements   ix

Introduction

Chapter 1   **Wither Middle East?**   1
                      Manochehr Dorraj

**The dynamics of Domestic Changes: The Domestic
Sources of Foreign policy**

Chapter 2   **The Post -Cold War Middle East and Its**   15
                      Foreign Policy Challenges
                      Manochehr Dorraj

Chapter 3   **The Fate of Human Rights in the Middle**   51
                      East and North Africa
                      Mahmood Monshipouri

Chapter 4   **Ideology and Foreign Policy in the Arab**   85
                      World: Jargon and Legitimacy
                      As'ad Abukhalil

Chapter 5   **Israeli Foreign Policy in the Era of Pax**   107
                      Americana
                      Stephen Zunes

Chapter 6   **Women and the Changing Political Dynamics**   147
                      in the Middle East and North Africa
                      Valentine Moghadam

The Changing Foreign policies of Great
Powers toward the region

Chapter 7   Refighting the Cold War: Containment as   173
             The Foundation of America's Post-Cold War
             Political-Military Posture in the Middle East
             Laura Drake

Chapter 8   Post- Soviet Russian Foreign Policy toward   211
             Middle East
             Mark Katz

Chapter 9   Political Economy of European Union   235
             Middle East Relations
             Anoushiravan Ehteshami

Chapter 10   Patterns of Reorientation in the Foreign   271
             Policies of Japan and China toward the
             Middle East in the Post-Cold War Diplomacy:
             A reflection on the regional determinants
             Touraj Noroozi

Index   297

About the Editor and the Contributors   305

About the Book   307

List of Tables

3.1 International Conventions 54

3.2 A Comparative Survey 56

3.3 Women and Political Participation 58

3.4 Gender Empowerment Measure 59

3.5 GDI Over Time: Ranks and Values, 1970-92 60

3.6 Background Characteristics of the Groups 62

9.1 Main Global Economic Players, mid-1990s 238

9.2 Foreign Direct Investment Flows to Developing Countries by Region, 1995 241

9.3 Inter-Arab Trade Relations, 1994 246

9.4 Euro-Mediterranean Trade, 1992 247

9.5 Military Profile of Main Non-EU Mediterranean Armed Forces, mid-1990s 256

Acknowledgements

I would like to express my gratitude to the contributors for their patience and cooperation. Special thanks is due to my friend and college Nader Entessar who started this project with me but because of his many other obligations and commitments could not finish it. Many of the chapters in this book benefited from his insights and editorial suggestions. I am grateful to Steve Sherwood for his editorial assistance, and to Juliet George and Gergely Takács for their help in the final preparation of the manuscript. I am thankful to vice chancellor Larry Adams for his financial assistance to defray some of the cost of the preparation of the manuscript, I would also like to thank Peter Cooper and Helen Hudson from the University Press of America for their cooperation and professionalism.

Manochehr Dorraj

Chapter 1

Wither Middle East?

Manochehr Dorraj

We shall not succeed in banishing
the curse that besets us, that of
being born too late for a great
political era, unless we understand
how to become the forerunners of
a greater one.

Max Weber

Introduction

The post-Cold War world is increasingly complicated, with delicate nuances and contradictions that defy the conventional wisdom and established paradigms. We have witnessed the unleashing of globalization and regionalism, economic integration and cultural particularism, homogenization and differentiation. The unwinding and unbecoming of the old institutions and structures have gone hand in hand with the birth of new ones that are not yet defined. Our shrinking and interdependent world has given rise to transnational organizations such as the European Union (EU), the North Atlantic Free Trade Association (NAFTA) and the Association of Southeast Asian Nations (ASEAN) that have brought the global economy closer together than any other time in the past, while simultaneously unleashing primordial loyalties and the unprecedented revival of religion, nationalism and ethnic identities and conflicts that are tearing it asunder. To grasp the essence of this explosive and contradictory hybrid requires a new thinking and a new understanding.[1]

These broad forces of change are by and large initiated by great powers' policies, the multinational corporations, and the unintended consequences of the technological revolution. It is also the case that as the Middle East becomes further integrated into the global economy, it becomes more vulnerable to the economy's reverberations. Seen in this light, Middle Eastern powers are primarily reactive players on the periphery of the global system. They neither have the resources, nor the capabilities, to set the agenda; they react to it. Having said this, it is also important to note the other side of this multivalanced reality. In an interdependent world, social transformations in the Middle East also impact the global politics in general and the policies of great powers in particular. Many western nations and Japan import more than fifty percent of their energy needs from the region. It is projected that in the future China and India would become major importers of Middle Eastern oil and gas as well.

Eight salient strategic issues have dominated the Middle Eastern political landscape in the post-Cold War era. First, the continuing challenge of populist Islam has rendered it as the main source of legitimacy and claim to authenticity in political discourse. Second, the demise of the Soviet Union and the independence of Muslim republics of Central Asia, and Russia's turn inward, have altered the regional power structure fundamentally. Third, the Gulf War of 1991 and its aftermath profoundly changed the regional balance of power and its geo-strategic map. Fourth, new political players, namely Japan and China have entered the political and economic life of the region and have ambition to assume a more active role in future. Fifth, The emergence of the European Union and its increasing willingness to chart a new course of foreign policy toward the region, distinct from its former Cold War ally, the United States, has provided many regional powers with more room for political maneuvers and opportunities that were unavailable during the Cold War. Sixth, the long and winding road to the Arab-Israeli peace process has left unresolved tensions surrounding that central imbroglio that for decades served as a catalyst for radicalization of regional politics. Seventh, the petroleum power and the vast oil reserves which, since the first discovery of oil in Masjid Suleyman, in Southern Iran in 1905, has continued to turn the region into a battleground for great powers' rivalries and competition for control and dominance of the black gold. Eighth, the Middle East has not been immune to the global forces of democratization. The region has had its own home-grown version of economic and political liberalization (albeit, manipulated and controlled), most notably in Jordan, Algeria, Egypt, Tunisia, and Iran with important consequences for development of civil society, human rights and non-governmental institutions, most prominently among them women's organizations.

The latest wave of Islamic revival is a part of global revival of religion which engulfed the region since the latter part of the 1960s and reached its zenith with the Iranian revolution of 1979. That event served as a major catalyst to inspire and invigorate Islamists throughout the Muslim World. The political potency of this neologism was dramatically demonstrated when Saddam Hussein, a secular nationalist (Ba'thist) who had fought Iran in a bloody battle for eight years under the guise of protecting the Arab World from the onslaught of Islamic Fundamentalism, wrapped himself in the flag of Islam in order to mobilize the Arab World against the Western coalition forces during the Gulf War of 1991. The Islamists have emerged as the most powerful force not only challenging their own secular regimes but also the US-led hegemonic power structure. Hence, the process of democratization, albeit limited and manipulated, has provided them with additional opportunities for growth and power as evidenced by political developments in Algeria, Turkey, Egypt and Jordan, to mention a few. This wave of Islamic revival was considered by some policy makers and pundits in the US to be the main threat to Western security, replacing the Communist threat in the post-Cold War era.

The disintegration of the former Soviet Union and the independence of Central Asian Muslim republics brought them back to the orbit of Middle Eastern political and economic systems. As evidenced by expanding trade and political ties, developments in the Middle East impact these republics, and their transformation in turn is increasingly important to the Middle Eastern states. The discovery of vast oil reserves in the Caspian Sea and the opening up of central Asian and Caucasus markets to the Middle East have provided them with unprecedented opportunities. Indeed, it may well be the case that the gravity of the regional politics may shift from the south (Persian Gulf area) to the north, as evidenced by increasing competition between Iran, Turkey, Egypt, Saudi Arabia and Israel for political influence in Central Asia and the Caucuses.

Hence, Russia is still very much interested in projecting its power in its southern periphery and playing a major role in the distribution of the Caspian basin energy resources. This may also partially explain why the Russians did not support the policy of dual containment and have tried to engage both Iran and Iraq through trade and diplomatic relations. As the Central Asian republics try to maneuver between their former imperial master to the north (Russia), which still regards Central Asia as the sphere of its influence, and their ancestral roots to the south (Middle East) which are eager to expand their power base in that region, they face a delicate balancing act: to maintain their autonomy and survive the uncharted waters of transition from a socialist command economy to a capitalist system.

The disintegration of the former Soviet Union and Russia's disengagement from Middle Eastern conflicts evidenced by its withdrawal from Afghanistan and the Arab-Israeli conflict also strengthened the political influence of the United States and the European Union. Abandoned by their former allies, many former Soviet client states such as Syria and the PLO now had to accommodate the West. Moreover, many regional powers no longer had the option of pitting one Superpower against another in order to enhance their bargaining position as they had done during the Cold War. Hence, Russia's turn inward created a power vacuum that allowed some of the Middle Eastern leaders with hegemonic ambitions to step in and fill the political vacuum. Saddam Hussein's invasion of Kuwait can be partially understood in this light.

The Persian Gulf War of 1991 profoundly changed political configurations in the region as well. First, the Gulf war in which one Arab nation had invaded another, for all practical purposes declared the end of Pan-Arabism as a salient political force. This reality was dramatically demonstrated when Saudi Arabia, Kuwait and other Arab monarchies of the Gulf rejected the offers of Egypt and Syria for military protection and instead opted for US and West European military alliances. Dictated by the exigencies of state survival, the Gulf War also broke the taboo of embracing the United States, although it did not diminish its political costs. After all, it was the US-led coalition forces who had liberated Kuwait from Iraqi invaders and protected Saudi Arabia against possible invasion from Saddam's forces. The war not only enhanced the power of the United States in the region and within OPEC, but it also brought some of the traditional conservative American allies (the Gulf monarchies) closer to the United States.

Thus, the American military presence was legitimized in the region and the United States and the European Union now enjoyed preferential access to the lucrative markets of the Gulf states. Another consequence of the Gulf War was the implementation of the dual containment policy, designed to isolate and contain Iran and Iraq during the Clinton administration. This policy is now regarded by many observers and analysts as ill-advised and short-sighted, detrimental to the region as well as the long-term US interests. Finally, the post-Gulf War era has witnessed new alliances in which Turkey and Israel have emerged as new strategic allies. Meanwhile the Saudi royal family's close association with the US government has further eroded its legitimacy, thus strengthening and bolstering the Saudi opposition. Indeed, the long-term fallout of the Gulf War and the political cost of the coalition's military victory have yet to unfold.

The fourth major development was the increasingly active economic and political role of Japan and China which is not only a sign of growing power of these two Asian giants, but also a sign of the increasing options available to the Middle East for political and economic trade and partnership. Due to the disappearance of the Soviet threat, reduced American pressure on Japan's diplomacy and its emergence as a major global economic power, Japan is willing to play a more active role in international arena. While Japan's primary ambition remains preferential access to the Middle Eastern markets and the security of an oil supply to safeguard its large import of Middle Eastern oil, China's bid for a Superpower role renders it more ambitious in terms of projection of its power in the region. While its professed Third Worldist sympathies strike a receptive cord in the Middle East, China has attempted to chart a less ideological course in its foreign policy in the post-Cold War era. Due to no legacy of direct colonial involvement in the politics of the region and their "independent" political postures, many political opportunities are present for these emerging powers to expand their influence in the region.

The fifth significant event was the emergence of European Union, increasingly in competition with the United States for political and economic supremacy, and the EU's willingness to define its interests separately, has given rise to a distinctively European policy toward the region. This is clearly evidenced by the EU's opposition to the Clinton administration's policy of dual containment but also in many other policy areas. Due to their close geographical proximity and expanded trade relations with Europe, Middle Eastern economies are further becoming integrated in European union. This may foretell a more active political role for the EU in future politics of the region. Hence, the ambition of some Middle Eastern powers, most notably Turkey, to join EU has influenced their choice in foreign policy. Turkey is eager to solidify its alliance with the EU, and partially in pursuit of this goal has sought strategic alliance with Israel. Turkey is also under pressure from the EU to improve its gross violation of the human rights of its Kurdish minority. Such external considerations of foreign and domestic policies are likely to become more significant as the EU's economic and political influence increases in the region.

Sixth, the unfolding of the Arab-Israeli peace process, highlighted by the Palestinian-Israeli peace Accords (1993) and followed by the Jordanian-Palestinian peace treaty (1994), manifested a turning point in the regional politics. Having seen the strongest army in the Arab world demolished by the coalition forces, and the PLO's position weakened by its support of Saddam Hussein during the Gulf War, Israel was now in a position to negotiate from the position of strength and sign a peace treaty that would protect its long-term security interests and end its status as a pariah state in the global community. Israel also hoped it would benefit from the windfall of the peace dividend by expanding trade with its Arab neighbors and enhancing its access to their markets. Israel, no longer fearing the Soviet support of its political opponents, in an age of Pax Americana and unconditional American support, clearly has the upper hand in peace negotiations with the Palestinians, Jordanians and Syrians. Hence, since the signing of the peace Accords, the peace dividend for Israel has been considerable. No longer preoccupied with the constant preparation for war, Israel has focused on expanding its economy. The peace process has also effectively ended Israeli isolation. No longer shunned by the global community as a pariah state, it now enjoys normalized political relations with the majority of the United Nations member countries. The United States, which played an active role in the peace process, hoped that the resolution of the Arab-Israeli conflict that for more than forty years had served as a catalyst radicalizing the regional politics, could now be defused and the security of the Israeli state would be safeguarded.

The seventh major catalyst for change is the role of petroleum in the political economy of the region. Petroleum is a strategic and politicized commodity in two distinct senses. First, as long as no cost-efficient and environmentally safe alternative sources of energy are available, oil and gas will continue to remain as the main source of energy. Second, the oil industry is nationalized throughout the region, thus it is controlled by the state and decisions regarding its production, sale, and distribution are political decisions, made by politicians. In some oil producing states as much as 90 percent of the state's foreign exchange comes from the petro-dollar. Approximately 70 percent of the world's proven oil reserves and over 40 percent of its natural gas reserves lie in an area between Southern Russia and Kazakistan to Saudi Arabia and the United Arab Emirates, combining the Caspian sea and the Persian Gulf regions. It is also projected that the growing energy needs of China, Japan, and India would have to be supplied by the Middle Eastern oil.[2]

While bereft of the Cold War mandate as the battleground of East-West contentious ideological interests, the immense oil and gas reserves of the region will continue to ensure its strategic significance. The Gulf War of 1991 would have never been fought if Kuwait did not possess more that 100 billion barrels of oil reserves. Saudi Arabia would not have enjoyed the unconditional American patronage despite its gross violation of human rights, if it was not for its distinction as the country with the largest oil reserves on earth. With the rise of technology and service industries, the strategic value of many natural resources and raw materials may have declined, but not oil. It is still the black gold. As long as this remains true, the Middle East will continue to be strategically significant and the competition for " the prize" will persist.

The power of petroleum makes the Gulf Cooperation Council countries (made of the Gulf monarchies) and Iran and Iraq's roles particularly significant in molding the strategic map of the region. These countries possess the largest portion of the oil and gas reserves within OPEC and are significant political players in regional politics. Thus, their future political course would have a profound impact on the political economy of the Middle East and the world. This reality renders the foreign policy of great powers toward these countries particularly significant in charting the course of future developments in the region. This in turn requires a more balanced and delicate foreign policy response that would overcome some of the shortcomings of the residual thinking of the Cold War containment paradigm.

Oil however, is a finite commodity and many oil producing countries are projected to run out of their oil in the next fifty years.[3] The trend in petroleum prices in the last decade has not been particularly encouraging to producing countries. They continue paying higher prices for the industrial and technological goods that they import and have seen the price of their oil decline since early 1980s. With the exception of the Gulf monarchies that have vast reserves and small populations, the rest of the region will suffer serious social and economic consequences if the present trend in diminishing oil incomes continues.

Another important feature of the changing political landscape in the region in the post-Cold War era is the steady growth of civil society, non-governmental organizations and the unfolding of a limited and manipulated process of democratization. Among the most notable developments representing empowerment of the civil society have been the development of an incipient but increasingly significant women's movement and human rights organizations. Since no genuine democratization is possible without empowerment of women, who have been historically excluded and oppressed throughout much of the region, women's organizations play a particularly important role in democratizing political life. With the increasing rate of literacy, the enlargement of the middle class, the global saliency of human rights, and in the face of the persistence of authoritarian regimes of different ideological persuasions, the Middle East has also witnessed a heightened interest in human rights issues and the growth of human rights organizations. Hence, the dialogue on civil society and democratization has found increasing currency throughout the region. However, the biggest regional imperative for democratization might be economic. The dictates of survival in an increasingly integrated global market might render democratization not as a nuisance, – as it is now perceived by many authoritarian leaders – but an inescapable necessity. The Middle East is competing with the rest of the world to attract foreign investment and capital. Due to chronic political instability, buttressed by arbitrary rule and lawlessness, the region's share of foreign investment so far has been meager. This in turn accentuates economic decline and exacerbates poverty and pauperization, which become an impetus for intensifying political instability even further. Seen in this light, for more astute political leaders of the region, democratization is not a luxury. It is a necessity for political and economic survival. These developments would undoubtedly have a profound and enduring impact on the future political dynamics. Political authoritarianism may be still the norm, but a more conscious and determined struggle against it is also a part of the new reality molding the political landscape. To be sure, the Middle East will carry the burden of its own cultural baggage and historical tradition as it struggles to democratize and chart its own political course toward a less arbitrary and repressive form of governance and political system. Many of the themes discussed above will be analyzed in depth in this volume. The book is divided into two parts. The first part comprises five chapters covering some of the regional developments in the post-Cold War era. The second part deals with the foreign policies of the United States, Russia, the European Union and China and Japan toward the region. These contributions provide a critical and nuanced analysis that is sensitive to the regional complexities as well as the context of foreign policy responses of the great powers. The contributors have attempted to link theoretical and historical considerations to the current realities. The essays contained in this volume demonstrate that the Middle East, contrary to Samuel Huntington's contention, is not out of step with history[4], but rather very much a part of it, shaped by it as well as molding it. These new realities have created a new political dynamic and have charted new political configurations. These regional realities, in turn, have impacted the relations among Middle Eastern countries, the global politics in general and the policy of great powers toward the region in particular. In order to chart the contours of the possible future political course in the Middle East, we must grasp and appreciate its present political dynamics. The emerging portrayal of the region sketched in this volume and the coming winds of change portend a future that is unpredictable and complex. To be sure, the future holds progress and regression, twists and turns, revival and rebirth. The synthesis is anything but simple. This complexity demands a new foreign policy response that is more sensitive to the regional realities as well as the aspirations of Middle Eastern people which are often diametrically different from the interests of their mostly corrupt and repressive leaders. What follows is a brief description of chapters in this book that would further discuss these issues.

In chapter two, Manochehr Dorraj charts the major contours of Middle Eastern politics in the Post-Cold War era. Having analyzed the shifts in global politics in the last decade, the chapter delineates the implications of these changes for the region with the emphasis on both the new opportunities as well as the shrinking options. The focus then shifts to the dynamics of the dominant trends in the regional landscape. Such issues as the shifting balance of power, the new security arrangements, the strength and the weaknesses of the Islamic challenge and the nuances of liberalization and retrenchment are analyzed. The chapter ends with a critical assessment of the Clinton administration's foreign policy toward the region.

In the next chapter, Professor Monshipouri presents an appraisal of the human rights situation in the Middle East by looking at such factors as regime types (traditional-authoritarian vs. authoritarian-distributive), state-civil society relations and different trade-offs and paradoxes (e.g., liberty vs. security and economic development vs. political development). Then, the author provides an empirical survey of the state of human rights in different countries of the region with special focus on the rights of women, ethnic minorities and refugees. He also briefly evaluates the tensions between Islam and democracy and expounds on prospects for democratization of the polity and improvement of human rights in select countries of the region.

The contribution of Professor Abukhalil investigates the determinants of foreign policy in Arab states. The author deviates from the standard norms, which characteristically attribute peculiar motivations for the political behavior of Arab regimes. The main focus of the chapter is on the relationship between ideology and foreign policy. Abukhalil downplays the role of ideology and suggests that ideology should be merely studied as the language of foreign policy, where Arab regimes – desperate for political legitimacy – incorporate the dominant terminology of the dominant ideology in order to conform to the popular mood of the population. Abukhalil illuminates the nuances of the cultural context of foreign policy decision-making. He focuses on the impact of Islamic political culture and Arab Nationalism on the style, language and substance of politics. Islamic rationalization of politics, he contends, is used to forge political legitimacy. He asserts that the political behavior of Arab regimes is driven more by pragmatic considerations and national interests rather than ideology. " Principles" are often sacrificed at the altar of state security and political legitimacy. This is particularly true in the post-Cold War era. If in the past rationalization of foreign policy was disguised under such lofty goals as "Arab unity, liberation of Palestine, and Islamic glory", since the Gulf war of 1991, there is a new policy dictated by the politics of expediency. Kuwait and Saudi Arabia had to forge a direct military alliance with the US and the United Kingdom in order to survive. It has become abundantly clear that promotion of each regime's interests are the main determinants of foreign policy.

In his contribution, Professor Zunes presents a critical analysis of the dynamics of Israeli foreign policy toward its neighbors with a special focus on US-Israeli connection. He expounds on the nature of new Israeli relations with its neighbors and the international community and the domestic and international determinants of Israeli foreign policies. The author contends that changes within Israel itself, among the Palestinians and elsewhere in the Middle East, have placed the Israelis at a crossroads in the development of their foreign policy goals and the options available to them. According to Zunes, Israel finds itself, for the first time, treated as a full member of the international community and no longer threatened by most of its former adversaries. Yet certain rigid residual attitudes, based on both Jewish and Israeli historical experiences – combined with a Superpower umbrella protecting the country militarily, economically and diplomatically from the consequences of its actions – has led to a failure of the Israeli leadership to make the compromises necessary to bring enduring peace and security to its people.

Professor Moghadam's contribution analyzes the gender dimension of changes that have swept the region (liberalization, Islamization, shifts in state-society relations and proliferation of non-governmental organizations). Her chapter draws attention to the growth of women's organizations in the region, contextualizing the phenomenon in terms of demographic, economic, political and international factors, discussing seven types of organizations that have emerged. She argues that women's organizations are the new political voice in the region, with implications for both status of women and societal democratization.

Professor Drake examines the applicability of Cold War containment doctrine to Post-Cold War regional settings of the Middle East. In this connection, she presents a penetrating critique of the Clinton administration's policy of dual containment. She contends that, similar to the "peace through strength" paradigm of the Cold War era, Washington is now implementing in the Middle East what amounts to a policy of peace through containment. It is not often realized, the author asserts, that the doctrine spans well beyond the containment of Iraq and Iran and envisions a comprehensive Middle East regional security system covering both the Gulf and the Arab-Israeli peace process, in which those states and non-state actors opposing the peace process constitute the primary objects of containment. While the dual containment doctrine holds that peace and containment are mutually reinforcing, Drake argues that by drawing artificial lines and barricades across the region and disregarding the regional realities, it promotes instability and conflict.

Professor Katz investigates the nuances of the Post-Soviet Russian foreign policy toward the Middle East with a focus on three specific points: 1) to identify Moscow's multiple goals in the region; 2) to analyze the extent to which they complement or conflict with one another, and 3) to assess Moscow's capacity for achieving them. Katz contends that in the Post-Cold War era, the politico-military aspects of Russian foreign policy have focused on the "Northern Tier" states — Turkey, Iran, and Afghanistan — which border on the former USSR and which have the greatest impact on it. Russian foreign policy toward these countries is undergoing important change as Moscow more actively seeks to revive Russia's role as a great power. Although by no means similar in scope or ambition to Soviet policy at the height of the Cold War, the emerging nationalist strain in Russia's Post-Cold War policy toward the region seems to be based on thought processes more similar to those prevalent in the Brezhnev era than in the Gorbachev one.

In his contribution on European Union-Middle East relations in the Post-Cold War era, Professor Ehteshami identifies five major developments that impact this relationship. First is the Iraqi invasion of Kuwait in 1990 and the Western/Soviet response to the Iraqi action. The second development was the Implosion of the Soviet Union a year later. The third development was the coming into force in Europe of the Maastricht treaty on 1 January 1993. The fourth important event was the Arab-Israeli peace process and the current and future role of the EU in it. The Expansion of the EU since 1995, with its political ramifications, is the fifth major factor identified by the author as pivotal development with consequences for EU-Middle East relations. The author expounds on the complexities and multifarious political dimensions of an ever more ambitious and assertive EU as its reach expands into the Mediterranean, Asia and the Middle East. Eheteshami asserts that Middle East, North Africa and Central Asia, which form a land mass between Europe and Asia are strategically significant to the long-term security of Eurasia. For this reason, despite the instability of Middle Eastern markets, it would continue to remain an area of particular interest to the EU in the near future.

In the final chapter, Professor Noroozi analyzes the changing foreign policies of Japan and China toward the Middle East in the Post-

Cold War era. The author dissects the patterns of realignment and reorientation by focusing on regional determinants of foreign policy. Noroozi identifies the main cornerstone of Japanese foreign policy toward the region as North-Atlanticism, a close alliance with the United States and Western Europe as exemplified by the Gulf War Coalition of 1991. Chinese foreign policy, on the other hand, has not favored either isolation or a thorough commitment to North-Atlanticist powers. Rather, China's policy has revolved around interdependence in economic and security areas of realignment. This is partially dictated by the Chinese dual and often conflicting need to modernize and acquire Western technology and expand its sphere of influence in parts of the world where anti-Western sentiment has created opportunities for China to exploit. Noroozi focuses on select issues such as oil, the Arab-Israeli peace process, Iran-Iraqi War (1980-1988), the Gulf War (1991), and their respective policies toward Iran to compare and contrast the evolving Japanese and Chinese foreign policies toward the region.

Notes

1. James H. Mittleman Editor, Globalization: Critical Reflections (Boulder and London: Lynne Rienner Publishers, 1996).

2. Gregory Kemp and Robert E. Harkavy, Strategic Geography and the Changing Middle East (Washington, D.C.: Brookings Institutions press, 1997). p.xiii

3. Daniel Yergin, The Prize: The Epic Quest For Oil , Money and Power (New York: Touchstone, 1993).

4. Samuel Hutington, The Clash of Civilizations: Remaking of World Order (New York: Touchstone Publishers, 1997). For critique of Hutington see Shireen Hunter, The Future Of Islam and The West: Clash of Civilizations or Peaceful Coexistence (Westport and London: Praeger Publishers, 1998).

Chapter 2

The Post-Cold War Middle East and Its Foreign Policy Challenges

Manochehr Dorraj

Introduction

The tumultuous events that marked the end of the Cold War changed the political map of the Middle East as well. The new realities of the region have put in motion a new set of dynamics that have imposed their own challenges. As has been mostly the case in the recent history of the region, the major global powers and the shift in their policies had a profound impact on the internal affairs of these countries. An appreciation of post-Cold War configurations is paramount to understanding the new regional politics. The first part of this chapter briefly assesses the shift in American and Russian foreign policies and the second part analyzes the impact of these changes on regional politics with a focus on select countries. The third part analyzes the myth and the reality of "the Islamic threat." In the next section the dilemmas of liberalization are assayed. The last part appraises the Clinton administration's foreign policy toward the region.

The Post-Cold War Era and the New Directions in American and Russian Foreign Policies

By the 1980's so far as US foreign policy makers were concerned, the two major lessons of Vietnam had been learned. First, swift victory and the minimal public resistance to the war must be assured. Reagan's invasion of Grenada and Bush's wars against Panama and Iraq are good examples. Second, American unilateralism of the past had to be replaced with an American-led coalition building to minimize the financial cost and provide a pretext of legitimacy and consensus. Both elements of new strategic thinking in post-Vietnam era were highlighted in the American-led coalition against Iraq in the Gulf war of 1991. While the United States provided the main bulk of the fighting force, Saudi Arabia, Kuwait, Japan and Germany paid the major portion of the cost of the war.[1]

The Gulf war of 1991 and its aftermath were a major watershed in the politics of the region. The war strengthened American influence. America's access to oil was more secure than ever before. Major oil producers of the Gulf including Saudi Arabia, Kuwait, and the Gulf Sheikhdoms were now more dependent on American military protection for their security than any other time in recent history. Thanks to demolition of Iraq, the strongest military threat to Israel, and the plummeting PLO's political fortune due to its support of Saddam Hussein during the Gulf war, Israel was now in a position to negotiate for peace from a position of strength. Hence, radical regimes such as Syria that stood defiant before, were co-opted during the Gulf war. Having lost the patronage of the former Soviet Union, Assad saw the Gulf War as an opportunity to settle the score with his nemesis, Saddam Hussein, and rapproch US and Western Europe.[2]

The post-Cold War era also ushered in a new attempt to assert American leadership in the face of demise of the former Soviet Union. Some scholars called the new reality a" unipolar moment" in which American power, institutions and values reigned Supreme.[3]   In the aftermath of the Gulf war, American goals in the region can be summarized as the following: preserving access to oil at low prices and enhancing the consumer-producer dialogue in terms favorable to American oil interests; preventing proliferation of weapons of mass destruction, especially in regard to radical regimes, protecting the interests of Israel and maintaining political stability in the region as a whole; and protecting the oil-rich Gulf Cooperation Council (GCC) countries and Egypt in particular, which remains the top priority. [4]

With the defeat of Iraq in 1991, American access to Middle Eastern oil and its influence in OPEC was further solidified. The policy of dual containment implemented by the Clinton administration to Isolate and militarily contain Iran and Iraq was designed to bolster the security of American allies, namely the GCC members in the region.

These developments ushered in an unprecedented political opportunity for America in which its power remained at its zenith and for the most part unchallenged. This, however, did not mean that America now had absolute power to chart the future course of the region. On the contrary, the post- Cold War era also revealed the limitations of American power. The former secretary of state, James Baker, for example, envisioned the new world order in the post-war Middle East to entail five points: First, to create a new regional security arrangement. Second, to reduce the arms race. Third, to narrow the gap between the rich and the poor nations in the Arab world through the creation of a regional bank for reconstruction. Fourth, to resolve the Israeli-Palestinian conflict. Fifth, to reduce American dependence on Middle Eastern oil drastically.[5] So far the new regional security arrangement has not materialized. In fact, the GCC countries are now more than ever dependent on American military protection. Saddam Hussein still remains in power in Iraq and several pro-Western Gulf nations including Saudi Arabia are facing increasing internal unrest. The arms race in the region has escalated. The United States alone sold $18 billions in arms to Saudi Arabia, Egypt, Kuwait, and the Gulf Arab states in 1992 and since 1991 the total US arms sales to the region have amounted to $90 billion. Iran has also been rearming its depleting arsenal since 1990 by buying Russian and Chinese weapons. The gap between the rich and the poor has widened and the plummeting oil revenues and population explosion are exacerbating this problem. The US dependence on Middle Eastern oil has increased since 1991 and it is projected to increase even more in the near future. The fragile Palestinian-Israeli peace accord is one of the few positive developments in the region.

With the ascendance of Gorbachev to power in 1985, the Soviet foreign policy changed dramatically. Deideologization of politics, peaceful resolution of conflict, decreasing regional and global conflict, reduction of the arms race and disengagement from Third World conflict constituted the major cornerstone of Gorbachev's foreign policy." The new thinking" allowed more pragmatic and flexible assessment of world politics. Now constructive alliance with "the class enemy" was possible as it was clearly indicated by Gorbachev's support for the anti Saddam coalition during the Gulf war of 1991. Gorbachev also perceived of improvement of East-West relations in the age of nuclear weapons as the central issue of our time. He argued that the Soviet Union so far has been bogged down in the periphery of the world. The key issue in the nuclear age however, is the improvement of superpowers' relations. In this context, the Third World, including the Middle East, assumed a secondary position in priorities of the Soviet and the post-Soviet foreign policy. Thus, conflict with the United States and her allies over the Third World should be avoided. The wisdom of creating financially costly dependencies such as Afghanistan and Cuba also came under question.[6] Instead, Moscow established relations with such former adversaries as Israel and Saudi Arabia and improved relations with Kuwait and Egypt. Such former Soviet client states as Syria, Libya, and the PLO, in the post-Soviet era had to find new sources of financial and military support. Hence, with the collapse of the Soviet Union, the Communist model of economic development based on a command economy, extensive nationalization and self-sufficiency increasingly lost luster in an interdependent world. Many countries in the Middle East including Algeria, Syria and Libya that looked upon the Soviet model sympathetically began to experiment with privatization and the free enterprise system. With the disintegration of the former Soviet Union, as Russia turns inward, attempting to mend its ailing economy, it is less inclined to be as actively involved in global and Middle Eastern affairs. This inward turn of Russia has created a vacuum for the regional powers to fill. Saddam Hussein's invasion of Kuwait can be partially explained in this term.

Another consequence of the Soviet disintegration is the emergence of the new Muslim Republics of the former Soviet Union with close historical and cultural ties to the Middle East. This new development has rekindled the ancient rivalries between the Turks and the Iranians for political influence in this region and has opened up new avenues of diplomatic and trade relations for the entire region. Hence, the discovery of the new oil reserves in the Caspian Sea has added to the strategic significance of the region. It has also provided the regional and Western countries with new opportunities for investment. Other regional powers such as Israel, Saudi Arabia and Egypt are also competing for influence in Central Asia. The opening up of Central Asia and the Caucuses has increased the complexity of the regional geo-political arena. Numerous trade and political associations have sprung up and the regional integration is well under way. As the two regions further integrate, their politics becomes more interconnected, with Russia still playing the dominant role in Central Asia and the

Caucuses and the US being the major global player in the Middle East. The old rivalry between the former ideological antagonists has not disappeared, it only has found a new form. For example, while the United States has antagonistic relations with Iran and Iraq and has imposed economic sanctions on them, Russia has cordial political relations and burgeoning trade ties with both.

Another ramification of the new reality in the post-Cold War era is the shrinking options of the region. Now many Middle Eastern countries find themselves competing with the former Soviet republics and East and Central Europe for Western loans and investments. Plagued with political instability and lacking in infrastructure and a trained labor force, Middle Eastern markets are not as competitive as the more developed and emerging markets of East and Central European societies. Hence, the Soviet threat having disappeared, the oil producing states notwithstanding, the region no longer holds the strategic significance that it enjoyed during the Cold War as the battleground of the two superpowers.

The Regional Politics in the Post-Cold War Era

The Cold War regional politics of Middle East was highlighted by the centrality of Arab-Israeli conflict and safeguarding the security of American allies most notably, Israel, Iran (prior to 1979), Turkey, Jordan, post-Nasser Egypt and Saudi Arabia. The Soviet Union, on the other hand, provided military and financial support to its regional allies, most notably, Syria, Libya, Iraq, Yemen, and the PLO. The two Superpowers played a direct role in maintaining a balance of power and safeguarding the security of their client states.

The Iranian Revolution of 1979 and the ensuing Islamic Revival abruptly altered this regional security order and forcefully introduced the Islamic factor into the politics of the region. Driven by revolutionary zeal and pan-Islamic sentiments, Iran under the leadership of Ayatollah Khomeini attempted to export its brand of populist Islam to other Muslim nations. This challenge to the supremacy of the bipolar system and the security of the regional allies on both sides alienated the superpowers, and they mobilized their resources to isolate and punish the Islamic Republic. The Iran-Iraqi war of 1980-1988 provided the United States and the Soviet Union with ample opportunity to do so. But it soon became clear that the Islamic revival in the Muslim world had a life and dynamism of its own and it was instigated primarily by such domestic factors as a sense of malaise, poverty, and political repression rather than the distant subversive hands of Tehran.

The next major event that fundamentally altered the regional political configurations, thus substantially changing the bipolar system was the collapse of Communism. By 1989 as Moscow sat passively watching the Berlin wall fall, it was clear that the Soviet Union had turned inward. By 1991, as the Soviet Union disintegrated, Russia was actively seeking to mend its ailing economy and disengage from Middle Eastern conflict. Now unrivaled, the United States was in a unique position to usher in a new era of Pax-Americana.

In the post-Cold War and post-Gulf War era, the strategy of the oil-rich Gulf Arab states is to forge alliance and to arm themselves. Eager to create a new regional security arrangement, in 1991 Washington sponsored a joint security alliance of Gulf Cooperation Council countries, Syria and Egypt. But this alliance did not take long to collapse. GCC countries felt more comfortable with the US military protection. They were not willing to pay the political cost of owing their security to their fellow Arabs with whom they have had a history of conflict and discord. Security pacts with the distant United States and Western Europe seemed a safer bet. After the Gulf War in which several Arab nations joined the American-led coalition to eject Saddam Hussein from Kuwait, each took the path of protecting and pursuing their own national interests. The collapse of the alliance was another indication that the idea of Pan-Arabism for all practical purposes was dead.

The main security concern of GCC countries is Iran and Iraq. As the two major powers of the Persian Gulf, the two are the main competitors for Saudi Arabia, the other major financial and political power in the region. With the military emasculation of Iraq, Iran, Saudi Arabia and Egypt have emerged as the three major powers that are competing for supremacy in the Gulf. While Iraq's secular regime has very little ideological appeal among the Saudi masses, Iran's populist Islam is much more appealing to the consciousness of the ordinary Saudis.

While during the reign of the Shah the two close regional allies of the United States, Iran and Saudi Arabia, maintained cordial relations, after the Iranian revolution of 1979, the relation between the two countries deteriorated considerably. With the Shi'ite uprising in the Eastern provinces and the attempt at the take over of the holy shrine in Mecca in 1981, the tensions between the two countries escalated. The

Saudis were scorned by Iranian clergy for their close embracement of US policies in the region. Hence, the populist Islam of Shi'ite Iran directly clashed with the establishment Islam of the Sunni Saudi monarchy.

The GCC was created in 1981 in the wake of looming dangers from the Iranian revolution and the spread of the Iran-Iraqi war. During the eight year Iran-Iraqi war, Saudi Arabia and Kuwait supported Iraq financially and militarily. In the post-Gulf War era, having seen their former Arab ally turn against them, the GCC countries have engaged in a balancing act. Many of them have rapproched Tehran as the major buffer to the threat from Baghdad. Saudi Arabia and Kuwait who had broken relations with Iran have reestablished relations. Qatar and Oman are supportive of a larger role for Iran in future regional security arrangements. Due to its rivalry with and mistrust of Iran and Iraq, Saudi Arabia does not favor their inclusion in any future security arrangements. Such exclusion also guarantees the uncontested leadership role of the Saudis within the GCC. By 1995, however, as the Saudi monarchy was challenged by a determined and increasingly militant Islamic opposition, the fingers were once again pointed to Tehran as the source of subversion.[7]

The GCC states are witnessing a period of economic stagnation and rising domestic political unrest. A young generation of educated technocrats and intellectuals has stepped into the political scene and they demand reform and a larger voice in the political process. Because the conservative monarchies of GCC refuse to open up the political process and allow genuine political participation, many members of this younger generation have either joined the Islamic opposition or other underground clandestine organizations. As the pressure on Saudi monarchy to further Islamicize the society mounts, it is likely that Saudis may want to temporarily distant themselves from Washington to weather the storm of Islamic challenge, just as Mubarak did in Egypt after Sadat's assassination in 1981. In fact, the recent warming up of Saudi Arabia to Iran may be understood in this context. Such temporary maneuvers, however, do not alter the long-term strategic alliance between the United States and the Saudi government, which is based on the Saudi's need for US military protection and the US need to have access to cheap Saudi oil and the lucrative Saudi market.

The GCC countries have demonstrated an active interest in the Arab-Israeli peace process as an overall contributor to the security of the region as a whole. They are also more likely to take a keen interest in security of Egypt with its close proximity to Arabian peninsula and possible ramifications of an Islamic state In Egypt for their own domestic affairs. [8]

In American strategic thinking, the security of GCC countries is linked to the successful resolution of Arab-Israeli conflict. This fact partially explains the active role the Bush administration played in the post-Gulf War period in initiating the Madrid negotiations in 1991 that ultimately under Clinton administration led to Palestinian-Israeli and Israeli-Jordanian peace accords. As one of the issues most responsible for the radicalization of the region for four decades, the successful resolution of Arab-Israeli dispute will diffuse a major source of political instability. Hence, due to the direct role of US in Arab-Israeli peace process, the success or failure of the peace accords will have a direct bearing on American prestige and political influence in the region. While the United States still firmly supports Israel, the strategic value of Israel in the overall context of US foreign policy in the post-Cold War era has diminished. With its military power uncontested, Israel is making peace with its Arab neighbors from position of strength, and seems more secure than at any time since its inception in 1948.

A country that has played a key role in Arab-Israeli peace process is Egypt. Under Mubarak, Egypt continued playing its traditional role of mediator between the Arab world and the external powers. As a close ally of the United States, Egypt "opens the Arab world to US interests". Egypt played a key role in Arab-Israeli rapprochement and peace settlement. Egypt is also a force of moderation against radical ideological currents of the region. Egypt played a leading role in forging the Arab coalition that was arrayed against Saddam Hussein during the Gulf War of 1991. Mubarak also used the Gulf War to cement the Saudi-Egyptian alliance. For these roles, instead, Egypt can count on US economic and military aid, subsidies, investment, and security cooperation. Since the late 1970's Egypt has received an annual amount of $2.1 billion that includes security and civil aid. Almost half of the Egyptian security budget comes from the United States. By 1997, the US aid to Egypt totaled to $49 billion. While by assuming a leadership role, Egypt tries to make itself indispensable to the US, the United States in turn finds Egypt a useful and reliable partner that enhances the achievement of its regional goals. [9] Sadat's separate peace with Israel, his close embracement of the US and his bombastic style led to Egypt's isolation in the Arab world. In contrast, Mubarak's shrewd diplomacy of maintaining some distance between Cairo and Washington and Tel Aviv, bringing the other nations to the peace process and playing a key mediatory role in Israeli- Palestinian peace accords has added to Egypt's clout in the Arab World. Egypt uses its alliance with the United States and its regional role as a facilitator and mediator to make itself indispensable to the Arab world as well. Lacking in substantial oil reserves, Egypt uses its political services to extract capital from oil-rich Gulf states. Under Mubarak, Egypt has managed to establish good relations with such conservative Arab regimes as Saudi Arabia and Kuwait as well as such radical regimes as Syria, Libya, and the PLO. But this balancing act of representing the often conflictual interests of America and the Arab world simultaneously is a very delicate one and is contingent upon legitimacy of Egyptian leadership role in the Arab World.[10]

Threatened by a potent Muslim opposition, Mubarak has tried to use Iran as a scapegoat to both discredit its Muslim opposition as the Pawns of Iranian intrigue and to detract from chronic domestic economic and political crisis that animates the opposition. Hence, Iran's call for creation of a Pan-Islamic order to combat Western domination is the main alternative to Egypt's pro-Western strategy in the region. Iran objects to its exclusion from an Egyptian-led Gulf security arrangement, arguing that as a major power in the Persian Gulf it should be considered a partner in such an arrangement. Egypt in turn feels uneasy about the Iranian military build up and its support of neighboring Sudan's Muslim Fundamentalist regime. Mubarak is concerned about the impact of Sudan's Islamic government on its own Muslim opposition. Egypt also sees Iran's denunciation of the Arab-Israeli peace process in which Mubarak played a key intermediary role, as an attempt to discredit his regime.[11] These conflicts are a part of the overall rivalry between these two ancient civilizations for supremacy in the region. Since Mr. khatami's ascendence to power in 1997 however, there has been a political rapprochment between the two countries and the tensions have eased.

The" Islamic Threat"

By the early 1990's, as the Islamic revival swept the Muslim World, it proved to be a much more tenacious and pervasive phenomenon than previously estimated by the observers. Islamists had won impressive electoral victories in Algeria, Egypt, Tunisia, Jordan and Turkey and through a military Coup d'etat they seized power in Sudan in 1989. In Algeria in particular, the Front for Islamic Salvation (FIS) came very close to seizing power after winning the parliamentary elections by impressive margins in 1991. In 1992, the Algerian generals annulled the elections and cracked down on the FIS, arresting and persecuting many of its leaders and supporters. Fearing the repercussions of an Islamic government in Algeria, the United States and French governments supported the generals. As the breadth and the depth of the Islamic movement revealed itself, the Soviet Union having ceased to exist, now the Communist threat was being replaced by a new menace from the East, namely, The Islamic threat.

The discovery of the Islamic threat conjures up the memory of Pan-Arabist "threat" posed by Nasser four decades earlier. But unlike nationalism, a secular ideology, Islam is a sacred faith that encompasses both private and social realms of life. As the source of spiritual guide and cultural authenticity, Islam plays a significant role in defining Muslim's identity and eliciting their abiding loyalty. Politicized in the age of ideology, by synthesizing the spiritual and the political, the Islamic revivalist movement has been transformed into a formidable political force. Capable of appealing to both the material and the spiritual impoverishment that plagues the Muslim world, many Islamists have raised political and economic demands on behalf of the poor. They have also addressed the moral malaise and the perceived vacuousness that a Western inspired commercial culture has brought to the Muslim world. This twin political and cultural challenge provides Islamists with an agenda to mobilize the masses against the status quo and pose Islam as the ideological alternative for reorganization of social and spiritual life. As the crisis of legitimacy of the authoritarian states intensified in the 1980's, the populist Islam emerged to challenge the secular states throughout the region. Alarmed by its populist demeanor and anti-Western rhetoric, Washington vilified militant Islam, labeling it as a terrorist movement. This confrontationist attitude combined with America's acquiescence toward Israeli state-sponsored terrorism angered many in the Muslim World. As Michael Hudson puts it,

When US president summons Middle East and World leaders to Sharm Al- Shaykh, in Egypt, to mount a campaign against terrorism, clearly he has in mind Islamist groups like HAMAS, Hizballah, and the Jama'at Islamiyyia (Islamic group), as well as terrorism sponsored by

the 'rogue' states like Iran, Iraq, Libya, and the Sudan. But when
America's chief regional ally deploys the massive military power of the
state to terrorize whole populations, and the United States excuses it,
public opinion throughout the Islamic Middle East naturally becomes
inflamed against America for employing a double standard.[12]

To be sure, the Muslim World has its share of terrorists, and there
are" Islamically" inspired terrorism as there are "Christian", "Jewish"
or" Hindu" inspired violence. But those who engage in acts of violence
under the guise of Islamic piety, constitute a small number of
exteremists who have received disproportionately large attention in
Western media. Consequently, by magnifying their deeds, an entire
people and their culture are projected negatively. In fact, the
overwhelming majority of Muslim leaders are not wild-eyed radicals or
terrorists. Many are populists and advocate the use of ballot box rather
than bullets to achieve their political goals. If the Islamic militancy of
the 1980's was highlighted by the hostage taking and car bombing, as
the political cost of violence proved to be too high and the world
around them changed, the Muslim activists of 1990's for the most part
have opted for electoral politics and civil disobedience. The Muslim
brotherhood in Egypt and Jordan, the FIS in Algeria (Before the Coup
d'etat of 1992), Al-Nahda (the Renaissance party) in Tunisia, Jama'at
Islami in Pakistan and the Welfare party in Turkey are examples. It is
primarily in countries where democratic rights have been suppressed
that the Islamists have resorted to violence. Lebanon, the West bank
and the occupied territories, and Saudi Arabia are a few examples. It is
under the repressive policies of a lawless state that extremism,
including Islamic extremism flourish. In fact, as several scholars have
noted, "Islamic Fundamentalism" is a reactive phenomenon. Far from
being expansionist, Muslims from Bosnia to Chechnya feel beleaguered
and victimized and a siege mentality pervades their ranks.[13]
Preoccupied with the stagnation and the malaise that has befallen them,
Muslim societies have very few resources or opportunities to seriously
threaten the West.

In the mold of the Cold War mentality, the new "threat," Islam is
depicted as a monolithic anti- Western monster led by Iran, scheming
to dominate the Muslim World, overthrow American allies and destroy
Israel. Given the meager resources of the Iranian government and its
Shi'ite ideology however, its ability to export its brand of Islamic
revolution to the mostly Sunni Muslim World remains limited and
seriously constrained. Conjuring up images of a long history of

confrontation between Islamic and Western nations, the new campaign also exploits fear and xenophobia. Thus, it often distorts and vilifies Islam and Muslims to justify the defense of authoritarian pro-Western regimes that are being challenged by their Islamic opposition. The terms "Islamic Fundamentalism" and terrorism have become synonymous in the lexicon of Western cultural industry and popular media. This campaign is spearheaded also under the pretext that militant Islam is antithetical to Western values and democracy. This contention clearly involves a double standard in which US closes her eyes to anti-democratic practices of its secular and Islamic allies and magnifies those of its political opponents. Saudi Arabia, a close ally of the US for example, is one of the most repressive Muslim regimes to be found anywhere. Nevertheless, it enjoys unconditional American support and patronage. In fact, America fought a major war to ensure the security of the Saudi "Muslim Fundamentalist" regime. Hence, the duplicity in American governments' adherence to democratic principles is evident when Washington is troubled by the prospects of democratic elections leading to the ascendance of Islamists in Algeria or Egypt. As Hadar aptly notes:

> There is a major contradiction between America's global democracy project and its Pax-Americana program in the Middle East. US policymakers know that democratically elected and popularly based governments – Islamic or otherwise – would be less inclined to bow to American wishes. It is not a coincidence that the governments in Jordan, Yemen and Algeria (before the military take over) were the most critical of US policy during the Persian Gulf crisis reflecting the general public mood in those countries. Hence the vicious circle: continued support for repressive regimes, exacerbated by America's alliance with Israel, only fans resentment and makes it more difficult for Washington to tolerate the idea of democratization and reforms in the region.[14]

Other scholars see a negative correlation between democratic reforms and US foreign aid policy. Zunes contends that the United States has reduced its economic and military aid to Arab countries that have experienced liberalization in recent years while increasing its support to such autocratic regimes as Saudi Arabia, Kuwait, Egypt and Morocco. The decreasing of aid to Jordan since it opened up its political system in early 1990's, the reduction and suspension of aid to Yemen, when the newly unified country held its first democratic election in 1990, and the increasing of aid to Israel in the 1980s, and Morocco when the country escalated its repressive policies in the occupied Western Sahara are presented as evidence to demonstrate the gap between the US government's rhetoric and its deeds.[15]One critic argues that the United States finds it much more convenient to deal with the non-democratic governments than the democratic ones. After all, "It is much simpler to manipulate a few ruling families – to secure fat orders for arms and ensure that oil prices remain low – than a wide variety of personalities and policies bound to be thrown up by a democratic system."[16] Instead of confrontation with militant Islam, Hadar and Zunes propose a policy of "constructive disengagement" and mutual understanding and accommodation. Only such a policy can bring long term peace and stability to the region. By supporting autocratic regimes that suppress their opponents including Islamists, America inadvertently helps to legitimize and strengthen the very extremist forces it seeks to suppress. Hence, Washington's current policy of containment of Islamic movements can be as costly as fighting Communism was and perhaps even more difficult. As Robin Wright has observed, "Challenging an ideology that is supported by a failed economic system is one thing; demonizing a centuries-old faith and culture is another. Moreover, as in the Cold War, the United States would have to cultivate some unsavory allies along the way. Many of the regimes most committed to blocking Islamist movements – ranging from Syria's Hafez Al-Assad to Libya's Muammar Al-Qaddafi – are also opposed to democracy."[17]

To defuse the tensions between the Muslim World and the West, the counterproductive campaign of vilification of militant Islam must be abandoned in favor of a positive dialogue. In fact, such dialogue has been initiated by the newly elected Iranian president Mr. muhammad Khatami. In his speech to Islamic Summit held in Tehran, December 8-11, 1997, Khatami stated, "our era is an era of preponderance of Western culture and civilization, whose understanding is imperative. Undoubtedly, we will succeed in moving forward.....if we....utilize the positive scientific, technological and social accomplishments of Western civilization, a stage we must inevitably go through to reach the future. Muslim World must understand the West in an unprejudiced way." [18] In a December 15, 1997 press conference, Khatami praised "the great American people" and challenged the US politicians to catch up with the changing times and reassess their acrimonious policies toward Iran.[19] In fact it is not too far-fetched to suggest that as the intransigent policies of the Islamic republic in its early years had a radicalizing impact throughout the Muslim world, the new accommodationist course in Tehran in due time may have a moderating impact in many parts of the Muslim World.

To break through the present impasse between Islamists and the West, the West should support the Islamic movements that seek to change their corrupt and repressive societies through humane and democratic means. The US government should express as much outrage at the Algerian government for their treatment of those who sought change through the ballot as it does against HAMAS for seeking change through the bullet. Only then can the US stand on the high moral ground necessary to exert influence and provide leadership. The Muslim world in the last decade has witnessed decisive US military action and confrontations with Iraq and Somalia and its inaction for five years in Bosnia (prior to NATO's involvement in 1996) and three years in Chechnya as scores of Muslims were massacred by their Serbian and Russian opponents. They also see the World Bank and IMF exhorting Egyptian and Indonesian governments to cut subsidies for food, fuel, health care, clothing and electricity, then it is obvious why many lay Muslims may regard those institutions and governments that support their repressive regimes and the austerity measures as evil.[20]

Finally, if the United States is committed to democracy and democratization in the region, in so far as all political systems are rooted in popular culture, then democracy cannot flourish by the negation of Islam but through its democratic interpretation. This reality renders the policy of constructive engagement urgent.

Dilemmas of Liberalization and Retrenchment

In the twentieth century, many populist leaders such as Mustafa Kamal Ataturk, Jamal abdul Nasser, Muammar al-Qaddafi, and Ruhollah Khomeini have employed populist politics to mobilize the masses and bestow nationalist legitimacy on their respective authoritarian regimes. While populist symbolism and rhetoric may be effective culturally, economically, in the face of global interdependence, its traditional schemes of self-sufficiency based on nationalization of industries and autonomous economic development have lost luster. The crisis of authoritarian populism combined with the global impact of democratization and a shrinking petro-dollar, induced many Middle Eastern regimes to grant concessions to their opposition and opt for controlled liberalization. This process, however, has been highly manipulated, and when the opposition threatens to seize power or poses a serious challenge, the insecure ruling elite resorts to repression and halts the process of liberalization as the events in Algeria and Egypt in the last decade so clearly demonstrate. Liberalization in its Middle Eastern context so far has been confined to some restricted openings in the political space, allowing associational life and tolerating electoral politics as long as the loyal opposition remains subdued and non-threatening.

In the last decades, despite the reluctance of many authoritarian regimes to democratize, independent non-governmental organizations have been steadily growing throughout the region and the discourse of pluralism, democracy, and civil society has become more prevalent, making the demand for political participation and Human rights more common. Due to the demonstration effect of democratization sweeping many parts of the Third World and East and Central Europe in the last decade, and the increasing cost of political repression; many Middle Eastern elites have opted for a new strategy of survival. They have implemented a policy of economic and political liberalization in an attempt to contain the forces of opposition and prevent revolution and turmoil. The response to the increasing demand for democratization throughout the Middle East has been mixed. Some regimes have attempted to appease the masses by giving symbolic concessions. The creation or expansion of advisory councils in the United Arab Emirates and Oman, and the elections for the national assembly that were held in Kuwait in 1992 are examples. In Turkey (until the banning of the islamic Rafah party in 1998) and Jordan, political Liberalization led to a large voice for the Islamic parties and allowed them to participate in the political process. By contrast, in Algeria, Tunisia, and Egypt, the secular regimes that felt threatened by their respective Muslim opposition engaged in retrenchment and repression.

This uneven wave of liberalization, albeit manipulated and controlled, which has engulfed the region has several crucial features. First, the process of economic and political liberalization has converged with Islamic revival and the resurgence of primordial loyalties. As events in Algeria, Tunisia, Jordan, Egypt and Turkey attest, Islamists have managed to use political openings to expand their influence and power. Second, liberalization has facilitated further growth of the incipient civil society in many parts of the region. The expansion of civil society in turn has pressured the elite to broaden the liberalization process. In countries where civil society remains weak and liberalization has not been institutionalized, it is often accompanied by periods of retrenchment and return of repression. Algeria is a tragic example. Third, while many countries in the region have opted for economic liberalization, they have avoided political liberalization. Initiation of economic reforms in Syria and Libya for example, have not been accompanied by political reforms. Fourth, the present wave of liberalization has not yet ushered in genuine social transformation or democratization, rather it has maintained authoritarian regimes in power by creating safety walves to release political and social pressures induced by poverty, unemployment, repression and the loss of political legitimacy. The essential pillars of democratic politics – contestation of state apparatus by opposition parties, peaceful transition of power and the rule of law – are not yet a part of the rules of the game in Middle Eastern liberalization experiment. Hence autonomous organizations such as voluntary associations, labor unions, syndicates and interest groups are regarded as a threat by the vast majority of Middle Eastern regimes. They are often either destroyed, infiltrated, or coopted.

In so far as political liberalization has been primarily confined to electoral politics, elections in and of themselves do not guarantee democracy or the rule of law. In fact, elections in societies where democratic institutions are weak or non-existent, and when they are not accompanied by social reforms, can become a meaningless practice that leads neither to empowerment nor to democracy or political accountability. Hence, the electoral system itself can be manipulated by excluding particular groups from participating, using the threat of punishment and the promise of reward to prohibit or encourage the people to vote or increase the rural representation in favor of more politicized urban sector. If such crisis as overpopulation, economic decline and increasing pauperization become more chronic, then short-term prospects for political liberalization are very bleak. This is however, one side of the story.

The Middle East is not an isolated island of obsolete traditions impenetrable to powerful forces of global change as the essentialists hold. Quite to the contrary, not possessing either the technological or political and military power to resist those forces renders it more vulnerable to them. The sense of malaise and stagnation articulated by many intellectuals of the region reveals that beneath the cries of Islamic authenticity lies an outward looking vision, the allure of the West,

where the new goods and gadgets, the new fads and ideas, and the
petro-dollar, all of which increasingly mediate Middle Eastern lives,
originate. To put it differently, most Middle Eastern nations are not in a
position to set the global agenda; they react to it from position of
weakness. While in the short term what seems to be at store for many
Middle Eastern countries is a kinder and gentler type of
authoritarianism and not democratization and democracy, as the forces
of globalization and their integrative trust further permeat the region,
the middle class will become a stronger player in social life and the
incipient civil society would gain strength. A new social contract
would then emerge between the ruler and the ruled in which political
inclusion and participation would be an acceptable rule of the game.
Hence, as the region becomes more integrated in the global market, to
remain viable, it has to concede to the demand for rationality,
efficiency, the rule of law and political stability. All of these are better
served by democratic systems. This, however, is not a linear process of
progress; to be sure, there would be twists and turns, progress and
regress, unwinding and unbecoming, liberalization and retrenchment
along the way. In the process, Middle Eastern political systems have to
resolve the conflictual interests of the elite and the mass and the other
contending interests of different groups as they attempt to define their
"democracies," something European democracies had to do over the
past two centuries. The Middle East will" liberalize," carrying its own
cultural baggage and historical tradition, and at the end Middle Eastern
"democracy" is likely to look like anything but its western counterpart.

Clinton Administration and the Middle East

The US policies toward the Middle East under the Clinton
administration represented both elements of continuity with the past as
well as new thinking and strategies. Like the administrations preceding
it, maintaining access to oil at low prices, and preserving the security of
Israel and the oil-rich Arab states in the Persian Gulf remains one of the
top priorities of the Clinton administration. Clinton also took an active
role in the implementation of the Arab-Israeli peace process by helping
the electoral victory of Yitzhak Rabin over Yitzahk Shamir. However,
it failed to ensure a victory for Rabin's successor, Peres. The Clinton
administration harbored none of the "oil sensitivities" of the Bush
administration and in its pro-Israeli policies and sentiments were much

more forceful and unapologetic. This was not the only thing that was new about Clinton's policy.

The centerpiece of Clinton's new thinking is encapsulated in the strategy of "dual containment." Introduced by Martin Indyk in 1993, the policy of dual containment is designed to marginalize, neutralize, isolate, and contain both Iran and Iraq, both of which are regarded as "backlash states" that are hostile to vital American interests in the region. Therefore, through "selective pressure," the US should seek "to transform them into constructive members of the international community". The US must also bolster relations with its regional allies in order to further diminish reliance on Iran and Iraq for security in the Persian Gulf.[21] This policy is also perceived to be linked to Arab-Israeli peace process. By isolating and weakening the two major opponents of Israel in the region, it is argued, the position of Israel will be solidified as the region's unchallenged hegemon.

There has been a conviction on the part of some of the American policymakers that Iran is the new Comintern of the Muslim World, responsible for the spread of Islamic militancy and terrorism.[22] Thus, economic sanctions, the administration's decision in 1995 to ban all US trade and investment with Iran, political pressures and the CIA's $19 million dollar campaign to destabilize Iraqi and Iranian governments were designed ultimately to crumble the Iranain state. In the same fashion that the collapse of the Soviet Union delivered a huge blow to the fortunes of Communism, during the period of 1992-1997, the Clinton administration hoped that the downfall of the Islamic Republic would put a halt to and ultimately extinguish the fires of Islamic militancy.[23] This schema, however, is too simplistic. East and Central Europe were brought to the Communist orbit by the intimidating force of the Red Army after the Second World War. The presence of their mighty neighbor to the north and its forceful military interventions in their domestic affairs (Hungary, 1956, and Czechoslovakia, 1968, to mention a few) reminded them of the cost of mutiny against Moscow. Iran clearly is not in a similar position. Hampered by a debt burden of $30 billion and an inadequate Third World technology, Iran neither has the financial nor military resources necessary to impose its will on its Muslim neighbors even if so aspired. Nor can she afford to do so politically given the tremendous costs associated with such a policy, which would definitely invite a military confrontation with the United States. If prior to the Gulf War of 1991, some Iranian leaders might have entertained some illusions about the outcome of such confrontation, having observed the fate of Saddam's army, they have a more realistic assessment of the limitations of their power. At a time when they are attempting to improve relations with the outside world, the Iranian leaders are less likely to engage in expansionist adventures beyond their borders that would certainly galvanize the public opinion against them. A realistic assessment of Iranian capabilities, resources, and policies indicates that the Iranian threat has been inflated beyond all proportions in order to justify the US military presence in the Persian Gulf.[24]

The roots of Islamic revival in the Muslim world are primarily due to domestic crisis, a sense of malaise and of the inequities of wealth and power. What has transpired in the post-Cold War era is not "a clash of civilizations," as Huntington has contended;[25] but rather a manifestation of global economic integration and the concomitant rise of cultural particularism. The two phenomena are linked organically and one buttresses the other. [26] Islamic revivalism is a part of the global phenomenon of the reemergence of primordial loyalties such as tribalism and nationalism. Thus, in the face of the universalizing and homogenizing logic of post-modern and post-industrial society, we witness the rise of religion, ethnicity, tribalism, and nationalism. The dynamics of Islamic revival go far beyond the intentions or actions of the Islamic Republic of Iran. Neither Tehran nor Washington can chart the future course of this movement or decisively mold its character. The forces that animate the Islamic revival are both global and domestic, traditional and modern; and for the most part these forces are unconscious and unintended consequences of the post-modern society. Tehran is a reactive player in this larger context of global forces. It neither has the resources nor the capability to set the agenda. It reacts to it.

The Clinton administration's dual containment strategy has also failed to bring about the desired end in Iraq. While U.N. sanctions have clearly hurt the Iraqi people, it is not clear if they have substantially undermined Saddam Hussein's regime. Iraqi opposition so far has proven unable to seriously challenge the regime. Despite some dissension in his family, Saddam seems to be resilient. Hence, since the memory of the Gulf War of 1991 still lingers on, it is not likely that Saddam Hussein would embark on another military adventure and engage in extra-territorial war any time soon. Iraq has been stripped of much of its former military might. The Iraqi army was devastated during the Desert Storm. According to one report, the morale in the army is low and many of its leading officers have been purged, the desertion rate is high, and the rumors of coup are rampant. Due to the imposition of sanctions much of the equipment that was destroyed during the Gulf War can not be replaced and spare parts are hard to find. Until the December of 1998, a U.N. force continued to oversee the destruction of non-conventional Iraqi weapons. These developments have seriously hampered Iraqi army's ability to engage in offensive operations beyond its borders.[27] With his domestic economic and political problems, diminished military capabilities, and the anticipation of a decisive retaliatory military response from the United States, Saddam Hussein, is more likely to be preoccupied with survival than expansion in the near future. Iraq also made a few conciliatory gestures indicating a willingness to establish a better relation with the West and its Arab neighbors. In 1994, for example, Iraq recognized Kuwait as a sovereign nation. In the same year Tariq Aziz, the Iraqi deputy Foreign minister, expressed that Iraq does not consider itself "a confrontational state vis-a-vis Israel. He added that Baghdad was open to reconciliation with Israel commensurate with progress between Israelis and Palestinians. Despite the public rhetoric, President Saddam Hussein desires a role in the regional peace process."[28] His harsh and bombastic public ststements notwithstanding, Saddam Hussien also repeatedly backed off in his 1998 showdowns with the United States over the United Nations' inspectors. And when he has taken his brinkmanship too far, he has been severely punished for his defiance as evidenced by the US and Great Britain's bombing of Iraq in December of 1998.

Dual containment also disregards the impact of the Gulf War of 1991 and the political realities of the last decade. As one of the protagonists of the doctrine, Anthony Lake has observed, the two Gulf Wars of the last decade (Iran-Iraqi war and Kuwaiti-Iraqi war) have substantially reduced the offensive military capabilities of both nations. The American-led military operation against Iraq has eliminated the timidity of regional security organizations over calling on Western support if threatened by any hostile action. Hence, relationships between economically powerful Gulf nations and other Middle Eastern countries, notably Egypt and the United States to a considerable measure, neutralizes the impact of Iran and Iraq as powers in the Middle East.[29] Yet this admission did not prevent Mr. Lake from making his condescending recommendation that the US should pressure these" back lash states" into becoming more constructive

members of the World community.[30] Putting "pressure" on Iran and
Iraq has translated into $ 90 billion worth of arms sale to American
allies, thus escalating the regional arms race and maintaining a military
force of 25,000 stationed in Saudi Arabia with the annual cost of $60
billion to be paid by US tax-payers and the Saudi regime. Indeed this
enormous expenditure has prompted some observers to wonder the
wisdom of spending between $30 to $60 billion a year for the defense
of the Gulf in order to protect the import into the United States of some
$30 billion worth of oil.[31] This statistic becomes even more remarkable
in light of the fact that most of the oil from the Gulf states goes to
Japan and Europe.

Dual containment has been criticized as a counterproductive and
self-defeating strategy that may ultimately achieve the opposite of what
was intended. One critic argues that the dual containment of Iran and
Iraq would not be possible without the cooperation of its counterpart.
Moreover, if any of the two countries are drastically weakened, they
become an inviting target for domination by the other, thus upsetting
the regional balance of power. Instead of pitting them against each
other, facing a common adversary, dual containment may bring Iran
and Iraq closer together. This strategy also lacks the active support of
American regional allies. It puts the main responsibility for the Gulf
security on the America's shoulders at a time when the United States
has very little influence to impact events in Iran and Iraq. Not having
any ties to Tehran and Baghdad also increases the possibility of direct
US military involvement in the region to protect the security of the
Gulf monarchies. This possibility increases the tensions between GCC
countries and Iran and Iraq. Many American allies including Egypt and
Turkey have questioned the imposition of continued sanctions on Iraq.
Oman, Qatar and Bahrain fear the consequences of Iraqi disintegration,
and have called for integration of Iraq into the Arab World.

According to International Action Center and the UNICEF the
number of Iraqi children dead under the age of 5 since the imposition of
the U.N. sanctions on Iraq is estimated to be 681,000 and the total
civilian dead is 1.4 million people. Saddam Hussein still remains in
power. The sanctions have not hurt him but they have devastated the
Iraqi people. This toll on human life and the suffering of the innocent
civilians poses major moral dilemmas before US foreign policy makers.
At the moment, it seems that the Clinton administration is willing to
keep the sanctions indefinitely despite its terrible consequences as long
as Saddam is alive. In the process, US has managed to alienate its

Western and Arab allies, who oppose the continuation of the sanctions. The Arab World clearly sees a double standard in US foreign policy. Whereby repeated Israeli violations of the U.N resolutions go unpunished, the Iraqi violations evoke harsh military responses. Netanyahu whose reckless policies has seriously undermined the American brokered peace process, continues to enjoy the Clinton administration's patronage and support. In fact, Iraqi expulsion of U.N. inspectors in November of 1997, and Saddam,s continued defiance of UN inspectors and the Arab World's reluctance to support Washington in its showdown with Iraq demonstrated American diminished influence with Arab countries. The Arab World is bitter about Clinton administration's heavy handed policy toward Iraq and its refusal to seriously press Netanyahu to abandon his intransigent policies.

Many GCC countries also see the isolation of Iran as an ill-advised policy. Instead, they support a policy of positive incentive that would rein Iran in rather than further alienating it. [32] They know that US military presence would not last forever and after the American forces leave the region, they still will have to live with their two powerful neighbors.   There are also indications that the policy of dual containment has brought Iran, Iraq, and Syria closer together.

With a population of seventy million and its strategic and economic significance as one of the two major powers of the Persian Gulf and the second largest Middle East oil producer after Saudi Arabia, Iran remains a significant political actor in the long-term security of the region. The global and regional developments of the last two decades have also convinced Iran of limitations of its own power. The domestic struggle between moderates and the hard liners over the substance and the form of rapprochement with the US not withstanding, the Iranian leadership seems to be willing to normalize relations with the United States. However, Khatami's leadership must first build bipartisan support for normalization of relations with the U.S Given the tenousness and the weaknesses of Mr. Khatami's leadership, achieving this goal has proven to be illusive so far. Khatami also needs to convince the different political constituencies in Iran of the concrete benefits and the windfall that would result from better relations with the US On this issue, the United States can help by engaging both factions of Iranian government in a dialogue toward normalization of relations and provide some positive incentives that would disarm the hard-liners intransigent policy.

Engagement of Iran would enhance the United States' influence in the region by enlisting Iran in regional security pacts. A fundamental change in US policy would put an end to the rift between European allies and Japan and the United States. The European community and Japan have large investments in and lucrative trade with Iran, so the current policy creates a tension between their economic interest and the American policy of pressuring them to boycott the Iranian market. [33] The European allies and Japan that have substantial trade relations with Iran, see American trade embargo and the policy of all sticks and no carrots as a self-defeating policy that would strengthen the position of radical hard liners within the Iranian government. They assert that only a policy of engagement would have a moderating impact on the Iranian regime. Such a policy would stand a better chance of eliciting Iranian cooperation on regional security issues as well. America's regional allies such as Turkey, Kuwait and the United Arab Emirates have also ignored American imposed economic sanctions and have expanded their trade relations with Iran. The participation of 1,500 companies from 54 countries in the 1996 Tehran international trade fair is trumpeted as another indication by Tehran that American imposed sanctions have not been successful in economic isolation of Iran.[34] Only Israel and Uzbakistan responded positively to the American economic sanctions on Iran. Major global powers such as Russia, Canada, Japan and China, for the most part, ignored the American call. In fact, some observers contend that the Iranian economy is in better shape than most regional powers that are the recipient of American aid.[35]

The Iranian revolution has run its course and the Iranian government is no longer seeking to actively export its revolution. In fact, Iranian leaders perceive their own behavior as conciliatory. They point out that it was Iraq that initiated the two extra-territorial wars of the region in the last two decades. In contrast, Iran has not displayed any belligerent conduct toward its neighbors. They refer to their responsible position during the Gulf War of 1991 and their instrumental role in releasing the Western hostages in Lebanon as indications of their positive political role in the region. [36]

As the PLO-Israeli peace process, despite its faltering moments, seems to be irreversible, the Islamic party HAMAS will be more pressured to negotiate with the PLO to join the political process. As soon as a Syrian- Israeli peace accord materializes or the relations between Tehran and Tel Aviv improves, it is very likely that Hizballah which has close relations with Syria and Iran would opt for a more accommodationist course toward Israel as well. Iran would also have to reassess its present oppositional stand toward the peace process if and when Syrian-Israeli peace accords become reality.[37] In fact, there were some movements in this direction. On July 29, 1996, Netanyahu praised Iran for its role in facilitating the swap of prisoners and bodies between Hezbollah and Israel through German mediation. With German and Russian mediation there are some low-key negotiations underway between Tehran and Tel Aviv. Israelis are questioning if their policy of an all-out confrontation with Iran has been productive. Initiatives that may signal provision of some positive incentive for Tehran to be more forthcoming toward Tel Aviv could be under way. Israel knows that Iran can help to moderate Hezbollah's policies. Iran for its part knows that improvement of relations with Israel is the key to normalization of its relations with Washington. Both sides have a lot at stake.

Some observers poignantly argue that as US engagement of revolutionary China ultimately had a moderating impact on Chinese government and proved to be beneficial to both sides, the same can be said in favor of engaging revolutionary Iran. While the US and Iran may disagree on many political issues, this should not prevent either side from pursuing a constructive relation, which serves the mutual interests of both sides.[38] Others, such as the former national security adviser to President Carter, Zbigniew Brzezinski, have argued that the US needs a "good strategic relationship with Iran in the long run if we are to have not only stability in the Persian Gulf, but access to Central Asia."[39]

Even before Clinton's reelection, as early as October 24, 1996, US Assistant Secretary of State Robert Pelletreau told a gathering of business executives in Dubai that "the current lack of dialogue with Tehran was unsatisfactory."[40] As the number of foreign policy analysts who called for a reassessment of dual containment strategy increased, at a time when both Russia and China were improving and expanding trade and diplomatic relations with Iran, the Clinton administration came under pressure to take a second look at its policy. With the election of the moderate leader, Muhammad Khatemi in May of 1997, and his inititive to improve relations with "great American people", the Clinton administration responded positively to overtures from Tehran.[41] Having won the presidential election by a landslide, Khatami clearly had a mandate for change. The Iranian people have overwhelmingly voted for reform and modification of hard line policies of the past that would end Iran's isolation. Having the public opinion behind him, Khatami decided to break from the past rhetoric of intransigence and confrontation and publically invited US government to establish a dialogue, something his predecessors, lacking his popular mandate, could not afford to do. The timing of Khatami's inititive was an opportune one, right after the December 8-11 1997 Islamic Summit in Tehran that included a number of close American allies including Saudi Arabia, Egypt, Kuwait, and Turkey. Iran's agenda in the Islamic Summit was two fold. First, to mend relations with its Arab neighbors. Second, to modify Iran's image as a pariah and establish her return to the mainstream politics of Middle East. While the conference passed a resolution condemning terrorism, it refrained from passing a resolution to condemn the Arab-Israeli peace process. In light of previous Iranian opposition to the peace process, this was a significant new development. These can be seen as two distinct conciliatory gestures toward the United States' government, designed to prompt a reassessment of its Iran policy.   Even before President Khatami's inititive, some of the major foreign policy experts and advisers such as Brent Scowcroft, Zbigniew Brezezinski and Richard Murphy had recommended abandoning the policy of dual containment in favor of a policy of differentiation between Iran and Iraq that would allow Washington to initiate a constructive dialogue with Iran, paving the way to normalization of relations in future.[42]They argued that Iran and the United States have mutual interest in access to Central Asia and both sides will benefit from expanded commercial and trade relations. A shift in the attitudes of some of the key foreign policy advisors as well as the new initiatives from president Khatemi induced the secretary of state Madeline Albright's speech of June 17,1998. Albright's speech was a positive overture to Iran, seeking a "road map to amity."[43] This was followed by President Clinton's offer of dialogue during the Iran-US soccer match in the World Cup. But given the campaign of public vilification, the lingering mistrust, and possible domestic political backlash, both sides are likely to proceed cautiously, behind the scenes and very low key.

Improvement of relations between Washington and Tehran has also prompted the Saudi regime to seek closer relations with Iran in order to bolster its Islamic legitimacy and safeguard against a possible backlash of its close embracement of Washington. As the Saudi government faces an increasingly active Islamic opposition, it hopes closer relations with Tehran will prevent possible Iranian alliance with its domestic Muslim opposition forces. Iran for its part hopes that better relations with Saudi Arabia, a close ally of the United States, will prove to the Americans and their European allies that Iran is not interested in subverting the Saudi regime and it can be relied upon as a partner in future regional security arrangements. While in 1996 Iran's relations with the GCC countries deteriorated, in 1997 after the diplomatic visits of Mr. Valayati, Iran's former foreign minister to the GCC nations, there has been considerable improvement in the relationship between Iran and its Arab Gulf neighbors. As a sign of apparent warming between Tehran and Ryiadth, the former President Rafsanjani went to Mecca on a pilgrimage in 1998. This trip was followed by President Khatami's trip to expand political and economic ties between the two nations in March 1999. Clearly, there is a distinct detente underway between the two countries. If the policy of containment is completely abandoned in near future, then the possibility of a future dialogue between the US and a defanged Saddam Hussein cannot be ruled out either.

Economic Imperatives and Foreign Policy

As the sole remaining military superpower in the post-Cold War era, the U.S and her allies no longer face an immediate security risk. America could now turn its attention to improving its economic competitiveness. As the source of power shifts from military power to economic power, even for American military power to remain relevant, America has to revitalize its economy. This new reality has reflected itself in the new thinking on foreign policy. Increasingly, geo-strategic considerations in US foreign policy have given way to geo-economics. Compared to previous administrations, under Clinton, businessmen and the executives of major corporations have a more substantial input in the process of foreign policymaking. While politico-military aspects of foreign policy still remain significant, foreign economic policy now constitutes a more significant element of overall strategy.

In the age of shrinking governmental budgets, political and military commitments have been minimized and pro-longed and costly wars and conflicts are avoided. Instead, expansion of free trade, access to new markets and creation of new jobs have assumed top priority in foreign policy making. Hence, in pursuit of cutting costs and forging legitimacy, unilateral actions of the past, manifested by US involvement in Vietnam for more than a decade, are now replaced by a preference for partnership and coalition building. This new thinking has been demonstrated in the major wars and conflicts that the United States has been involved in since the end of the Cold War. The Gulf War of 1991, the Somalian civil war of 1992 and the ethnic war in former Yugoslavia (1990-1996), are all salient examples. Moreover, the imposition of sanctions and peace keeping and peace making missions are deemed to be less costly and more conducive to the overall US strategy in the post-Cold War era.

With the Soviet threat no more, American access to oil secured, and a strong Israel at peace with its Arab neighbors, the Middle East no longer demands the urgent attention of the US as it did during the Cold War. If in the past Middle East conflicts invited superpower intervention and were internationalized as several Arab-Israeli wars of the past attest, now these conflicts are localized. As one scholar has put it: "Washington's role could now be confined to serving as a military insurance agency and diplomatic fire brigade-ensuring that Iran and Iraq are marginalized and safeguarding the peace process from potential Arab-Israeli tensions".[44] Middle East conflicts are now regarded as one of many conflicts that plague the Third World. This new strategy is dubbed as "low cost Pax-Americana"[45], where American involvement requires the least commitment of financial and military resources. With the American position in the region being the strongest it has been in decades, America can now turn its attention to troubles brewing in the former Soviet Union and East and Central Europe. America can also turn its attention to more pressing issues such as improving its economic competitiveness and wining the trade wars. In fact, America's strength in the Middle East may become an asset in the trade war. As the economic competition among the three trading blocks (EU, NAFTA and ASEAN) escalates, America may use the vulnerability of Europe and Japan to the flow of oil from Middle East in order to manipulate the supply of oil "as a way of pressuring the EU to cut agricultural subsidies and trying to force Japan to open its markets to American products."[46]

With the emerging markets of the former Soviet Republics and East and Central Europe and unprecedented opportunities presented by economic growth in China and East Asia, America can easily afford to ignore its loss of Iranian or Iraqi markets and "squeeze them" until they display "acceptable behavior" and come to the negotiation table on its terms.[47] This has been clearly the Clinton administration's economic rationale behind the dual containment strategy. Enfeebled and vulnerable economically and militarily, Iran and Iraq may find that the arena for their political maneuvering has shrunk and their options are few. They can no longer pit one superpower against another as they did during the Cold War. Therefore, it is plausible that the governments in Baghdad and Tehran may have to choose a more accommodationist course of action as has been evinced in Iran by president Khatemi's initiatives already.

As the Middle East loses its former strategic significance, bereft of ideological mandate of the Cold War, America's definition of its national interest in the region also becomes increasingly "domesticated" and the domestic imperatives take command in formulation of foreign policy. The most influential political actors and interests in Washington set the agenda of American foreign policy and increasingly, geo-economic considerations are replacing geo-political ones. America's close alliance with Saudi Arabia, for example, has translated into lucrative business contracts for American companies. The signing of $7.5 billion deal between Boeing and McDonald Douglas in 1995 and $4 billion contract with AT&T to modernize Saudi telecommunication systems are indicative of this trend.[48] Indeed part of the rationale for maintaining a force of 25,000 at the cost of $60 billion a year is deemed to be "preferential access" to the lucrative Persian Gulf markets.[49]

But the potential instability of the region also renders Pax-Americana vulnerable and the present "unipolar moment" as a passing phase. A combination of depleting Saudi financial assets,[50] and increasing level of education unmatched by financial opportunities, and some political opening for dialogue and criticism since 1991 has culminated in the birth of the Islamic opposition that is now challenging the Saudi Monarchy.[51] The small traditional sheikhdoms of the Persian Gulf have also experienced their share of turmoil since the Gulf War of 1991. The government in Baharain had to resort to force to put down a pro-democracy movement in 1994 and is being challenged by a suppressed Shi'ite opposition. Qatar experienced an inner family Coup d'etat in 1995, when the crown prince Hamid bin Khalifa al Thani ousted his father and declared himself the new leader.

The Egyptian Government of Hosni Mubarak with its chronic economic and demographic problems is being challenged by Islamic forces. Iran and Iraq face political isolation, economic crisis and an uncertain future. The future projections for many oil producing nations with smaller reserves is also not very promising. If the price of oil does not increase substantially in the next decade, and the present rate of population growth, production, and consumption continues, by the year 2020 many oil producing nations of the region would be net importers of oil to satisfy their domestic energy needs. Petroleum and petro dollar have provided a vital economic resource for a region that as of yet has not developed a viable industrial or agricultural output that can replace the oil income. If the above prediction turns out to be correct, in light of the fact that most countries of the region which are net importers of food stuff and have been financing their purchases with income from oil, then the more profound economic and political crisis of the region may yet be ahead.

Thus, the status quo upon which the Pax-Americana is based may not endure long and new crises and conflicts may emerge to challenge its foundations. This fragility is indicative of the fact that any enduring security arrangement requires full participation of major powers of the Gulf region, including Iran and Iraq. As long as security in the Gulf is perceived as a balancing act primarily designed to safeguard Western interests and protect the conservative monarchies of the region, in the eyes of the popular masses it would lack legitimacy and would remain tenuous.

Conclusion

It is ironic that in the age of the fall of paradigms imposed by the dizzying pace of change in the late twentieth century, many US policymakers are still looking for a neat paradigm to deal with foreign political systems. In their preoccupation with quick and simple formulas and solutions and their distaste for complexity and nuance, some bureaucrats and policymakers have conjured up the ghost of the Truman Doctrine of containment, applying it to the Middle East. While the Cold War has ended, the Cold War mentality persists. The dual containment is reminiscent of Cold War thinking. In the post-Cold War era when peaceful resolution of conflict, peace making, and peace building have become a growth industry, national and international interests must also be redefined as a cooperative endeavor. Security must no longer be conceived as a zero sum game in which one side must lose if the other is to win. Rather, it should be conceived as a mutually beneficial process in which both sides stand to gain from commonly agreed security arrangements. As Max Weber in his inaugural lecture of 1895 asserted, "we shall not succeed in banishing the curse that besets us, that of being born too late for a great political era, unless we understand how to become the forerunners of a greater one."[52] The Clinton administration's dual containment strategy lags behind the new thinking required for the new realities of the post-Cold War era. Released from the burden of the Cold War, America has ample opportunity to use its vast resources to redefine global politics in a positive, innovative, and more humane fashion. The politically explosive and conflictual nature of the Middle East provides America with a unique opportunity to implement this new policy.

In its attempt to broaden the base of the new security arrangement in the region, the US has courted Syria. Washington has also sought a peace settlement between Syria and Israel. But to build enduring peace and stability in the region, Washington needs to normalize relations with and enlist the support of Iran as well. The secretary Albright's speech of June 17, 1998 and offering of an olive branch to Iranian leaders is a positive step that needs to be followed by bolder initiatives on both sides in order to break through the barriers of mistrust and mutual vilification of the last nineteen years. As the largest oil producer after Saudi Arabia in OPEC and the gateway to Central Asia, Iran remains indispensable for any long-term security arrangements in the Middle East. The US must also lift the sanctions against Iraq, ensure that the territorial integrity of Iraq remains intact, and bring Iraq gradually back to the Arab World. This may not be as easily achievable with Saddam Hussein still in charge, but at present there are no other alternatives and there are no indications that he may depart from the political scene any time soon. A policy of all sticks and no carrots limits the options and flexibility in American foreign policy and leaves very few incentives for the leaders of Iran and Iraq to modify their behavior. Hence, in the long run, the security of GCC and Egypt will also be better served and regional tensions would decrease by abandoning the policy of dual containment in favor of a more balanced policy of constuctive engagement.

Notes

1. Manochehr Dorraj, "The New Word Order: Prospects for the Third World", Hamid Zanganeh, ed, Islam, Iran and World Stability, (New York: St. Martin's press, 1994), pp. 13-40.
2. Tareq Y. Ismael and Jacqueline S. Ismael, eds, The Gulf War and the New World Order, (Gainesville: University Press of Florida, 1994), pp.1-21.

3. Phebe Marr, "Strategies for an Era of Uncertainty: The US Policy Agenda", Phebe Marr and William Lewis, eds. Riding the Tiger: Middle East Challenge After the Cold War, (Boulder: Westview Press, 1993), p.213.

4. Ibid., pp.219-234.

5. Jerry Sanders, "History and World Order: Framing the Past to Shape the Future", Harry Kreisler, ed, Confrontation in the Gulf, (Berkley: Institute of International Studies, University of California, 1992), pp.157-158.

6. Mikhail Gorbachev, A Time for Peace, (New York: Richardson and Steirman, 1986). See also Perestroika: New Thinking for Our Country and the World, (New York: Harper&Row,1987).

7. Said K. Aburish, The Rise, Corruption and Coming Fall of the House of Saud, (New York: St. Martin's press, 1995).

8. Gregory Aftandilian, Egypt's Bid for Arab Leadership: Implications for US Foreign Policy, (New York: Council on foreign relations press, 1993), p. 10.

9. Nasrin Jewell and Raymond A. Hinnebusch, "Iran, Egypt, and The Middle East State System in the post-Gulf War New World Order", Critique, Spring 1993, No.2, pp.3-4.

10. Ibid.

11. Ibid., p.10

12. Michael Hudson, "To Play the Hegemon: Fifty Years of US Policy Toward the Middle East", The Middle East Journal , Vol. 50, No.3, Summer 1996, p.341.

13. Graham Fuller and Ian Lesser, A Sense of Siege: Geopolitics of Islam and the West, (Boulder: Westview Press, 1995).

14. Leon T. Hadar, "What Green Peril"?, Foreign Affairs, Spring 1993, p. 40.

15. Stephen Zunes, "Hazardous Hegemony: The United States in the Midlle East", Current History , January 1997, p.23.

16. Dilip Hiro, "The Gulf Between the Ruler and the Ruled", New Statesman and Society, February 28, 1993. As cited by Zunes, Ibid., p.24.

17. Robin Wright, "Islam, Democracy and the West", Foreign Affairs, Summer 1992, p. 25.

18. Fort Worth Star-Telegram, December 10, 1997, p. 16.

19. Fort Worth Star-Telegram, December 15, 1997, p. 11.

20. Stanlet Reed, "The Battle for Egypt", Foreign Affairs, Vol.72, No.4, 1993, p.99.

21. Anthony Lake, "Confronting Backlash States", Foreign Affairs: Agenda 1995, pp.141-143.

22. The former secretary of state Warren Christopher for example, was particularly outspoken in advocating a hard line toward Tehran. See Elaine Sciolino "Christopher signals a tougher US line toward Iran", The New York Times , 31 March 1993. For a critical appraisal of this policy see Ellen Laipson, Garry Sick and Richard Cottam, "Symposium: US Policy Toward Iran: From Containment to Relentless Pursuit", Middle East Policy, Vol. 15, September 1995, No. 1&2, pp.1-21.

23. One analyst summarizes the sentiment of many observers of Middle Eastern and Iranian politics very well:
"Many are bemused by the way Washington has developed an unhealthy obsession with Iran, demonising it and attributing to it any and all unexplained outrages. with support only from Israel and Uzbakistan, the US has been willing to alienate its allies, endanger its international ties and undermine free trade policies. It has put its prestige on the line, watching Europe draw up counter-legislation and NATO allies such as Turkey complete a massive gas supply deal despite US pressure."   Vahe Petrossian, "US escalates war of words against Iran", Middle East Economic Digest, Vol. 40, No. 35, 30 August 1996, p.2.

24. Michael Dunn, " Five Years After Desert Storm", Middle East Policy , Vol. 15, No.3, March 1996, p. 35.

25. Samuel Huntington, "The Clash of Civilizations?", Foreign Affairs, Summer 1993.

26. Benjamin R. Barber, Jihad vs. McWorld: How Globalism and Tribalism are Reshaping the World ,(New York: Ballantine Books, 1996).

27. Michael Dunn, Op.cit.

28. Rolin G. Mainuddin, Joseph R. Aicher, Jr. and Jeffrey M. Elliot, "From Alliance to Collective Security: Rethinking the Gulf Cooperation Council", Middle East Policy, Vol. 15, No.3, March 1996, p.46.

29. Anthony Lake, Op.cit., pp. 143-145.

30. Ibid.

31. Graham Fuller and Ian lesser, "Persian Gulf Myths", Foreign Affairs, May/June 1997, p.43.

32. F. Gregory Gause III, "The Illogic of Dual Containment", Foreign Affairs: Agenda 1995, pp. 150-160.

33. Alon Ben-Meir, "The Dual Containment Strategy is no Longer Viable", Middle East Policy, Vol. 15,No. 3, March 1996, pp. 63-64.

34. Jahangir Amuzegar, "Adjusting to Sanctions", Foreign Affairs , Vol.76, No.3, May/ June 1997, pp.31-41.

35. Ibid., p.39.

36. Alon Ben-Meir, op. cit., p.59.

37. Ibid., pp.64-65.

38. Ibid.

39. "Iran: second look in second term?" Middle East Economic Digest , Vol. 40, No. 46, 15, November 1996, p.2.

40. Ibid.

41. The congressional reaction to Khatami's electoral victory however, was not encouraging. In 1997 several members of congress released a letter to president Clinton signed by 222 US house members, calling on the administration to keep its tough sanction policy against Iran and do more to encourage Europeans to join in this effort to isolate Iran economically. These members believed that the election of Muhammad Khatami brought Iran no closer to changing its policies. In the same spirit, the House Speaker, Newt Gingrich reportedly said that "since the collapse of the Soviet Union and the former Warsaw pact, Iran now poses the biggest security threat to Europe." Fort Worth Star-Telegram, December 15, 1997, p. 11.

42. Brent Scowcroft, Zbigniew Brezizinsky, Richard Murphy, "Differentiated Containment" , Foreign Affairs, Vol. 76,   No. 3,   April 1997, pp. 20-30.

43. The New York Times, Thursday, June 18,1998, p.1.

44. Leo Hadar , "America's Moment in the Middle East", Current History, Vol. 95, No.597, January 1996, p.2.

45. Ibid. p.3.

46. Ibid. p.5.

47. Anthony Lake, op. cit., pp. 140-149.

48. Hadar, op. cit., p. 5.

49. Fuller&Lesser, "Persian Gulf Myths", op. cit., p.45.

50. Saudi Arabia which boasted of an asset of $120 billion prior to the Gulf War, by 1995 had only an asset of $60 billion. The Gulf War is estimated to have cost the Saudis $70 billions.

51. Madawi Al-Rasheed , "Saudi Arabia's Islamic opposition", Current history, Vol. 95, No. 597, January 1996, pp. 16-22. See also Michael Collins Dunn ,"Is

the sky falling? Saudi Arabia's Economic problems and political stability",
Middle East Policy, Vol. 3, No. 4, April 1995, pp. 29-41.

52. Max Weber, Gesammelte Politische Schriften, 3rd.ed., johannes
Winckelmann,ed. (Tubingen: Mohr Siebeck, 1971), p.24. As cited by Charles
S. Maier, "Democracy and its Discontents", Foreign Affairs: Agenda 1995,
p.40.

Chapter 3

The Fate of Human Rights in the Middle East and North Africa

Mahmood Monshipouri

Introduction

The legacy of authoritarianism, stunted civility, and patriarchy in the Middle East and North Africa is in question. The struggle for human rights, however, is stymied by a wide array of structural, institutional, and cultural forces. Since the 1970s, Islamic revivalism has added a twist to the issues of human rights in the region. In those Middle Eastern and North African countries where political openings have expanded civil society and promoted some democratic measures, Islamic movements have been the main beneficiaries of change. These countries' nascent democratization has never moved beyond the electoral stage to embrace a viable system of human rights and the rule of law. In some cases (especially in North Africa) elections results have been nullified.

The reconstruction of political Islam in response to the failure of secular nationalist regimes has led Islamic groups into political struggle against the status quo. Because they question the ethos of both liberal democracy and secular nationalism, these revivalists movements appear intent on challenging the modernizing, secular elite while renewing the basic Islamic values, ideologies, and codex. In response to this challenge, secular regimes have defended secularization in the name of human rights. They argue that women and minorities have been beneficiaries of their secular programs, as has civil society as a whole. Instead of taking a Western comparative perspective, which typically combines history and cultural-religious anthropology, this chapter adopts an empirical approach toward understanding the region's human rights conditions. To this end, the chapter examines the relationship between civil-political rights and socioeconomic conditions, the rights of women, the rights of minorities, the refugee problem, the role of Islam in the promotion of democracy, and the future of Islamism, civil society, and democracy. First, however, a brief note on the definition of human rights and an overview of the ratification or accession to human rights conventions by the region's countries is provided in the following section.

Definition of Human Rights

The concept of *human rights* continues to be a contested term. The Western World refers to the rights enunciated in the Universal Declaration of Human Rights (UDHR) as internationally recognized human rights. The UDHR include civil and political rights as well as economic, social, and cultural rights. The Western traditions, however, have emphasized the necessity of civil-political rights to the actual enjoyment of the other rights. That is to say, the freedom of thought, conscience, religion, expression, association, political participation, and equal protection under the law are widely regarded as essential to the realization of economic, social, and cultural rights.

The Muslim World, on the other hand, tends to underscore the importance of economic, social, and cultural rights: the right to work, the right to strike, to social security, and to an adequate standard of living; and the right to physical and mental health, education, and participation in cultural life, and to benefit from scientific, literary, or artistic production. Many Muslim countries have pressed for a so-called "third generation" of rights – sometimes known as "solidarity rights." These include the rights to development, to a healthy environment, to peace, to humanitarian aid, and to the benefits of an international common heritage.

Scholarly works within the two worlds reflect this conceptual division. Whereas Western scholars tend to stress the primacy of civil-political rights, the Muslim observers rate socioeconomic and cultural rights as equally important. A limited but growing number of Western

scholars reject a dichotomy between political and economic rights.[1] At
both theoretical and empirical levels, Muslim countries continue to rely
in practice on nativistic approaches to human dignity and equality.
Given that human rights and human dignity are interrelated concepts, it
can be argued that since Islamic societies recognize human dignity,
they have some conceptions of human rights, however different they
may be from their Western counterparts.

Many in the Muslim world argue that human rights legislation has
failed to respect their culture, customs, and legal traditions and that it
has interfered in their internal affairs. They insist that Muslim nations
must be allowed to stress economic development over human rights. It
is, however, safe to say that certain standards of human rights must be
realized and implemented, regardless of the diversity of historical,
cultural, and politico-economic conditions among societies. Genocide,
torture, mass starvation, racial discrimination, and the denial of
people's right to self-determination are *grave* violations of human
rights that must be denounced under all circumstances. Increasingly,
points of convergence on a broad range of rights, including rights to
political participation, are emerging. The Muslim world is not and will
not be immune from such global challenges.

International Human Rights Conventions

Many Middle Eastern and North African countries have ratified or
acceded to human rights conventions. Of the 21 countries under
scrutiny here (see Table One), eight countries are a party neither to the
International Covenant on Civil and Political Rights (ICCPR) nor to the
International Covenant on Economic, Social, and Cultural Rights
(ICESCR). These include Bahrain, Kuwait, Oman, Pakistan, Qatar,
Saudi Arabia, Turkey, and United Arab Emirates. Nearly half of the
region's countries have ratified or signed the Convention Against
Torture and other Cruel, Inhuman and Degrading Treatment or
Punishment. These include Algeria, Egypt, Israel, Jordan, Libya,
Morocco, Sudan (signed but not yet ratified), Tunisia, Turkey, and
Yemen (see Table One). The following countries have also ratified
both the Convention relating to the Status of Refugees (1951) and the
Protocol relating to the Status of Refugees (1967): Algeria, Egypt, Iran,
Israel, Sudan, Tunisia, Turkey, and Yemen.[2]

Country·	ICCPR	ICESCR	Convention against Torture and other Cruel, Inhuman or Degrading Treatment or Punishment
Algeria	x	x	x
Bahrain	-	-	-
Egypt	x	x	x
Iran	x	x	-
Iraq	x	x	-
Israel	x	x	x
Jordan	x	x	x
Kuwait	-	-	-
Lebanon	x	x	-
Libya	x	x	x
Morocco	x	x	x
Oman	-	-	-
Pakistan	-	-	-
Qatar	-	-	-
Saudi Arabia	-	-	-
Sudan	x	x	s
Syria	x	x	-
Tunisia	x	x	x
Turkey	-	-	x
UAE	-	-	-
Yemen	x	x	x

Table One: International Conventions
*s   denotes that country has signed but not yet ratified.
*x   denotes that country is a party, either through ratification, accession or succession.
Source: *Amnesty International: The 1995 Report on Human Rights Around the World*, Alameda, CA: Hunter House, 1995, pp. 334-342.

Civil-Political Rights and Socioeconomic Conditions

The link between civil-political rights and socioeconomic conditions has been widely discussed, explored, and analyzed. No consensus, however, exists as to the exact nature of this relationship. An effort to compare the degrees of political freedoms with socioeconomic conditions in the Middle East and North Africa reveals interesting results. The human development index (HDI) of the United Nations Development Programme (UNDP) provides a measure of socioeconomic conditions in the Middle Eastern countries. The HDI measures whether people lead a long and healthy life (life expectancy), are educated and knowledgeable (adult literacy), and enjoy a decent standard of living (per capita income).

Only three countries (Israel, Jordan, and Turkey) show good records in both human development and civil-political rights (see Table Two). With the exception of Sudan, which is a dreadfully poor country, some of these countries with relatively high indices of human development do not display equivalent human rights records. These include Algeria, Iran, Iraq, Libya, Qatar, Saudi Arabia, and Syria. Several of these countries (Iraq, Libya, Saudi Arabia, Sudan, and Syria) are ranked among the 20 worst rated countries from the viewpoint of civil-political rights.[3]

Yemen and Sudan have the worst human development indices in the region; yet, they differ on comparative measures of freedom. Sudan's leaders have not allowed general elections since 1989, when General Omar Hassan Ahmad al-Bashir led a military coup that overthrew the pro-Western civilian, elected government of Sadiq al Mahdi. Yemen's initial drive toward reunification and the expansion of civil society led to a considerable improvement in civil rights, the results of which were disrupted by ensuing civil war.

Several important conclusions can be drawn from the comparisons in Table Two. First, it is clear that internal dynamics of different states play an important role in determining the state of human rights in these countries. The political leaders of these states ultimately determine the state of human rights. The type of political structure in states such as authoritarian and premodern (Sudan) or democratic and modern (Turkey) predicts the degree of human rights better than the HDI. The link between socioeconomic progress and civil-political rights is not *causal* in that countries with better HDI have not necessarily demonstrated better records in civil-political rights arenas. This is consistent with the assertion that civil and political rights develop independently of social and economic conditions and even rights.[4] Only when progress measured by the HDI is blended with a balanced and steady economic and political liberalization can the HDI be regarded as a vehicle for measuring human rights.

Country	HDI	PR	CL	Freedom Ratings
	1992			1992
Algeria	0.73	7	6	Not Free
Bahrain	0.86	6	5	Partly Free
Egypt	0.61	5	6	Partly Free
Iran	0.77	6	6	Not Free
Iraq	0.62	7	7	Not Free
Israel	0.91	2	2	Free
Jordan	0.76	3	3	Partly Free
Kuwait	0.82	5	5	Partly Free
Lebanon	0.68	5	4	Partly Free
Libya	0.77	7	7	Not Free
Morocco	0.55	6	5	Partly Free
Oman	0.72	6	5	Partly Free
Pakistan	0.48	4	5	Partly Free
Qatar	0.84	7	6	Not Free
Saudi Arabia	0.76	7	7	Not Free
Sudan	0.38	7	7	Not Free
Syria	0.76	7	7	Not Free
Tunisia	0.76	6	5	Partly Free
Turkey	0.79	2	4	Partly Free
UAE	0.86	6	5	Partly Free
Yemen	0.42	6	4	Partly Free

Table Two: A Comparative Survey
Sources: For UNDP Human Development Index (HDI), see *UNDP Human Development Report, 1995. United Nations, 1995.* pp. 155-157. For political rights (PR), civil liberties (CL), and Freedom Ratings, see *Freedom in the World: The Annual Survey of Political Rights and Civil Liberties, 1992-1993,* New York: The Freedom House, 1993, pp. 620-621.

The Status of Women: Gender Equality in Perspective

The elimination of discrimination based on gender is the moral kernel of human rights for women. Violations of women's rights are widespread in the region. In Saudi Arabia, which represents an extreme case of such abuses, women do not have identification cards and are barred from travelling alone without permission from a male relative. They are also limited to jobs in teaching, nursing and journalistic writing. The Arab states of the Middle East have the least political participation by women of any region.[5] In 1994, women held only 4% of the seats in Parliaments and had one percent of the ministerial positions. On the average, in the least developed countries, women held 6% of the seats in Parliaments and had 5% of the ministerial positions (see Table Three).[6]

The status of women in modern Middle Eastern and North African countries seems, to some degree, unrelated to religion. Those who have thoroughly examined the premodern *Shari'a*, make a persuasive case that male interpreters have distorted the *Shari'a* because of vested interests in preserving the patriarchal system.[7] Nikki R. Keddie, a prominent historian, finds that the Quranic provisions for women's rights have followed selectively instances connected with several patriarchal tribal practices, including rules of inheritance, veiling, seclusion, divorce and polygamy. The mere existence of such provisions has in practice meant no assurance of their actual realization.[8] The status of women, Walid Saif concurs, has altered in the course of Muslim history and has been molded by a male dominated society and culture. This, Saif adds, has not only influenced *fiqh* (Islamic jurisprudence) in different ways, but also resulted in many Muslims confusing some inherited traditional cultural values with Islamic values.[9] In short, male prejudice and the force of habit account for poor status of women in these countries.

In Pakistan, great strides have been made in enhancing women's status: five percent of jobs have been earmarked for women in all government and government-controlled organizations. For the first time in the country's history, female judges have been appointed to supreme courts. Police stations exclusively by women have been set up. A comprehensive Social Action Programme has been launched to improve literacy and health care in the rural areas.[10] In Turkey, legal measures are being adopted to eliminate violence against women.[11]

	Local Municipalities		Parliamentary Upper and Lower		Executive
	Female Council Members	Female Mayors	Share of Seats held by women		Women at Ministerial Level
	(%)	(%)	(%)	(%)	
	1990-94	1990-94	(as of 30/6/1994)	(as of 31/5/1994)	
Algeria	..	..	12	7	4
Bahrain	..	..	--	--	0
Egypt	1	..	10	2	4
Iran	..	..	9	3	0
Iraq	..	..	27	11	0
Israel	11	0	11	9	9
Jordan	..	..	3	3	3
Kuwait	..	..	0	0	0
Lebanon	..	0	3	2	0
Libya	..	..	..	..	0
Morocco	0	..	2	1	0
Oman	..	..	--	--	0
Pakistan	..	..	5	2	4
Qatar	..	..	--	--	0
S. Arabia	..	..	--	--	0
Sudan	..	..	14	5	0
Syria	..	..	21	8	7
Tunisia	14	0	11	7	4
Turkey	1	0	8	2	5
UAE	..	..	0	0	0
Yemen	11	..	2	1	0

Table Three: Women and Political Participation
Source: *Human Development Report 1995*, pp. 60-62.

Gender Empowerment Measure

The gender empowerment measure (GEM) focuses on economic, political, and professional participation by women. It specifically examines whether women and men are able to actively participate in economic and political life. It differs from the gender-related development index (GDI), which is concerned primarily with basic capabilities and living standards. The GEM concentrates on three variables: per capita income in PPP dollars, the share of jobs classified as professional, technical, administrative, or managerial which are held by women, and the share of parliamentary seats held by women. The GEM for 116 countries with comparable data shows that Turkey, Kuwait, and the United Arab Emirates have very low GEM values compared with their GDI values. Similarly, Turkey and many Arab states rank much lower in the GEM than they do in real GDP per capita. The United Arab Emirates ranks third in real GDP per capita among 116 countries, but 94 in the GEM. Kuwait ranks 32 in GDP per capita and 93 in the GEM (see Table Four). This owes much to the fact that neither country has any women in parliament. In the United Arab Emirates, women hold fewer than 2% of the administrative and managerial positions and receive only 7% of the earned income.[12]

	Gender Empowerment Measure	Seats held in Parliament	Administrators & Managers	Professional & Technical Workers	Earned Income Share
		1994	1992	1992	
GEM rank	(GEM)	(% women)	(% women)	(% women)	(% women)
47 Iraq	0.386	10.800	12.700	43.900	17.700
81 Syria	0.285	8.400	5.600	26.400	11.300
85 Morocco	0.271	0.600	25.600	24.100	16.400
87 Algeria	0.266	6.700	5.900	27.600	7.500
91 Tunisia	0.254	6.800	7.300	17.600	19.500
93 Kuwait	0.241	0.000	5.200	36.800	18.400
94 UAE	0.239	0.000	1.600	25.100	6.800
95 Iran	0.237	3.500	3.500	32.600	14.900
96 Egypt	0.237	2.200	10.400	28.300	8.200
98 Turkey	0.234	1.800	4.300	31.900	30.200
99 Jordan	0.230	2.500	5.400	33.800	9.800
102 Sudan	0.219	4.600	2.400	28.800	18.500
103 Lebanon	0.212	2.300	2.100	37.800	21.800
114 Pakistan	0.153	1.600	2.900	18.400	10.200

Table Four: Gender Empowerment Measure
Data was available for the above countries.
Source: *World Development Report 1995*, pp. 84-85.

GEM means more GDI and more political development. Above all, its logic shatters traditional roles for women in the overall process of change. It is a challenge to Bedowin tribal habits and the region's long tradition of authoritarianism. In sum, empowering women is a sure way to link economic growth with human development. The issues of gender and development cannot be separated if we are to better explore ways to empower women in socioeconomic and political arenas.

Gender-related Development Index

The gender-related development index (GDI) measures achievement in the same basic capabilities as the HDI does, but takes note of inequalities between women and men. The greater the disparity between genders in a nation, the lower a country's GDI will be when compared with its HDI. Arab states have made the fastest progress in the last two decades by many indicators of human development, especially in literacy for women. Nevertheless, much investment in basic human capabilities is needed before women can catch up with men.[13]   In the United Arab Emirates, the literacy rate in 1970 was 9% for women and 27% for men. In 1992, the rates were almost equal, at 77%. Except for Kuwait, Egypt, and Sudan, all the Arab states rose in rank (see Table Five). Most of the Arab states registered impressive increases in GDI value during 1970-1992 ranging from 70% to 130% (see Table Five).

Rank	GDI Percentage Change in value		Rank	Minus Rank
	1970	1992	in 1970	in 1992
58 Algeria	0.252	0.508	101	6
39 Bahrain	0.383	0.689	79	6
63 Egypt	0.261	0.453	74	-1
47 Iran	0.301	0.611	103	9
55 Iraq	0.263	0.523	99	5
35 Kuwait	0.475	0.716	51	-3
64 Morocco	0.223	0.450	102	3
69 Pakistan	0.196	0.360	84	1
56 S. Arabia	0.242	0.514	113	10
73 Sudan	0.189	0.332	76	-2
51 Syria	0.306	0.571	87	3
42 Tunisia	0.274	0.641	135	16
31 Turkey	0.381	0.774	95	15
40 UAE	0.352	0.674	92	8

Table Five: GDI Over Time: Ranks and Values, 1970-92
HDI and GDI ranks have been calculated for 79 countries. A positive difference in rank means an improvement from 1970 to 1992 relative to other countries. Data was only available for the above Middle Eastern and North African countries.
Source: *World Development Report 1995*, p. 80.

However, as noted earlier, the Arab States' record in improving women's access to economic opportunities is not impressive. In 1970, women's share of earned income in the United Arab Emirates was 4%, and in 1992, it was 7%. The corresponding shares for Bahrain are 5% and 12%, for Saudi Arabia 5% and 7%. In Tunisia, women's share of earned income rose from 12.5% to 25%. Tunisia's average adjusted income rose tenfold, Saudi Arabia's fivefold, and Bahrain's threefold. In many of these countries, changes in income account for less of the rise in the GDI than the changes in educational attainment or life expectancy. In Saudi Arabia, the change in income explains 24% of the rise in the GDI, the change in education 43% and the change in life expectancy 33%.[14]

The Minorities

The region's main ethnic minority groups are Kurds (22.5 million), Armenians (5 million), Palestinians (5.5 million), Turkamens (4 million), and Berbers (18 million). Some smaller ethnic groups include Circassians, Laz, and Georgians. The main religious minority groups consist of Shi'is, Druzes, Alevis, Nusayris or Alawites, Christians, including Eastern Orthodox Churches, Roman Catholics and Protestants, Jews, and some smaller religious sects, including Yazidis, Ahmadis, and Baha'is.[15] Minority groups in the Middle East, Ted Robert Gurr finds, are subject to more severe political discrimination than those of any other region and are second only to Latin America in severity of economic discrimination. Politically, differentials among groups are the highest of any world region: "Palestinian and Kurdish ethnonationalists and Shi'is are excluded from political power and participation in a number of states because their demands threaten the state-building ethos of nationalist elites. The Baha'is in Iran and the Ahmadi and Hindu minorities in Pakistan face political restrictions on sectarian grounds."[16] The economic differentials and discrimination are clearly a function of political and religious cleavages. Likewise, minorities in this region register high to very high on indicators of ecological and demographic pressure.[17]

This contrasts, Gurr adds, with the situation in North Africa. The most active communal groups of the region, the Berbers of Algeria and Morocco, have enjoyed cultural interests, political incorporation, and economic improvement. The North African states have also promoted "greater religious tolerance." The Coptic Christians of Egypt are a prosperous and influential religious minority in a Muslim society, although subject to some political restrictions. The same applies to the Jewish community in Morocco.[18] Problems are most acute in the core of the Arab world; there is less inequality and greater accommodation among communal groups in North Africa and Pakistan.[19] In Sudan, however, black African Christian and animist southerners, via the Sudan People's Liberation Army (SPLA), have fought against the imposition of strict Islamic law (*Shari'a*) by the northern, predominantly Arabic government.[20] There are thirty-one politically active minorities in the Middle East and North Africa, and they have, since post-war period, caused considerable communal protest and rebellion (see Table Six).

COUNTRY	NAME	POP90	PROP90	TYPE1	TYPE2
Algeria	Berbers	5400	0.2100	INDIG	.
Egypt	Copts	4780	0.0850	SECT	.
Iran	Azerbaijanis	14330	0.2600	ETHNA	.
Iran	Baha'is	475	0.0086	SECT	.
Iran	Bakthiaris	900	0.0165	ETHNA	INDIG
Iran	Baluchis	950	0.0170	ETHNA	INDIG
Iran	Kurds	5000	0.0905	ETHNA	INDIG
Iran	Turkmens	795	0.0145	ETHNA	INDIG
Iran	Arabs	950	0.0173	ETHNA	.
Iraq	Kurds	4150	0.2200	ETHNA	INDIG
Iraq	Shi'ites	9800	0.5200	ETHCL	SECT
Iraq	Sunni Arabs	3950	0.2100	COMCO	.
Israel	Arabs	800	0.1310	ETHCL	SECT
Israel OT*	Palestinians	1600	0.2620	ETHNA	SECT
Jordan	Palestinians	1070	0.3500	ETHNA	.
Lebanon	Druze	170	0.0445	SECT	COMCO
Lebanon	Maronite Christians	1360	0.3558	SECT	COMCO
Lebanon	Palestinians	430	0.1125	ETHNA	SECT
Lebanon	Shi'is	1085	0.2839	SECT	COMCO
Lebanon	Sunnis	780	0.2041	SECT	COMCO
Morocco	Berbers	9700	0.3700	INDIG	.
Morocco	Saharawis	160	0.0060	ETHNA	INDIG
Pakistan	Ahmadis	3960	0.0350	ETHC	SECT
Pakistan	Baluchis	4640	0.0410	ETHNA	INDIG
Pakistan	Hindus	1800	0.0160	SECT	.
Pakistan	Pashtuns	14710	0.1300	INDIG	COMCO
Pakistan	Sindhis	11540	0.1020	COMCO	.
Saudi Arabia	Shi'is	500	0.0300	ETHCL	SECT
Syria	Alawis	1620	0.1300	SECT	COMCO
Turkey	Kurds	10180	0.1800	ETHJNA	INDIG
Turkey	Roma	620	0.0110	ETHCL	.

Table Six: Background Characteristics of the Groups

*Israel's Occupied Territories, the West Bank and Gaza Strip.
POP90: Best 1990 estimate of group population.
PROP90: Best 1990 estimate of group size as proportion of country population.
TYPE1: Primary classification of group:
    ETHNA= Ethnonationalists
    INDIG= Indigenous people
    ETHCL= Ethnoclass
    SECT=Militant sect
    COMCO= Communal contender
TYPE2: Secondary classification of group (same categories as TYPE1).
Source: Ted Robert Gurr, *Minorities at Risk: A Global View of Ethnopolitical Conflicts*, Washington, D.C.: United States Institute of Peace press, 1993, pp. 332-333.

The fate of two minorities, the Kurds and the Palestinians, has dominated the Middle Eastern political agenda in the 1980s and 1990s.[21] Iraq, Turkey, and Israel have faced the biggest challenge. The Iraqi and Turkish states' refusal to come to terms with the realities of their Kurdish minorities is costing them dearly. In 1994, Turkey spent an estimated $8.2 billion – one fifth of the state's budget – on the war against the Kurdish insurgency. Additionally, repression has increasingly pushed Turkish Kurds into the ranks of the Kurdistan Workers Party (PKK) and of Islamic radicalism; both are unfavorable to democracy.[22]

While the Kurds' destiny remains precarious and unresolved, the Palestinians are entering a new process aimed at implementing a peace. The Oslo Agreement of September 13, 1993, set in motion a dynamic of peace in the Middle East not only between the PLO and Israel but also between Jordan and Israel. Oslo 2 was signed on September 28, 1995. It has led to the Israeli redeployment, the election of an 88-member Palestinian Council, the release of prisoners, and the modifications of the Palestinian Covenant, water resource allocations, and could resolve disputes about the religious sites. These agreements are bound to nudge the Palestinians and Israelis along the path to a sustained peace, and will have far-reaching implications for the Palestinians' human rights. The move from limited administrative autonomy toward the actual sovereignty will have a direct impact on the Palestinians' overall human rights conditions. The ascension to power of the right-wing Likud Party in June 1996 elections in Israel is unlikely to undermine the Palestinians' legitimate claim to self-rule. The Netanhayu government must find a way to reconcile Israelis' security concerns with th Palestinians' human rights if it intends to resume peace talks in the region.   Granting Palestinians the right to self-rule is the surest way to avoid further political violence and strain on the peace process.

The Refugee Problem

During the last quarter of the twentieth century, many Palestinians, Kurds, Afghanis, and Iraqi Shi'a Muslims have been forced to abandon their homes.   They have been denied their fundamental rights and suffered serious human rights violations.   The refugee problem has become a source of regional tensions and instability.

In Iraq, Amnesty International reports, the government's relentless crackdown on the Shi'a Muslim population in the south caused many Iraqi Shi'a Muslims to flee across the border into Iran.   Over 20,000 Iraqis remained in refugees camps in Saudi Arabia, fearful of returning to Iraq following the 1991 Gulf War.   Some of these refugees had frequently suffered gross violations of human rights.   Since 1991, hundreds had forcibly returned to Iraq, despite the enormity of the risk they face there.   Many thousands of asylum-seekers from Iran and Iraq have fled to Turkey in recent years, but Turkey has limited its formal obligations under the 1951 Convention to refugees coming from Europe.   The situation for non-European refugees and asylum-seekers has become critically alarming: some had been forced to return to the countries from which they have fled and others have been intimidated by the Turkish police.[23]

This section focuses only on the Palestinian and Kurdish refugee problems.   The Palestinian and Kurdish refugee problem remains one of the region's most complex and intractable issues.   It is evident that Palestinian refugee problem cannot be resolved in isolation from the overall settlement of the Arab-Israeli conflict; likewise, Kurdish refugee issue cannot be dealt with effectively in the absence of a genuine commitment by the regional actors and the international community.

The Palestinian Refugees

Estimates of the total number of Palestinian refugees vary.   Outside the occupied territories, large concentrations of Palestinians are located in Jordan, Lebanon, Kuwait (before the Gulf War), Syria, and Saudi Arabia.   Projected percentages of Palestinians in the total population of

Middle Eastern countries for the year 2000 indicate that Jordan (46.2%), Kuwait (32.4%), and Lebanon (11.4%) continue to be the home to the largest Palestinians refugees.[24] In 1995, the total number of the Palestinian refugees registered with the United Nations Relief and Works Agency for Palestine Refugees (UNRWA) was 2,797,179, of whom there were 1,072,561 refugees in Jordan, 479,023 in West Bank, 603,380 in Gaza, 328,176 in Lebanon, and 314,039 in Syria.[25]

In addition to those registered as refugees with UNRWA, many Palestinians lived in other Arab countries. They were not classified as refugees and were unable to obtain local citizenship; their tangible economic improvement notwithstanding, as non-citizens they felt insecure. While some Palestinians have achieved the highest economic, political, and social status abroad, others have been at the bottom of the social scale, providing unskilled labor for the economies of the countries in which they have resided. Overall, however, the level of education and literacy among Palestinians is one of the highest in the Middle East.[26]

The Gulf War in 1990-91 led to a new crisis when many Palestinians were forced to leave several of the Gulf states. The largest departure was from Kuwait. By December 1990, Don Peretz writes, the Palestinian-Jordanian refugee population constituted about one-third of the total number of refugees who came from the Gulf. The refugee influx threatened Jordan's development plans and altered its economic goals from promoting growth to minimizing the deterioration of living standards and quality of life. The cost of this adjustment has been estimated by Jordanian authorities at between $3.7 and $4.5 billion.[27]

Since 1991, the right of return to Israel has been the Palestinians' major concern in the peace process. The implementation of such a right, Peretz adds, would combine repatriation in its broadest sense with resettlement in new homes; compensation would play a major role in realizing this right.[28] The Refugee Working Group, one of the five multilateral Committees established to deal with functional problems as part of the Madrid Middle East peace process, has thus far circumvented long-term political matters like compensation, repatriation or resettlement. Instead, Peretz notes, it has focused on such issues as improving refugees' quality of life. The compensation issue has been deferred to be dealt with as a part of the refugee problem in the so-called "final status negotiations" between the PLO and Israel. Ultimately, the resolution of the compensation issue will hinge on where the refugees are settled, the future of Arab Jerusalem, location of the boundaries between Israel and the Palestinian state, and the fate of Jewish settler property in the territory that will become part of Palestine.[29]

The Kurdish Refugees

Kurdish self-determination in the region has remained a quest with a problematic future. Iraqi's defeat by the US-led coalition in the 1991 Gulf War gave the Kurds another opportunity to pursue their goal of an independent homeland. However, the Kurdish assault against Iraqi President Saddam Hussain, largely enticed by President George Bush's call during the war, was crushed by Saddam's forces. A mass flight of Kurds from Iraqi Kurdistan ensued in Spring 1991. Approximately one and half million Kurds fled their homes.[30] U.N. Resolution 688 on April 5, 1991, authorized international humanitarian intervention on behalf of the Kurdish people in Iraq. Many observers stressed the necessity of stronger U.N. involvement in the protection of all asylum-seekers and refugees.[31]

The Iraqi refugee crisis can also be traced to chemical attacks of the 1980s. Although the use of chemical weapons against the Kurds by Iraqi forces in August 1988 was condemned by the international community, no punitive actions were taken against Iraq. Some observers have persuasively argued that such chemical attacks tantamount to the acts of genocide, noting that the use of these weapons against civilian targets, the systematic destruction of all life in large swathes of Kurdistan, the deportation of the Kurdish people, and the extirpation of forestry and agriculture in the region fall within the purview of the Genocide convention.[32]

The current Kurdish problem in Turkey has serious implications for Turkey's relations with Europe, the United States, and other regional players with similar refugee problem. The Kurdish crisis could jeopardize Turkey's relations with Europe and America and limit its role as a stabilizing force in the region. Civil violence and terroristic acts by the Kurdish Workers Party (PKK) could hinder foreign investment and erode its tourist industry, complicating Turkey's long-range economic plans. Given that a stable Turkey can remain committed to its Western orientation, the resolution of the Kurdish crisis is imperative.[33]

No solution, however, appears to be in sight in Turkey, where thousands of Kurds have been forcibly removed from their homes. While some have resettled elsewhere, others have struggled to find a place to reside. Many have fled to Western Europe.[34] Amnesty International has frequently reported that human rights violations are widespread and systematic. Extrajudicial executions of those opposing government policies are frequent. The Turkish army, in their conflict with the illegal PKK, is waging a "low intensity" war, aiming at terrorizing Kurdish population. Other international human rights groups concur with the Amnesty International that torture is institutionalized in Turkish police stations.[35] By the mid-1994, according to one source, some 15,000 Kurdish refugees had fled to Iraq in order to escape Turkish military attacks on their villages. The refugees did risk getting caught in hostilities between rival Kurdish factions, but they nonetheless felt more secure in Iraq than in Turkish Kurdistan.[36]

The Renewed Importance of Religion

The resurgence of Islam as a political movement has focused much attention on the nature of theocratic state as well as on a basic question, "Is Islam compatible with pluralist democracy?" To answer this question, it is necessary to put into perspective role of religion in society. The evidence linking religion to constructive social change is mixed at best. William C. Shepherd offers a typical view. He writes that religions, by rendering tribal folkways sacred, limit social change and incite ethnocentrism. He adds, however, that "religions also function to dull the hard edges of individual egocentrism and to encourage the social cooperation vital to civilization at all."[37] It is evident that religions in the Third World, while having very different histories, have been influential in promoting mass mobilization and politicization.

Donald Eugene Smith writes that "the religious factor has been relatively more important in the mass mobilization of Hindu, Buddhist, and Muslim societies.... For four and a half centuries, Latin American rulers and ruled have shared a common Catholic faith. By contrast, nationalist struggles in Asia and Africa took the form of Hindu, Buddhist, and Muslim mass movements in the opposition to Christian colonial governments."[38] Religion has typically upheld the status quo, but the evolution of "liberation theology" in the Third World and the mobilizing role of religious bodies to challenge injustice in the Middle East and Latin America point to a radical role for religion.

Ted Robert Gurr, who documents 233 politically active communal groups in ninety-three countries, examines the connection between religion and ethnic strife. In response to the question "How serious is religiously based communal conflict?" Gurr finds that religious rifts are at most a contributing factor in communal conflicts; hardly, if ever, are they the principal cause.[39]   Gurr's broad findings suggest that "groups defined wholly or in part along lines of religious cleavage accounted for one-quarter of the magnitude of rebellions in the 1980s by all groups in the study."[40]

Gurr's analysis contradicts, generally if not exclusively, arguments made by Samuel P. Huntington, who accords religion the central role in his so-called "Clash of Civilization" worldview.   Huntington maintains that world politics is entering a new phase, in which the fundamental source of conflict in the post-Cold War world will be, not primarily economic or ideological, but cultural.   To the extent that religion is one of the most fundamental characteristics of culture, there is a kernel of truth in Huntington's argument.   To argue, however, as does Huntington, that the fault lines between civilizations will be the battle lines of the future is to invite controversy.   In fact, some scholars believe that a return to clerically prescribed Islam is not a viable alternative to capitalism as a *social system*.   They argue that the idea that the West is in rivalry with the Islamic world, as it was with the Communist world is simply absurd.[41]

Some Muslim scholars have focused on the obstructionist role of religious elites and traditional cultural systems, arguing that religion cannot be blamed for the lack of liberty, justice, dignity, and equality that all human beings may have experienced in different historical junctures. Mohammed Arkoun's observation is perceptive:

> Religions have performed significant educative and therapeutic functions over the centuries, but their effectiveness has always been limited either by misuse at the hands of clerics or by weaknesses inherent in traditional cultural systems. One cannot, indeed, judge the effect of religious teachings on the emancipation of human conditions without evaluating the cultures that have refined, diffused, and applied those teachings.[42]

A thorough examination of the world's religions demonstrates that some religious values can mesh with universal human rights and democratic values. Clearly, Heather Deegan writes, certain political features identified as "democratic," such as elections, upholding national assembly, political participation, and the use of the referendum, have been, and indeed, still are, employed in Islamic states like Iran.[43] To be sure, all religions of the world have some precepts that are compatible with democracy and individual rights and some that are not. Egalitarianism, charitable obligations, personal responsibility, and collective moral standards are elements that are consistent with the protection of human rights and the promotion of pluralistic structures. As Heiner Bielefeldt has argued, although human rights do not arise immediately from religious traditions, they are not entirely foreign to those traditions that have recognized the notion of human dignity. With regard to human rights, Bielefeldt maintains that "a critical reconciliation between the competing requirements of particular religious traditions and modern international human rights standards might be conceivable."[44]

Many religious doctrines inhibit the exercise of certain human rights and the effective functioning of democracy. For instance, orthodox Christianity and Judaism accept social hierarchy. Orthodox Islam limits apostasy and gender equality. Consensual – not adversarial – governing patterns exist in confucianist societies. Buddhism perceives social roles and expectations based on gender distinctions in Southeast Asian traditions. And Hinduism requires submissive attitudes of women. All of these indicate the incongruities at work.

The key question concerns the reconciliation of religious premises and burgeoning modern demands for the protection and promotion of human rights: "Is it possible to harmonize religious morals with the necessities of a modern, dynamic society?" Some common ground seems to be both logically and intuitively possible. Ann Elizabeth Mayer argues that one cannot foretell the position that a person will take concerning a human rights problem solely on the basis of the person's religious affiliation. This is true for members of all faiths.[45] The linkage between religion, the protection of human rights, and the adoption of democratic reforms is complicated. The topic demands further, more detailed, theoretical and empirical treatment.

Islamism, Civil Society, and Democratic Reform

With the Cold War over and the Arab-Israelis peace process on a sustainable track, efforts to resurrect civil society in the Middle East have gained a new momentum. Politics in the Middle East has not been immune to the global resurgence of democracy. The global democratic revolution has touched the Middle East and North Africa in many ways and evoked critically significant questions regarding the region's political transformation. Demands for greater pluralism, for good governance, and for economic and political reforms have been on the rise. These demands have coincided with the rise of Islamism. The rise in Islamism, the construction and expansion of civil society, and democratization in the region are not discreet phenomenon. They can be placed along a continuum.

The Islamic Resurgence

Since the Islamic Revolution in Iran in 1979, the Islamists have become a potent political force and vigorous ideological influence on the domestic scenes of the Muslim countries. Often barred from running candidates in public elections, the Islamists have targeted civil society, including trade unions and professional associations in these countries. These intrusions into civil society, some have argued, dim the prospects for democratization.[46] Others have regarded Islamism, which has bedrock support because of these countries' domestic ills, as a historical inevitability that could, as a mass movement, lead to an alternative to the autocratic regimes in the region.[47]

The recent Islamic movements have developed a penchant for a pragmatic political involvement.[48] They have, to a large measure, relied on the verdict of the ballot box. Nevertheless, the radical ideologies of some of the Islamists have alienated the reform-minded nationalist groups and blocked the process of national accommodation and reconciliation. The Algerian experiment with democratization during 1991-1992 revealed a flawed transition from single-party to democratic politics. Without constructing a civic and democratic pact between opposing factions and parties, democratic transitions are doomed to failure.[49] One participant in the Rome Platform, negotiated in January 1995 between different Algerian secular and religious groups, observed that Algeria'a rulers were as unwilling in 1995 as in 1962 to allow civil society to manage its own affairs. In fact, the army's refusal to confer legitimacy on the Rome Platform as a basis for further discussion underscored the exclusion of civil society from the decision-making process.[50]

The peaceful Algerian presidential election of mid-November 1995, which was denounced and boycotted by the Islamic Salvation Front (FIS), has paved the future negotiations with opposition forces such as the FIS. The election of "incumbent" President Liamine Zeroul brought mounting pressure on him to signal his commitment to political change in the near future.[51]   Rebah Kebir, the exiled leader of outlawed FIS, has proposed direct talks with President Zeroul to find a solution to Algeria's civil strife.   Kebir called Zeroul a legitimate negotiator.[52] It remains to be seen whether any positive political change will flow from this election.   In 1993-94, parliamentary elections took place in Jordan, Morocco, and Yemen, but election results did not bring to power Islamists.

The upsurge of the Islamist challenge and the broadening of their activities are now inexorably connected to the construction or expansion of civil societies in the region.   In some cases, Islamic movements have represented the only viable way to oppose the authoritarian governments of the region.   Islamization programs have also generated transitions from an authoritarian monarchy to a modern Islamic state (Iran) and from a relatively democratic government to a military government insistent on the implementation of full Islamic law (Sudan).

In these two countries, Islamization produced different results.   In the case of Iran, some types of civil-political rights have been restricted, causing a backlash by religious minorities and women against the government.   In Sudan, since the Bashir government came to power in 1989, the Sudanese Human Rights Organization has been forcibly dissolved and secular associations have been dismantled. Among the systematic violations of human rights cited by the International Arab Bar association, whose secretariat has on several occasions visited Khartoum, were the elimination of trade unions, the massive arrest of trade union leaders, and extra-legal coercion to dominate the judiciary.[53]

Contending Discourses on Civil Society

Two competing paradigms of politics have characterized the future of state-society relationship in the region.   While one paradigm expects the dominance of state over society, the other stresses the existence of a balance between the two.   Those who argue that the state dominates society in the region have noted that in the Middle East, unlike the

West, civil society – that is the clubs, organizations, associations, and groups that function as a buffer between state power and the life of the citizen – is often poorly developed and managed. As a result, the state, directed by entrenched political elites and espoused by powerful civilian and military bureaucracies, maintains exclusive power.[54] Recently, however, there has been burgeoning support for the second paradigm. Respect for tolerance and diversity, as well as active governmental role in protecting and promoting human rights have been on the rise in much of the region.

The conflict inherent in the dual objectives of political Islam, namely, the expansion of civil society and the control of the state, has renewed a classic debate concerning the confusions between secular civil society and religious civil society. Some have asked whether the notion of civil society is too historically and culturally specific. One analyst has suggested that we need to focus our attention on the functions of civil society, rather than the organizations that normally constitute civil society. These organizations are often absent in Islamic societies, even though citizens and communities address their interests and grievances vis-à-vis government policies through a wide range of social interactions that could clearly fit the characterization of civil society.[55]

Undeniably, civil society's capacity to challenge the state in the Muslim world is increasing as more citizens strive for some political say in government. In the post-Khomeini era, Iran has seen economic liberalization, pragmatic politics, electoral politics, and the upholding of the rights of a national assembly. Increasingly, the Iranian state faces a potential challenge from civil society, making it necessary for the Iranian government to either modify its behavior or to risk even further alienation from its own population.[56] Turkey has returned to parliamentary democracy; Jordan had held reasonably fair elections; the *Intifadah* has led to the sprawling of civil and social organizations and a viable chance of holding regular elections in the West Bank and Gaza Strip in the near future.

Economic and Political Reform

The interplay between the two processes of economic and political reform in the Middle East has in point of historical fact been paradoxical. Although there exists a broad consensus that economic liberalization and political liberalization are interactive processes, the link between the two processes cannot be determined precisely. It is unclear which process is consistently more significant. Moreover, the relationship between the two processes is immensely complex. The partial economic liberalization undertaken in several Middle Eastern and North African countries supports the view that it is unlikely that these regimes will voluntarily institute genuine and long-term economic reform; to do so would seriously endanger their political longevity.[57]

While examining reform in the region, David Pool points out that the sequences of economic and political liberalization vary and that both processes sometimes embolden authoritarian political elite.[58] Economic liberalization may reinforce or re-introduce autocratic regimes. Likewise, political liberalization can have a negative effect, retarding, if not blocking, economic liberalization. In Turkey and Egypt, where the longer experiments with economic and political reform have transpired, it is possible to discern a pattern:

> Economic liberalization sets constraints on political liberalization, and although a degree of political liberalization can facilitate the introduction of economic reform measures, the social and political consequences of such measures put limits on the extent of political reform. As a result of this symbiosis and dialectical tension between the two processes, economic liberalization is marked by progress and regress and political liberalization is authoritarian, cautious and controlled.[59]

Some Third World specialists attribute political liberalization in the most rapidly liberalizing countries largely to economic decay, arguing that the persistent problems of poverty, inequality, and social injustice have led to democratic openings. Paradoxically, yet understandably, it is economic decay – not prosperity – that has culminated in democratic openings in much of the Third World.[60] James Bill and Robert Springborg describe two different paradoxes: paradox one – economic growth and political decay – and paradox two – economic decay and political growth. In the end, Bill and Springborg conclude, political systems will be profoundly affected by the course of economic liberalization since "if economic growth is rapid and private sectors of national economies prosper, resources beyond the control of the state will be available to reinforce political liberalization. The state's retreat from the economy would be paralleled by the expansion of civil society."[61]

The complex interplay between these processes, if not properly managed, leads to the collapse of political regimes. It is ironic that the political and social problems that arise from the implementation of economic liberalization programs (e.g., structural adjustment) can only be effectively resolved by a strong and stable regime. Any heavy-handed approach curtails democratic measures considerably – at least in short to medium terms. Furthermore, economic liberalization, by widening the disparities between the rich and the poor that are primarily caused by structural problems, will provoke religious and tribal radicalism. It is not surprising that Islamism has in recent decades thrived on anger about structural adjustments and their impacts on the dreadfully powerless of the region: the poor, women, and children.

Prospects for Democracy

The version of democracy in Middle Eastern and North African countries that is widely accepted is *populism*, not *constitutionalism*. Drawing our attention to this critical distinction, Jean Leca points out the two major principles of *populism*. The will of the people, which is identified with justice and morality, prevails over any institutional norm. The leaders are good only to the extent they are directly related to the people, over and above the intermediary elites – that is, intellectuals, experts, and technocrats. *Populism* , Leca writes, provides the linkage between the masses and politics. The state's legitimacy is tied to its ability to fight poverty and help the citizens. The democratic state's duties stem from its citizens' rights, not from its benevolent or god-fearing prince.[62]

As important as the distinction between *populism* and *constitutionalism* is, Leca admits, the key elements in any operative democracy are the forces of a viable civil society.[63] But even if one can argue that civil society is sufficiently well-grounded to serve as a platform for the development of democracy in some parts of the Middle East and North Africa, countervailing forces pose serious challenge to implementing and underpinning democracy in the region.

One problem results from structural constraints and anomalies such as poverty, overpopulation, tribalism, patriarchy, regional disparities, and ethnic strife and factionalism. Another problem involves actor-related obstacles like the strategic choices of leaders. In addition, there are regional problems like the arms race, border disputes, and interstate conflicts. There are also international obstacles such as the massive infusion of military aid and arms into the region. All of these dim prospects for any move toward democracy in the region. As Lisa Anderson has argued, due largely to records of reliability and compliance, the region's governments have garnered fairly consistent international tolerance, and often active support. The latter is nowadays justified in the name of peace. But as long as peace is pursued as a tool for revenue-enhancement, its achievement will lessen rather than promote the likelihood of increased domestic accountability and democracy.[64]

In the case of Egypt since Camp David, Anderson adds, Sadat's political clampdown demonstrated that liberal domestic policies were not necessarily a precondition for continued aid.[65] The infusions of foreign revenues, whether from superpowers or international creditors, have proved unfavorable to political liberalization and democratization. In sum, the availability of external revenues has controlled economic reforms and development throughout the Middle East and North Africa.[66]

Structural obstacles such as state-building and economic development -- not religion or ideology -- seem to constitute the essential obstacles to the implementation of democratic measures in the region.[67] It is grossly inaccurate to argue that *Shari'a* is thus inherently anti-democratic and antithetical to the codes of civil society.[68] Without underestimating the role of structural factors, it can be argued that the region's lack of pluralistic structures owes much to the state security apparatus, intrusive state penetration in society, and corrupt leadership.[69]

Two major discussions have intensified the debate about the prospects of democracy in the region. First, it is argued that in the absence of national consensus about the outcome of electoral process, democratic mechanisms such as elections can be disruptive and counterproductive. Moreover, the implementation of economic and political reforms with equal vigor and intensity can seriously jeopardize democratic practices. The Algerian debacle demonstrated that the fast-track democratization can unleash anti-democratic forces. Secondly, there is no consensus that the region's authoritarian regimes (e.g., Iraq and Sudan) could effectively defuse subnational regional, ethnic, linguistic, and religious divisions by moving toward democracy. The value of democracy in resolving intrastate and communal conflicts in these countries is still in question. Democratization is likely to precipitate both protest and rebellion, culminating in civil war or the reimposition of autocratic rule.[70] Hence paradoxical and problematic nature of democracy in the region. Precisely how such paradoxes and problems will be dealt with is hard to predict. The tension between increasing demands for participation and governmental resistance to those demands is real. If political repression continues to be a government's sole response, then political regimes will most likely collapse at some point. Repression alone will not stop the proliferation of Islamic movements. Democratization in the Middle East and North Africa will provide space for the Islamic movements to enter the political process. The nagging question, however, remains: "How can such a process be effectively managed along with the much touted economic and political liberalization programs?" The answer may lie in leaders' strategic choices. Eventually, democracy needs democrats – that is, "rational" and "reasonable" agents.[71] To improve the state of human rights in this region, other states ought to specifically gear their support toward indigenous democrats. Graham Fuller's observation is poignantly relevant: "US Support for democracy – a long-term policy goal that has sometimes suffered under the choices imposed by the Cold War – is the most effective instrument for helping deradicalize Islamic extremism."[72]

Conclusion

This study's findings have lent support to the idea that the link between socioeconomic progress and civil-political rights is not *causal*. The countries with better human development index (HDI), such as Bahrain, United Arab Emirates, Oman, Algeria, and Saudi Arabia, have not necessarily registered decent records with regard to civil-political rights. The Arab states of the Middle East have the lowest degrees of political participation by women in the world. Nevertheless, these countries (with few exceptions) have made the fastest strides in the last two decades in accelerating women's literacy. The Arab states' record in improving women's access to economic opportunities has not been impressive. The status of women's rights in the modern Middle East and North Africa is not determined solely by religious traditions.

Minority groups have been subject to severe political and economic discrimination in the Middle East. The region's main minorities (Palestinians, Kurds, Ahmadis, and Baha'is) register high on indicators of ecological and demographic pressure. The situation in North Africa is palpably better. The Berbers have enjoyed cultural interests, political inclusion, and economic improvement. Greater religious tolerance and accommodation and lesser inequality among communal groups in North Africa stand in stark contrast with the Middle East.

The connection between religion and ethnic strife is not apparent. Religious values, depending on whether they are based on enlightened or orthodox interpretations, can mesh or clash with universal human rights. A reconciliation between Islamic perspectives and modern international human rights standards is conceivable. Civil society's capacity to challenge the state is increasing throughout the region as citizens strive for more political say in government. Civil and social organizations have grown considerably faster in recent years in Iran, Jordan, Turkey, and among the Palestinians than in the past. Economic and political reforms, however, have not kept the pace. The complex interplay between economic and political liberalization has made it impossible to predict with certainty which process is consistently more significant.

The prospects for democracy have also been complicated by infusions of foreign aid and revenue from foreign countries. In fact, the availability of foreign aid, oil revenue, and credit has conditioned economic and political reforms in much of the region. The operative value of democracy in resolving ethnopolitical conflicts in certain cases (e.g., Iraq and Sudan) has come under increasing attack. The fate of human rights in the Middle East and North Africa remains hostage to many paradoxical forces and situations. Efforts to manage constructive change present a daunting task for the region's leaders. Any improvement in the region's human rights conditions hinges not only upon the actions of the rational and reasonable agents from within but also upon genuine support for these actions by external forces. In the post-Cold War world, such conditions are hard to come by. It should prove well worth the attempt for human rights scholars to continue efforts to find and describe the conditions under which good governance can thrive.

Notes

1.   See Morton E. Winston, ed., The Philosophy of Human Rights, (Belmont, CA: Wadsworth Publishing Company, 1989); Jack Donnelly, Universal Human Rights in Theory and Practice, (Ithaca: Cornell university press, 1989); and David P. Forsythe, The Internationalization of Human Rights, (Lexington, Massachusetts: Lexington Books, 1991).

2.   Amnesty International Report 1995, (Alameda, CA: Hunter House, 1995), pp. 334-342.

3.   See Adrian Karatnycky, "The Comparative Survey of Freedom 1993-1994: Freedom in Retreat," Freedom in the World: The Annual Survey of Political Rights and Civil Liberties 1993-1994, (New York: The Freedom House, 1994), pp. 3-9; see p. 5.

4.   Michael Haas, Improving Human Rights, (Westport, CT: Praeger Publishers, 1994), pp. 61-63; see also Jack Donnelly, "The 'Right to Development': How Not to Link Human Rights and Development," in Claude E. Welch, Jr. And Ronald I. Meltzer, eds., Human Rights and Development in Africa, (Albany: State University of New York, 1984), pp. 261-283.

5.   The percentage of share of seats held by women in parliament (as of 30/6/1994) was 4 in the Arab states, 19 in East Asia, 10 in Latin America and the Caribbean, 5 in South Asia, 9 in South-East Asia and the Pacific, 8 in Sub-Saharan Africa, 6 in the least developed countries on the average, 14 in European Union, 35 in the Nordic countries, and 13 in OECD. Similarly, the share of women at ministerial level (as of 31/5/1994) was 1 percent in the Arab states, 6 percent in East Asia, 8 percent in Latin America and the Caribbean, 3 percent in South Asia, 3 percent in South-East Asia and the Pacific, 6 percent in Sub-Saharan Africa, 5 percent in the Least developed countries on the average, 16 percent in European Union, 31 percent in the Nordic countries, and 15 percent in OECD. See Human Development Report, 1995, p. 62.

6. Human Development Report 1995, published by the United Nations Development Programme (UNDP), (New York: Oxford University Press, 1995), p. 62.

7. Ann Elizabeth Mayer, Islam and Human Rights: Tradition and Politics, (Boulder, CO: Westview Press, 1991), see especially chapter 6.

8. Nikki R. Keddie, "The Rights of Women in Contemporary Islam," in Leroy S. Rounder, ed., Human Rights and the World's Religions, (Notre Dame, IN: University of Notre Dame Press, 1988), pp. 76-93; seep. 82.

9. Walid Saif, "Human Rights and Islamic Revivalism," Islam and Chrisitian Muslim Relations, Vol. 5, No. 1, 1994, pp. 57-65; see p. 63.

10. Human Development Report 1995, p. 112.

11. Ibid., p. 115.

12. Ibid., p. 86.

13. Ibid., p. 78.

14. Ibid., p. 81.

15. David McDowall, Minorities in the Middle East, (London: The Minority Rights Group, 1992).

16. Ted Robert Gurr, Minorities at Risk: A Global View of Ethnopolitical Conflicts, (Washington, D.C.:United States Institute of Peace Press, 1993), p. 67.

17. Ibid.

18. Ibid., p. 68.

19. Barbara Harff, "Minorities, Rebellion, and Repression in North Africa and the Middle East," in Ted Robert Gurr, Minorities at Risk, pp. 217-251; see p. 217.

20. See Marj Humphrey, "Herod Lives: The Story From Sudan," Commonweal, Vol. CXXI, No. 22, December 16, 1994, pp. 8-10.

21. Substantial evidence now exists that warrant a U.N. Supervised investigation into the charge that, in 1988, the Saddam Hussein government deported tens of thousands of Kurds to southern Iraq where they were massacred and buried in mass graves. Some have called for a large-scale forensic investigation aimed at trying to locate and excavate the putative graves. See Middle East Watch, "Unquiet Graves: The Search for the Disappeared in Iraqi Kurdistan," New York, 1992, p. 28.

22. See David A. Korn, "The Middle East: A Dynamic of Peace--and Terror," in Adrian Karatnycky, et. Al., Freedom in the World: The Annual Survey of Political Rights and Civil Liberties, 1994-1995, (New York: Freedom House, 1995), pp. 31-39; see p. 39.

23. Amnesty International: The 1995 Report on Human Rights Around the World, (Alameda, CA: Hunter House, 1995), p. 26.

24. See Don Peretz, Palestinians, Refugees, and the Middle East Peace Process, (Washington, DC: United States Institute of Peace Press, 1993), p. 17.

25. See UNHCR, The State of the World's Refugees 1995: In Search of Solutions, (New York: Oxford University Press, 1995), p. 254.

26. Don Peretz, op. cit., p. 22.

27. Ibid., pp. 47 and 102.

28. Ibid., p. 75.

29. Don Peretz, Palestinian Refugee Compensation, (Washington, DC: The Center for Policy Analysis on Palestine, May 1995), pp. 17-18.

30. David McDowall, The Kurds: A Nation Denied, (London: Minority Rights Publications, 1992), p. 127.

31. Ibid., p. 128.

32. Ibid., p. 131.

33. James Brown, "The Turkish Imbroglio: Its Kurds," Annals, AAPSS, Vol. 541, September 1995, pp. 116-129.

34. David McDowall, op. cit., p. 127.

35. Derek Summerfield, "Turkey and the Kurds: A Grave Human Rights Picture," The Lancet, Vol. 344, No. 8919, August 6, 1994, pp. 350-351.

36. Conor Foley, "Letter From Kurdistan," New Stateman and Society, Vol. 7, No. 308, June 24, 1994, p. 11.

37. William C. Shepherd, "Cultural Relativism, Physical Anthropology and Religion," Journal of the Scientific Study of Religion, Vol. 19, No. 2. 1980, pp. 159-172; see p. 169.

38. Donald Eugene Smith, Religion and Political Modernization, (New Haven: Yale University Press, 1974), p. 23.

39. Ted Robert Gurr, Minorities at Risk: A Global View of Ethnopolitical Conflicts, (Washington, D.C.: US Institute of Peace Press, 1993), p. 317.

40. Ibid., p. 318.

41. Simon Bromley, Rethinking Middle East Politics, (Austin, TX: University of Texas Press, 1994), pp. 181-182.

42. Mohammed Arkoun, Rethinking Islam: Common Questions, Uncommon Answers, Translated and edited by Robert D. Lee (Boulder, CO: Westview Press, 1994), p. 113.

43. Heather Deegan, The Middle East and the Problems of Democracy, (Boulder, CO: Lynne Rienner Publishers, 1994), p. 127.

44. Heiner Bielefeldt, "Muslim Voices in the Human Rights Debate," Human Rights Quarterly, Vol. 17, No. 4, November 1995, pp. 587-617; see p. 601.

45. Ann Elizabeth Mayer, Islam and Human Rights: Tradition and Politics, (Boulder, CO: Westview Press, 1991).

46. For a pessimistic perspectives on the waves of Islamism, see David A. Korn, "The Middle East: Moment of Illusion, or Hope?" and Adrain Karatnychy, Freedom in the World: The Annual Survey of Political Rights and Civil Liberties, 1993-1994, pp. 30-40.

47. Hosni Mubarak's campaign against Islamic radicalism has become too indiscriminate and brutal. It is alarming to see Egypt embark on Algeria's path. Mubarak attempts to defeat a mass movement, which is rooted in disillusion with a corrupt governing class, by using indiscriminating force.   See Economist, February 4, 1994, p. 15.

48. See, for example, Hasan Turabi, "Islam, Democracy, the State and the West," Middle East Policy, Vol. 1, No. 3, 1992, pp. 49-61.

49. See Mahmood Monshipouri, Democratization, Liberalization, and Human Rights in the Third World, (Boulder, CO: Lynne Rienner Publishers, 1995); see especially chapter four. See also Robert Mortimer, "Islamists, Soldiers, and Democrats: The Second Algerian War," Middle East Journal, Vol. 50, No. 1, Winter 1996, pp. 18-39.

50. Robert Mortimer, "Islamists, Soldiers, and Democrats: The Second Algerian War," p. 38.

51. The Christian Science Monitor, November 20, 1995, p. 14.

52. The Christian Science Monitor, November 21, 1995, p. 2.

53. J. Millard Burr and Robert O. Collins, Requiem for the Sudan: War, Drought, and Disaster Relief on the Nile, (Boulder, CO: Westview Press, 1995), p. 255.

54. For more on this perspective, see the literature reviewed in James A. Bill and Robert Springborg, Politics in the Middle East, fourth Edition (New York: Harper Collins College Publishers, 1994), pp. 23-24.

55. Jillian Schwedler, ed., Toward Civil Society in the Middle East? A Primer, (Boulder, CO: Lynne Rienner Publishers, 1995), p. 16.

56. For a stimulating discussion on this subject, see Farhad Kazemi, "Models of Iranian Politics, the Road to the Islamic Revolution, and the Challenge of Civil Society," World Politics, Vol. 47, No. 4, pp. 555-574.

57. Henri Barkey, "Can the Middle East Compete?" in Larry Diamond and Marc F. Plattner, eds., Economic Reform and Democracy, (Baltimore: The Johns Hopkins University Press, 1995), pp. 167-181; see p. 175.

58. David Pool, "The Links Between Economic and Political Liberalization," in Tim Niblock and Emma Murphy, eds., Economic and Political Liberalization in the Middle East, (London: British Academic Press, 1993), pp. 40-54; see p. 49.

59. Ibid.

60. Robert Pinkney, Democracy in the Third World, (Boulder, CO: Lynne Rienner Publishers, 1994).

61. James A. Bill and Robert Springborg, Politics in the Middle East, fourth ed. (New York: Harper Collins College Publishers, 1994), pp. 413-452; see p. 450.

62. Jean Leca, "Democratization in the Arab World: Uncertainty, Vulnerability and Legitimacy, A Tentative Conceptualization and Some Hypotheses," in Ghassan Salamé, ed., Democracy Without Democrats? The Renewal of Politics in the Muslim World, (New York: I.B. Tauris Publishers, 1994), pp. 48-83; see p. 56.

63. Ibid., p. 59.

64. Lisa Anderson, "Peace and Democracy in the Middle East: The Constraints of Soft Budgets," Journal of International Affairs, Vol. 49, No. 1, Summer 1995, pp. 25-44; see pp. 33-35.

65. Ibid., p. 40.

66. For an empirical support of this thesis in the cases of Turkey, Morocco, Egypt, and Kuwait, see Bradley L. Glasser, "External Capital and Political Liberalizations: A Typology of Middle Eastern Development in the 1980s and 1990s," Journal of International Affairs, Vol. 49, No. 1, Summer 1995, pp. 45-73.

67. Simon Bromley, "The Prospects for Democracy in the Middle East," in David Held, ed., Prospects for Democracy: North, South, East, West, (Stanford, CA: Stanford University Press, 1993), pp. 380-406.

68. For an illuminating discussion on this subject, see Saad Eddin Ibrahim, "Civil Society and Prospects of Democratization in the Arab World," in Augustus Richard Norton, ed., Civil Society in the Middle East, (New York: E.J. Brill, 1995), Vol. 1, pp. 27-54.

69. See Jill Crystal, "Authoritarianism and Its Adversaries in the Arab World," World Politics, Vol. 46, No. 2, January 1994, pp. 262-289; also see John P. Entelis, "Islam, Democracy, and the State: The Reemergence of Authoritarian Politics in Algeria," in John Ruedy, ed., Islamism and Secularism in North Africa, (New York: St. Martin's Press, 1994), pp. 219-251. For an interesting story on the cash crisis, debt, questions about the royal succession, lack of reforms, and the corruption in the royal family in Saudi Arabia, see Leslie and Andrew Cockburn, "Royal Mess," The New Yorker, Vol. LXX, No. 39, November 28, 1994, pp. 54-90.

70. Ted Robert Gurr, op. cit., p. 138.

71. See Ghassan Salamé, ed., Democracy Without Democrats? The Renewal of Political in the Muslim World, (London: I. B. Tauris Publishers, 1994).

72. Graham E. Fuller, "Islamic Fundamentalism," in Richard K. Betts, ed., Conflict After the Cold War: Arguments on Causes of War and Peace, (New York: Macmillan Publishing Company, 1994), pp. 386-393; see p. 392.

Chapter 4

Ideology and Foreign Policy in the Arab World: Jargon and Legitimacy

As'ad Abukhalil

Introduction

The study of ideology in relation to foreign policy has been influenced by the ideological struggle between the Soviet Union and the US The view that the struggle between the two superpowers was rooted in ideological differences is not universally held although advocates of both sides stressed the ostensibly superior moral foundations of one over the other. In accordance with the school of Realism in International Relations theory, it can be argued that classic calculations of power politics were the actual determinant of the American-Soviet rivalry. Not that no ideological arguments were tossed back and forth; but the language of lofty ideals was convenient to camouflage concrete state – not national – interests. Thus, the Cold War could be looked at as a case of Realism parading as Idealism, as interests hiding behind principles.

When the Soviet Union and the US were fighting through proxies in various parts of the world they needed to justify their involvement through an invocation of ideals: the causes of peace and freedom were often stressed. Explanations in the West of Soviet foreign policy behavior through references to non-ideological factors were dismissed and the US wanted to attribute its actions around the world to its ostensible monopoly over the cause of global struggle for freedom.

It is in this context of the Cold War and its legacy that the subject of ideology and foreign policy needs to be examined. The relationship between ideology and foreign policy was seen as applicable only to "foreign" and "aggressive" states. It has been easy for US policy makers and academics to dismiss the foreign policy of the former U.S.S.R., or present-day Iran, as the result of ideological objectives. Ideology itself was a dirty word; it was reserved to describe the detested concepts of socialism and communism. The US political experience was considered above ideology and above classes, and class and ideology were often intertwined in the official and public imagination until the advent of the Iranian Revolution when religion and ideology became closely associated.

Michael Brecher maintained that ideology and power become intertwined only with the "coming of Fascism, Nazism and Communism,"[1] as if the international system was based on peace, harmony, and mutual respect before that. But colonialism was never of concern to classic International Relations theory because it dealt with countries and peoples that were outside the zone of "western civilization," which – for a long time – was the only recognized civilization worthy of academic examination. Indeed, the word "ideology" was so stigmatized that anti-colonial struggle was labeled "ideological,"[2] as if the word is sufficient to discredit the cause of national liberation. Yet, Western struggle for independence was not conceived as ideological perhaps because the non-European desire for freedom was not taken seriously, or was seen as part of a hostile – hostile to the West that is – conspiracy to harm Western interests. The Reagan administration, for example, looked at regional crises in the Third World in terms of an international communist conspiracy. Discourse on "international terrorism" characterized foreign policy debates.[3]

One scholar refuses to accept the universal appeal of ideology. He suggests that all discourse on ideology can be traced back to the German tradition. As evidence, he reminds readers that the foremost authority on ideology, Karl Mannheim, was himself "the product of that tradition."[4] This same author, considers US foreign policy different from all other in that it alone aims at "the preservation of the status quo."[5] It is doubtful that he is unaware of American successful and failed attempts at changing regimes all over the world. Those changes, of course, from the American ideological perspective – and it does exist – conform to global peace and order. This explains why American intervention around the world is attributed to motivations of altruistic pacification by "the policeman of the world." Of course, debates exist over whether the US should intervene or not, but not over whether its intervention per se is actually innocent policing of the world. There are status quos that the US supports and others that it tries to demolish, by force if necessary. Support for the status quo exists when the present furthers the interests of the US, but never when it poses a threat to it.

Surprisingly, or perhaps unsurprisingly, Hans Morgenthau rejects the exclusion of the American experience from discussion of ideology and foreign policy. He states: "American foreign policy, from the very beginning of American history, has been justified and rationalized by ideologies."[6] For Henry Kissinger morality and ideology, what ever they are, should take a back seat to "the need for survival."[7] In an earlier work, he exclusively associates ideology with the revolutionary and imperialist goals of the Soviet Union and China.[8] Others in the US dismiss the concept of ideology out of hand as an "irretrievably fallen word."[9]

Richard Cottam, the author of a sophisticated book on foreign policy motivation, concedes that ideology, or "ideological messianism," applies to the study of American foreign policy. But he then proceeds to belittle its impact by arguing that it resembled (in the American case) "British cultural messianism."[10] The object of cultural messianism, according to Cottam – of course – and not to its victims around the world, is to "elevate the colonial subject."[11] The Egyptians and the Algerians would have been better off without this elevation judging from the struggle they launched against European colonialism. Advocates of colonialism, or cultural messianism or whatever fancy title is given to the subjugation project of the non-European world, may respond by saying that the colonized did not know their best interests, that they were irrational. Cottam falls into the same resistance to the use of the ideological label in referring to American foreign policy, because the dreaded word is reserved to the enemy Soviet Empire.

Yet, the debate over the political salience of ideology as a determinant of foreign policy should not lead to its total rejection as an element in contemporary political analysis. If evidence exists that American voters' "understanding and use of ideological thinking are minimal at best,"[12] it should not be applied to cases from other countries to nullify the relevance of ideologies. Democratization in different continents is not producing one-party, one-ideology dominance. Instead, political diversity and a multiplicity of ideas and parties is now synonymous with the new situations of political pluralism. The Arab world is no exception, as will be argued throughout this piece.

The collapse of the USSR has marginalized ideology further, relegating it to the historical accounts of the twentieth century. American victory in the Gulf War and the rise of pro-Western regimes in the former Soviet Bloc have led to the celebration of the American era, or to "the end of history." It is now assumed that US global supremacy is not only good but historically predestined because America possesses that eternal truth. It alone monopolizes the virtues of freedom and peace, despite the wars that America has caused and fought and despite its violation of human rights around the world, regardless whether it is direct or indirect through the support of oppressive regimes.

What is Left of Ideology in the Arab World

Ideology in the Middle East has never been a subject of academic study perhaps because Islam has been emphasized at the expense of all other ideas. Not even Arab nationalism at the height of its appeal generated the same volume of study that Islam now generates. Some Western specialists of Arab nationalism, notably Sylvia Haim and Elie Kedourie, saw in Arab nationalism, or Pan-Arabism as it has been labeled, an imitation of European fascism and Nazism. Furthermore, the study of ideology was neglected because the Arab people, and the Muslim people too, were seen as a monolithic bloc which is easily shaped and molded by people in power. Thus, attention was paid to leaders' statements and declarations but not to popular opinion and preferences. The cold war era did produce a time of concern about communism but the people of the region were not considered to be a factor in the spread of communism. Instead, the fear was centered on Soviet manipulation of local leaders and parties.

The end of the 20th century has witnessed a revival of fundamentalism within Judaism, Christianity, and Islam. In the Arab world, Western attention to the rise of Islamic fundamentalism is approaching the level of public hysteria. The old fear of communism has been discarded and various forms of Islamophobia now prevail. The attention to Islam in the region is not new, of course, and the West was historically sympathetic to Islamic tendencies in the region especially when they were targeted against Nasir and communism in the 1950s and 1960s. Islam of the past, however, was anti-Nasir and anti-communist, while present-day Islam declares its enmity to the US

The discussion of ideologies in the Arab world often lead to an assessment of Islam and Arab nationalism, the two most important ideas, according to the various people who studied the region. While Arab nationalism is now dismissed from scholarship and policy debates[13], it remains a motivational ideology for many in the Arab world.[14] The subject of ideology in the Arab world will not be addressed here[15]; it is important, however, to assess the role and making of ideology. That ideas influence people in their lives, and that those ideas change over time is not challenged as a thesis for analysis of Western societies. This thesis has to be persuasively argued when one deals with the Arab world due to the lasting impact of Theologocentrism, of the exclusive analytical attention to Islam.

One also need to question some of the assumptions of Western approaches to the study of Islam and nationalism in the Arab world. When Arab nationalism was being dismissed from Arab political trends in the 1970s the US was finding little threat in Nasser's legacy. Attention to nationalism during the 1950s and 1960s was devoid of understanding of the underlying causes of Arab political upheavals. Nationalism was erroneously equated with socialism and Soviet influence was consistently exaggerated perhaps to rationalize American intervention in the Middle East and to justify the series of arms sales to "friendly Arab regimes." The collapse of the USSR shifted American focus from an obsession with Soviet expansionism to the discovery of the menacing role of Islam in Arab politics. Islam, however, is far from holding an exclusive monopoly over people's minds and hearts. The spectrum of Arab ideological choices remains broad and diverse.

Democratization in a small number of Arab countries over the last several years has revealed the presence of non-religious ideas in people's minds, despite the general primary attraction of Islamic ideologization. Islamic fundamentalists in Lebanon, Jordan, and Yemen compete with other effective political movements, ranging from traditional tribal forces to leftist Marxist parties. Even in Algeria before the military crackdown had a number of non-religious-oriented parties that were voted in by the electorate. The Islamic fundamentalists are not the only political players in the region and their enemies have not disappeared despite intimidation by the state and advocates of the imposition of Islamic laws.

More interesting than the enumeration of ideas in the Arab world is the process of the production of ideas. How do ideas become popular and how do other decline in appeal? How are ideas articulated and who shapes the jargon of ideology? Is the process of ideological "culture industry," to borrow a term from the Frankfurt School, tied to the apparatus of the state or is it sometimes controlled by opposition forces? Those questions should be raised while discussing the relationship between ideology and foreign policy in the region. While theologocentrism is rejected as a methodological tool, Islam will be considered but under the very rubric of ideology to underline the ideological nature of Islamic fundamentalist movements. The reference to ideologies needs to be grounded in the distinction by Karl Mannheim between ideology and utopia.[16] If ideologies, to follow Mannheim's terminology, denote a belief system that rationalizes an existing order, then ideologies are all but dead in the Arab world. Support for an existing order does not exist, which refutes the assumption of Arab popular irrationality. How could existing orders be supported in light of the presence of oppressive rule throughout the region? Utopias, in reference to what does not actually exist but to what should exist, appeal to all those who have lost hope in the present and aspire to future salvation, in whatever form, secular or fundamentalist. Utopias have no ties to state apparatuses that engage in the torture of citizens.

One can also note the diversity of ideological choices by relying on publishing trends and readers' preferences. Publishers in Lebanon and Morocco report a recent decline in the readership of Islamic political literature. The classical works of the Islamic tradition are available at reduced prices in "popular" editions. Yet, the sale of books on the West and "secular" writings in general remain in demand in more than one country.[17] Marxist and secular authors, like Sadiq Jalal Al-`Adhm and Fatimah Marnisi, continue to outsell religious authors. Furthermore, popular culture in the Middle East has been more secularized than is often assumed in the West.

Determinants of Foreign Policy in the Arab World

1. Language and Islam

Ideology plays a role in foreign policy making in the region. But before one elaborates on that statement one is obliged to explain briefly the foreign policy making system of the Arab world. While differences, sometimes major differences, exist between the various Arab regimes one is able to offer generalizations by virtue of the common regimes' antipathy to democratic rule. The regimes collectively and individually fear popular participation and they particularly reject the expansion of the foreign policy making elite or even the regularization of the foreign policy process. Democratization in Jordan and Lebanon, for example, did not affect the monopolization of foreign policy by the King in Jordan and by the ruling troika in Lebanon. Very little is known about how foreign policy is reached in Arab capitals and the study of the subject often resembles a guessing game, not unlike the study of past Soviet foreign policy. Unlike the Soviet Union, Arab regimes do not pretend to abide by a fixed set of principles and doctrines in their policies. Ideological ambiguities characterize the ruling world of ideas in the region, where on one day Islam and on another Arab nationalism seem to be the norm. Saddam Husayn's reliance on Islamic dogma may not be as sudden as is suggested in the Western press although it represented a shift in the regime's foreign policy orientation and jargon.

There are many reasons for the unchanging nature of foreign policy making in the Arab world. Political legitimacy, which has never been solely based on Islam, has been carefully constructed and maintained. The centrality of the Palestinian question among Arabs and the widespread popular antipathy to the US have restrained official public discussion of foreign policy. Pro-Western regimes need military and/or financial support from the US despite popular opposition to Western political support for Israel. Moreover, Arab regimes have been forced to take popular sentiments into considerations when planning and delivering public statements on the Arab-Israeli question. For a long time, meetings between Arab and Israeli officials took place in utmost secrecy; the people in most Arab countries remain unsupportive of official or private interaction with the Jewish state. Similarly, Gulf regimes could not publicize the extent to which they have been closely aligned with the US and American military presence in Saudi Arabia is still referred to as a presence of some unidentified "friendly forces."

In dealing with the ideological roots of foreign policy one is obliged to clarify what one means by the term within the context of the Arab world. Does ideology, for example, include whatever is promoted by political parties and regimes as ideology? When ideologies were fashionable in the political life of the Arab world in the 1950s and 1960s, collections of speeches and utterances were presented as ideologies. The Palestinian Fath movement never developed a coherent set of objectives or principles and yet it published its statements and declarations as evidence of its ideological constitution. Any religio-political or political rationalization of the status quo or of a desired future order will be accepted as ideology. The lines between religion and ideology can be obscured by the invention of a new Islam, an Islam that responds – not to the needs of individuals for comfort, hope, and understanding but – to the needs of the state for survival and security. The apparatus of power is no more satisfied with general assumptions of popular consent based on toleration of the succession process that followed detested colonial rule. The appeal of ideas, not necessarily based on tribal lineage or traditional manliness, requires the production of a new belief system. Its novelty is not contradicted by its Islamic motifs.

The connection of language to politics is close, the former being the designation of policies often hiding and often unmasking intentions. For Theodor Adorno "language is actually ideology."[18] The role of ideology in the study of the foreign policy of the Soviet Union was often exaggerated although Zbigniew Brezezinski, unlike other Soviet experts at the time, cautioned against attributing all sources of Soviet foreign policy orientation to communist ideology.[19] In the Arab world, the change of the language of foreign policy is an indication of the association between language itself and ideology. The latter is so vaguely defined and so loosely presented that leaders have been able to adjust themselves to the changing moods of their populations.

The role of language in foreign policy discussion should deal with its relationship to Islam. Bernard Lewis, in his work on Islamic political terminology[20], typically ignores the diversity in Muslim lives, experiences, and political behavior. For him, there is such a thing as "the political language of Islam," even though Muslims express their views, feelings, and their Islam through different languages. The symbols and motifs of Islamic expressions cannot be reduced to one standard. Furthermore, the role of language, as device to examine the thoughts of a people, should not be exaggerated, as Lewis has done. He, for example, considers the late arrival of the Arabic word for freedom, to mean more than the negation of slavery, an evidence for the absence of the notion of freedom from the minds of Arabs. That Arabs did not develop the word for sex and sexuality until this century does not, of course, imply that they have abstained from thinking about, or practicing, sex. The development of a language has to go through the restrictive guidelines set by political and clerical authorities.

It will not be argued here that language determines foreign policy but that ideology does not necessarily determine foreign policy. What is considered ideological determinants of foreign policy orientations in the Arab world should be understood as the necessary communicative apparatus of the state. The power of the state is not only branched through the various arms of the government but it also is spread through words. Those words have to be continuously revised and changed in order not to be left behind popular attitudes. In the absence of electoral standards of legitimacy, Arab governments have to rely on guessing the feel of the populace. Those who decide to ignore the clash between the stance of the government and the popular mood could face the fate of Anwar Sadat.

The governments need to stress the impact of words in their policy making because they fear the use of Islam and its terminology against them. Islamic fundamentalists use Qur'anic language to dismiss the ruling regimes and to call for new "Islamic" governments. Ruling groups develop a body of words that marry general terms of Islam with maslahat ad-dawlah (interest of the state). In foreign policy, the use of Islamic terms of reference is particularly effective especially if Muhammad's wars with Jewish tribes in Arabia is used to discredit Arab peace efforts with Israel. Arab governments also rely on political literature in order to fill the gap produced by the absence of free media. Reliance on foreign broadcasts have often made Arab rulers nervous; they often complain to American and British diplomats about commentaries carried on BBC and Voice of America. Little emphasis was put on candid dialogue with the constituency especially when rulers feared internal threats and coup attempts.

Islam does not present itself to Arab regimes as a body of teachings or as a collection of daily rituals, as important as those teachings and rituals are for purposes of absorption into the official discourse. Islam means first and foremost a common bond between the rulers and the ruled, between those for whom Islam is a luxury and those for whom Islam is a daily necessity in the face of earthly hardships. Islam for regimes is a political imperative in light of the physical and mental isolation of governments from the people under their rule, it is the one pretension that may preserve the tie of mutual recognition between the parties. The state needs Islam not so much to inspire its policies but to convince the people that policies spring from the same source of people's philosophical outlook. For one side Islam is an excuse, for the other it is the explanation. For the governments, Islam is an obvious means of political exploitation and ideological articulation, while Islam for the people remains an ill-defined sources of moral identification.

The use of Islam in foreign policy discourse is, of course, not new. It goes back all the way to the day of the early Islamic caliphate when rulers had to obtain the support of wary people by providing a moral continuity between Muhammad's rule and theirs. Muslim rulers rationalized their power through the invocation of Islamic terms, symbols, and motifs. The net effect was not necessarily popular conviction and consent, but cynicism emanating from the relegation of Islam to matters of power politics. Thus, when the third Rightly-Guided Caliph `Uthman spent ten thousands dirham on the expansion of the Prophet's Mosque people said: "He is expanding [the Prophet's] mosque and straying from his path."[21] The exaggeration of the effectiveness of governmental exploitation of Islam for political purposes reached its peak in Western scholarship dealing with Islamic law and its relevance to the modern world.

For a long time, analysis of contemporary Middle East politics could not be conducted without the customary reference to the Islamic global split of Dar al-Islam (abode of Islam) and Dar al-Harb (abode of war)[22], and no mention was made of the third legal category, observed since Muhammad's time and known as Dar as-Sulh (abode of concord). This application of ancient and obsolete notions of governance only perpetuated the myth of Islamic determinants of foreign policy. But this distinction between the two worlds was devised long after Muhammad's death and it represented the political interests of new insecure states. The presentation of permanent struggle between two ostensible worlds, of vaguely defined entities, helped in preserving the mobilizing mood of the empire. It also was useful in the wars of expansion, the relationship of which to Islam was purely propagandistic. References to the two abodes appear only in the classical legal literature and in Orientalist writings on Islam.

Modern Arab governments have incorporated into their legal systems influences from Western legal codes in areas of commerce and diplomacy. The role of Islam in diplomacy is minimal in present-day Arab world although foreign policy statements are full with religious citations. Governments do not deviate from the established pattern of Islamic political terminology, which characterized political discourse soon after the death of the Prophet.

It is in this realm of political jargon that Islam was, and remains, a strong presence. The Gulf War contained vivid examples by all the Arab parties to the conflict of the role of Islam, as a language and ideology. When the crown prince of Kuwait announced the news of the Iraqi invasion he did not refer to Kuwait as Kuwait but as "the Kuwait of Islam and Arabism."[23] On the other side, Saddam did not wait long before he ordered the Islamic phrase "God is Great" be imposed on the Iraqi flag. In Saudi Arabia the announcement of the decision to invite the American forces to the kingdom was accompanied by an official statement by the subservient body of clerics who stressed that "the Qur'an and the Prophetic path indicated the necessity of preparedness and timely precautions."[24]

The invocation of Islamic language in the form of Qur'anic citations and Hadith quotations is as old as the practice of government in Islam. The practice was briefly interrupted in the 1950s and 1960s when the fashionable language was social justice and Arab nationalism. Nasir, however, would fluctuate in his speeches depending not only on his audience but also on the moment of history. The influence of religion increased in his speeches after his defeat in 1967 while the discourse of the Ba'th became less and less secular especially after the overthrow of the regime of Salah Jadid in Syria in 1970. The regime of Salah Jadid tried, but not for too long, a version of secularism that simply ignores the presence of religion in social life. Furthermore, the Islamic character of Nasir's enemies in the Gulf region discredited the role of Islam in politics. Nasir was often sarcastic in his speeches about the Islamic proclamations emanating from Saudi Arabia.

It may be argued that the need for the Islamic rationalization of politics in general and foreign policy in particular is due to the dependence of most Arab regimes on external sponsors. In the era of the Cold War, most Arab countries were closely associated with one of the two superpowers. Those who were aligned with the Soviet Union had to assert their respect for Islam, in their language and political rituals, for fear of alienating a population that is assumed to be generally pious. The pro-Western governments, on the other hand, had to deal with the perceptions of their regimes as servants of detested Western powers. For Saudi Arabia, the association with the West, and with the US in particular, was problematic because the very moral foundations of the regime were rooted in an extremist, puritanical sect of Islam. The marriage with the US clashed with the declared cultural antagonism to "Western lifestyles."

The association between official foreign policy and ideology is closely related to the realm of the "culture industry," to where ideas are produced for mass consumption and political legitimization. The purpose behind the culture industry to keep the masses linked to the state through a system of mutually understood symbols. The Islamic culture industry today, for example, is intended to generate a degree of public identification with the state in light of the underground production of Islamic ideas. The state utilizes the realm of cultural production to adjust to the changing moods of its population especially when the popularity of Islamic ideas rose sharply after 1979. Foreign policy becomes particularly important here because it reveals the manners and conduct of behavior of Islamic states with other non-Islamic states. It also reflects state attitudes to the Arab-Israeli conflict, which is visible in every facet of Arab foreign policy formulation.

The Islamic culture industry contains officially sanctioned Islamic institutions and bodies that are on the payroll of the government. The state generates carefully controlled edicts that aid in the government's efforts of political rationalization and legitimization. It embodies the fatwa-issuing arms of the state apparatus. The legitimacy of those bodies came increasingly under attack in the late 1970s when Khumayni publicized the dichotomy between the Sultan's clerics and the people's clerics. In Egypt and elsewhere in the Arab world a new generation of clerics, with superficial or no affiliations with the state, expressed views and opinions that clashed with official fatwas.

The language of Islam, which is not monolithic given the diverse interests and characteristics of Islamic Arab governments, serves the regime well because it derives from the Qur'an itself, the one source that knows no dispute over its moral centrality. Sadat, for example, had to increase the references to the Qur'an and Hadith after his trip to Jerusalem because the legitimacy of the regime was diminished and because he was on the defensive. He had to borrow more symbols and jargons from the source of the Islamic Idea. Similarly, the rise of Islamic fundamentalist threats throughout the region and the participation of Arab armies on the side of the US during the Gulf War have increased the need for Islamic language in foreign policy although the foreign policy itself became more pro-Western. In other words, moments of legitimacy crisis increase Islamic rationalization of foreign policy. Governments feel more need for the assertion of an Islamic identity. Iraq and Saudi Arabia both resorted to heavy Islamic rationalization during the cold war. In the absence of reliable public opinion surveys in those countries, one cannot judge the relative effectiveness of propaganda campaigns.

The use of Islam in foreign policy language is not restricted to governments alone. Opposition groups, especially those which base their ideologies on Islamic terms of reference, also use Islam in their political discourse to discredit the governments that they oppose. This political war between governments and opposition groups has escalated the struggle over the "soul of Islam." Various competing factions and groups speak in the name of "the true Islam." Emphasis on authenticity, a fashionable word in contemporary Arab political literature, represents the absence of a central course of arbitration. The conflict is not settled and it spills over to the various facets of social and political life.

2. Arab Solidarity as a Form of Regime Protection

The era of Arab nationalism is still misunderstood. It is often treated as a phase, as a mere shift in the Arab collective mood. The death of Nasir confirmed the transitory nature of the idea. In reality, the idea of Arab nationalism never meant the same thing for the governments and their subject people. Arab nationalism was, and is, incongruent with state interests because of its prescriptive disruptive connotations. It requires for its satisfaction a total elimination of the current state system and its transformation into a new one all-encompassing Arab state. No transitory solutions of alliances and pacts could satisfy the aspirations of Arab nationalists who put into question the very existence of modern nation-states. Their project, however, clashed with the requirements of self-preservation among rulers protecting precarious, and in most cases, newly created entities. Arab nationalism was not an ideology of the elite imposed on the masses, and was not a mass ideology founding its way to the top. It came about as a result of intellectual dissatisfaction with the Ottoman Empire and with its ability to adapt to Western reformist ideas. The appeal of the idea among the masses was based on a desire to reverse the acts of colonial powers, especially when the creation of the Arab entity resonated in the historical memory of a population taught the glory of the Arab/Islamic past.

Yet, Arab regimes were able to incorporate the themes of Arab nationalist ideologies in their discourse without abandoning their sensitivity to the Islamic question. The solution was formulated through a marriage between the two, Kuwait becomes at once a state of "Islam and Arabism." The listener, the citizen, may pick and choose from the available menu of ideologies provided to her/him by government rhetoric. Those who restricted menu choices, like Saudi Arabia, had less popular appeal outside their own borders but they compensated through the provision of social and economic benefits to welfare state recipients. Those who broadened menu choices, or changed them with time, like Yasir Arafat and the Nasserist movement, suffered from ideological incoherence, which often translates into organizational factionalism and ineffectiveness.

Arab regimes talked, and still talk, about Arab ties of brotherhood (mention of sisterhood may offend honor-conscious clerics of the government) but they did not have Arab nationalism in mind. Instead, a system of state solidarity, expressed superficially through public statement and official visits, was reached to avoid the consequences of real unionist commitments that even the verbally zealous Qadhdhafi found hard to keep. The end of the U.A.R. experience put an end to Arab official expectations of a reconciliation between Arab nationalist aspirations – articulated popularly – and preservations of existing regimes. The Ba`th did not expect that unity with Nasir's Egypt was a prelude to organizational suicide, on which Nasir was insistent. To appease the populace the regimes had to maintain rhetorical references to Arabism – less and less to Arab unity itself as a goal – while pledging cooperation and coordination with "fellow Arab brothers" (sisters are forgotten in the official discourse).

That Arab nationalism is not a determinant of foreign policy of Arab states should not dismiss the political salience of the idea from Middle East analysis. The continued attention to its incorporation in official jargon reflects its appeal among the public. Nor is Arab cooperation and coordination, as loosely as it is defined and used, a determinant of foreign policy orientation. The Syrian-Israeli, Palestinian-Israeli, and Jordanian-Israeli tracks in the on-going peace negotiations were separate from one another in pace and in substance.

The negotiating teams approached "peace talks" from the perspectives of narrow regime interests despite promises of coordination. The three Arab negotiating teams often surprised each other with statements and developments, and in fact competed – in the case of the Palestinian and Jordanian teams – for the speediest resolution of thorny issues in hope of pleasing the American administration, which is always too eager to take credit for progress that is not of its own making.

As things stand today, the efforts of Arab solidarity are used to further the leadership role of one Arab state or another. The Egyptian government of Husni Mubarak has played an important role in urging the Arab governments to coordinate their efforts before proceeding in their relationships and negotiations with Israel and the West. It is used to undermine the efforts of one government (like Jordan) to monopolize closeness with an outside power (like Israel or the US). Arab solidarity was also championed by Saddam in his war against Iran in order to extract concessions and financial grants from his Arab brethren. It does not, however, reflect a plan of regional unification, nor does it stand as an alternative to former plans of phased Arab unity. This is understood by the Arab people who rarely take seriously talks of Arab coordination and who are aware that many Arab governments are closer to non-Arab countries than they are to one another. It is arguable that Jordan's relations with Israel are today better than Jordan's relations with any other Arab country and with the Palestinians who constitute close to 70 percent of the Jordanian population.

3. The Fear of Erring on the Palestinian Question

It can not be claimed that Arab governments were in fact ever committed to a resolution of the Palestinian problem. If anything the longevity of the Palestinian problem provided Arab regimes from the maghrib to the mashriq with the golden opportunity of building overreaching military-intelligence apparatuses all in the name of working towards the liberation of Palestine. In the 1950s and the 1960s, when Arab masses were less cynical than what they were turned into after 1967, military expenditure was one of the resources of legitimacy. People must have believed that military solutions are necessary for the final resolution of the Palestinian problem. Political violence, in whosever hands, was seen as a political and national imperative. The belief in the efficacy of political violence does not stem from some peculiar political culture, or from a unique genetic makeup, as has been alleged in the body of classical orientalism and its modern outgrowth, but from a reading of the region's history. Colonial powers imposed their will by force and created new states by force; the idea of popular consent was shelved and disregarded. National will and individual will have been crushed by force by regimes in the contemporary history of the region, or by the US in the Gulf War.

Post-independence regimes, along with the PLO, compensated for their weaknesses and lack of political accountability by promoting political violence as the most successful method in international affairs. The Vietnamese experience, as an illustration of third world military success against the mighty armed forces of the US, was used by third world regimes to rationalize their focus on military/intelligence construction.

Arab regimes were concerned in their foreign policies with the consequences of the Arab-Israeli conflict, they were even more concerned with the impact of unchecked rise of Palestinian nationalism. The very creation of the PLO, with unusual Saudi and Egyptian cooperation at the time, was the direct result of the growing independence of the nascent Palestinian political movement, represented by the Fath movement. The independence of the Palestinian national movement, which Arab regimes successfully aborted, could have dragged Arab regimes into unwanted confrontations with Israeli, just as the verbal wars between the Ba`th and Nasir dragged three Arab regimes into the 1967 war although only one of them was truly interested in fighting Israel.

The Palestinian question today has been marginalized from the rhetoric and practice of Arab regimes. The peace accord between the PLO and Israel allowed Arab regimes to seek at different paces peace and normalization with Israel. The new Arab official acceptance of Israel does not imply a change of Arab popular sentiments on the Palestinian question. Arab regimes are only calculating that peace with Israel is more rewarding economically and politically than the ostensible state of war. The results of the Gulf War changed the way Arab regimes deal with their own people; it made them less dishonest about their intentions vis-a-vis Israel and the US They now assume that they can get away with a strong identification with the West. Nasir had earlier set different standards of regional interaction and jargon whereby no government – not even Saudi Arabia and Jordan – was expected to align itself openly and untimidly with the US Arab regimes fear less popular disturbances and unexpected coups d'etat, and when those occur, whether in Jordan or in Qatar, they are the product of domestic issues or ruling family squabbles.

The salience of the Palestinian question has often clashed with dictates of regional and international alliances. The fear of Israeli involvement during the Gulf War affected Arab official attitudes to the war coalition. They wanted to join the war efforts to please the US administration but were afraid of potential Israeli intervention that would make their participation look like an alliance with the Jewish state. The US, aware of those Arab sentiments, pressed Israel to stay out of the war even when key Israeli leaders were eager to bomb Iraq.

4. Security and Stability

While the ideological determinants have been emphasized in Western writings about the Middle East, Arab regimes often formulate their policies on the basis of immediate needs and situations. Arab regimes tend to seek a preservation of the existing regional system, causing little disturbances in the balance of forces unless one can achieve success with little risk of retribution. Saudi Arabia's foreign policy, for example, is far from the widely spread "myth of non-alignment"[25] but the royal family avoids overly ambitious attempts at expanding influence. The precariousness of royal family rules in the Gulf region has deterred those regimes from radical adventures in the regional system. Of course, any direct threat to their rule or influence would be met by firmness and force, as the events leading up to the Gulf War have shown. The Saudi Royal family tolerated Saddam's adventures in the Middle East but was unwilling to accept his threat to monarchist rule in the region. Similarly, Saudi Arabia was willing to achieve a peaceful understanding with Nasir in the 1960s as long as he was willing to end his efforts at overthrowing the rule of the Saud family.

In the past, Arab regimes could not admit to their people that their own security and survival were the most decisive determinants of their foreign policies; they had to hide their interests behind the flowery rhetoric of Arab unity, liberation of Palestine, and Islamic glory. Violence and threats of violence in Arab people's lives allowed the governments to instill respect for the rule of law, as illegitimate and as unjust as it may be in the eyes of the citizens. The people of Syria, for example, feared the death of Hafidh Al-Asad in the 1980s during his illness, not so much due to emotional attachment or political identification but for fear of the unknown, of the president's tested brother, Rif at. Present-day Arab regimes have been in power for decades and have achieved for their people a measure of predictable pattern of autocracy and oppression. Any sudden change in the political system would cause confusion and panic especially when regional history is full of violent changes of government. The predictability of oppressive rule rationalizes fear and suffering; it does not legitimize power even if it facilitates its extension and prolongation.

Towards that purpose, Arab regimes have made the survival of their populations dependent on their own survival. This method of political communication between the rulers and the ruled is not new; Islamic thinkers like al-Ghazzali often warned of the evil of fitnah (sedition) which only helped to perpetuate the rule of the unjust. The price of achieving justice was exaggerated and measured in blood. Acceptance of current rulers became less costly, or was portrayed as less costly, than the price of change.

The protracted Lebanese civil war, the on-going civil war in Algeria, and the seemingly unending conflict in Sudan, all were used by Arab governments to discredit the process of change and democratization. It was argued that change, unless designed and managed from above, would harm the people. Only the continuity of the regimes could guarantee the safety of the ever fearful population. The government of Bahrain dissolved the parliament as soon as the Lebanese civil war started, and it told its subject population that it was sparing it the agony of civil wars.

The Gulf War allowed Arab governments to use the Iraqi invasion of Kuwait as one of the dangers looming over the population's horizons. Security arrangements with the US are no more the taboo they used to be because they are now portrayed as a protection of the very survival of the country, not merely of the royal family. The Iraqi government after all erased the very legal existence of Kuwait, which ironically helped to solidify the Kuwait national front against the Iraqi invasion of the country. The security argument, however, may be more convincing in the Gulf region than it is in other parts of the Arab world where security does not exist anyway and where security is meaningless to the poor masses. The citizens of the Gulf have something to protect, not only the wealth of the rich but the real material benefits derived from citizenship. The people of Yemen have much less to protect and defend especially when the government has failed in providing either security or prosperity.

Conclusion

What is to be emphasized is that the foreign policy making in the Arab world is less different from policy making procedures in other countries. Official propaganda declarations should be taken less seriously and the dismissal of domestic determinants of foreign policy is intended to serve the legitimacy of the ruling regimes.[26] Domestic influences are discredited because they are associated with regimes' interests and calculations. It is rare to associate domestic concerns with the interests of citizens in the region. Fixation with foreign policy in the Arab world was only a sign of the intellectual and political bankruptcy of Arab rulers. Foreign policy is the realm of long term promises and declarations, it allows rulers to divert attention from the domestic situation. Few Arab rulers, probably with the exception of the Egyptian president who knows that he can ignore the local scene and sentiments at his own peril in the wake of Sadat's assassination, dwell in their speeches on domestic issues. The speeches of King Husayn, Hafidh Al-Asad, Saddam Husayn, King Hasan II, King Fahd and Mu`ammar Qadhdhafi focus on Islam and Arab-Israeli questions, domestic issues are left to weak and ineffective prime ministers whose missions are to take the blame for whatever goes wrong internally. Successes have to be attributed to the genius of the leader, the hero and the savior.

The study of foreign policy in Arab states is marred by a variety of factors. Ministers in the region, especially those dealing with foreign policy and national security, operate in the utmost of secrecy. Declassification of documents is still unknown in the region, and only the trusted loyalists are given access to state documents and official interviews. Furthermore, this very problem of secrecy of deliberations and foreign policy creates another problem: researchers and analysts wound up paying too much attention to official discourse to compensate for the scarcity of resources. If the study of officialdom is difficult, the study of the masses is even harder. Citizens are either prevented from expressing their views freely or public opinion surveys in places like Lebanon, Jordan, and Egypt are not conducted according to the standards of academic social science. Certain questions cannot be asked and certain assumptions have to be made, or the entire survey project would not be permitted. The role of Islam in political behavior, for example, remains a mystery and the appeal of Arab nationalism will not be properly understood without a comprehensive Arab-wide public opinion survey.

These methodological problems, however, do not justify the pervasive misconceptions in the West about Arab foreign policy orientation and their making. They should not perpetrate the theologyocentric school or the school that focus on ideological determinants of foreign policy. Instead, foreign policy needs to be studied with special references to the internal political situation in each country under study. Moreover, official discourse has to be critically analyzed, but not necessarily believed literally.

Recent events on the Arab-Israeli front have exposed the vulnerability of Arab regimes, many of which have been all too eager to mend fences with the Jewish state and please the American administration. American foreign policy has always been predicated on the willingness to reward those regimes (like communist Rumania or Sadat's Egypt) that are willing to violate national conventions or regional political standards in fostering ties with Israel. Qatar was the eager emirate that was insistent of proceeding towards peace with Israel in total disregard of the timetable and priorities of the Gulf Cooperation Council. Those independent decisions are often rationalized, if not totally denied in the state media, by asserting the "independent will of the nation." The nation and the citizen become one when the government needs to respond to criticisms and challenges from other states and when defeat is suffered by the armed forces. The so-called Iraqi victory against Iran in the first Gulf War was that of Saddam alone (known in official propaganda as Qadisiyyat Saddam), but the defeat of Iraq in the second Gulf War was one that was to be shared by the entire nation either as a testimony to the inescapable will of God or as a necessary stance of national unity in the face of external conspiracies.

Notes

1. See Michael Brecher, "The Subordinate State System of Southern Asia," in James Rosenau, ed., International Politics and Foreign Policy, (New York: Free Press, 1969), p. 155.

2. See Walter Carlsnaes, Ideology and Foreign Policy, (Oxford: Basil Blackwell, 1986), p. 2.

3. Two influential works were: Claire Sterling, The Terror Network: The Secret War of International Terrorism, (New York: Rinehart, and Winston, 1981); and Binyamin Netanyahu, Terrorism: How the West Can Win, (NY: Farrar, 1986).

4. Vojtech Mastny, "Ideology and Foreign Policy in Historical Perspective," in George Schwab, ed., Ideology and Foreign Policy: A Global Perspective, (New York: Cyrc Press, 1978), p. 8.

5. Ibid, p. 12.

6. Hans Morgenthau, "The Organic Relationship between Ideology and Political Reality," in Ibid, p. 120.

7. From a 1977 lecture at New York University cited in Stanley Kober, "Idealpolitik," in Richard Betts, ed., Conflict after the Cold War: Arguments on Causes of War and Peace, (NY: Macmillan, 1994), p. 251.

8. See Henry Kissinger, Nuclear Weapons and Foreign Policy, (New York: Harper, 1957).

9. Cited in Walter Carlsnaes, Ideology, p. 3.

10. Richard Cottam, Foreign Policy Motivation: A General Theory and A Case Study, (Pittsburgh: University of Pittsburgh Press, 1977), p. 40.

11. Ibid, p. 39.

12. Richard Niemi, and Herbert Weisberg, eds., Classics in Voting Behavior (Washington, D.C.: Congressional Quarterly Press, 1993), p. 50.

13. For the obituary of and debate about Arab nationalism, see Tawfic Farad, ed., Pan-Arabism and Arab Nationalism, (Boulder: Westview Press, 1987).

14. For a fuller elaboration on this theme, see As`ad AbuKhalil, "A New Arab Ideology? The Rejuvenation of Arab Nationalism," The Middle East Journal, Vol. 46, No. 1 (Winter 1992).

15. For a descriptive summary of Arab ideological ideas, see Paul Salem, Bitter Legacy: Ideology and Politics in the Arab World, (Syracuse: Syracuse University Press, 1994).

16. Karl Mannheim, Ideology and Utopia, (New York: Harcourt Brace, 1936).

17. Information about sales of books is obtained from booksellers in Morocco and Lebanon.

18. Theodor Adorno, The Jargon of Authenticity, (Evanston: Northwestern University Press, 1973), p. xxi.

19. See Zbigniew Brezezinski, Ideology and Power in Soviet Politics, (New York: Praeger, 1967), ch. 5.

20. Bernard Lewis, The Political Language of Islam, (Chicago: University of Chicago Press, 1988).

21. Reported by Al-Baladhuri in his Ansab as quoted in `Alawi, Hadi, Al-Mustatraf Al-Jadid, (Damascus: Markaz al-Abhath wa-l-Dirasat al-Ishtirakiyyah fi-l-`Alam al-`Arabi, u.d.), p. 51.

22. See Elie Kedourie, Politics in the Middle East, (Oxford: Oxford University Press, 1992), p. 2.

23. See Uktubar, August 12, 1990.

24. As cited in Al-Majmu`ah Al-I`lamiyyah, Malaffat Badhdad, (Badhdad Files), (Jiddah: Al-Majmu`ah Al-I`lamiyyah, 1411 D.H.), p. 57.

25. Ghassan Salamah, As-Siyasa-l-Kharijiyyah-s-Sa`udiyyah mundhu `am 1945, (Saudi Foreign Policy since 1945), (Beirut: Ma`had Al-Inma' al-`Arabi, 1980), p. 279.

26. See in this respect Bashshar Al-Ja`fari, As-Siyasa-l-Kharijiyya-s-Suriyyah 1946-1982, (Syrian Foreign Policy 1946-1982), (Damascus: Dar Tlas, 1987).

Chapter 5

Israeli Foreign Policy in the Era of Pax Americana

Stephen Zunes

Introduction

Israel is entering a new era in its relationships with its Middle Eastern neighbors and the international community. The forces shaping these new relationships are far more significant than the often-overstated ideological differences between the two major political blocs in Israeli politics: the center-left Labor and the right-wing Likud. What transcends domestic Israeli politics is the role Israel plays in the post-Cold War international system dominated by the United States, which treats Israel as its key ally in a region seen as crucial for American interests. Yet changes within Israel itself, among the Palestinians and elsewhere in the Middle East have also placed the Israelis at a crossroads in the development of their foreign policy goals and the options available to them.

Internal Dynamics

Due in part to an electoral system based on proportional representation, Israeli foreign policy is driven more by public opinion than is the foreign policy of many countries. In addition, unlike the United States, with its strong sense of security made possible by wide oceans and friendly neighbors, the Israeli public has never enjoyed the luxury of placing foreign policy issues low on its scale of political concerns. As a result, public opinion can be a decisive factor in foreign policy options available to the government. At the same time, it would be a mistake to put forward a naively pluralistic model of foreign policy formulation in Israel, in part due to the fact that Israeli public opinion, like public opinion elsewhere, is subject to manipulation by those in power.

The overriding sentiment among the Israeli public regarding its foreign relations is that of fear. While the actual threat to Israel's survival posed by its Arab neighbors has been and continues to be exaggerated, there is no question that there have indeed been powerful forces in the Middle East which have sought the destruction of the Jewish state. In addition, there has always been an assumption in Israel – also highly dubious, but sincerely and widely believed – that if Israel was ever defeated militarily, there would be a systematic slaughter of virtually the entire Jewish population.[1] Decades of terrorist attacks against innocent Jewish civilians have seemed to only confirm such assumptions.

This fear and mistrust has much deeper roots, however. The very survival of the Jewish people has been under constant threat for centuries. The Holocaust was just the most extreme of the periodic waves of persecution over the generations which has left a deep-seated level of terror in large sections of the world's Jewish population. This internalized manifestation of anti-Semitism makes consistently rational strategic and diplomatic decisions on the part of Israelis extremely difficult even in the best of circumstances. For those in positions with a political, ideological or financial stake in encouraging such fears for personal gain, the exploitation of such widespread feelings of paranoia, isolation and imminent destruction among the Israeli public is not difficult.[2]

Related to this is the deeply-rooted sense by many Jews – again, based on historical experience – that no non-Jew can be trusted, and that even those seemingly willing to cooperate on some level will eventually turn on them. As a result, the worldview of virtually Israel's entire foreign policy elite across the political spectrum, as well as for much of the population, is essentially Hobbesian in nature. If one's very survival is seen to be at stake, there is little aptitude for adherence to international law, universal standards of human rights, U.N. Security Council resolutions, or similar principles, particularly if you have the world's most powerful nation protecting you from the consequences of non-compliance. The widely-held assumptions in Israel of realpolitik has rather profound implications for Israeli foreign relations, which in part explains the rather presumptuous nature of many Israeli demands in peace negotiations, the tradition of grossly disproportionate responses in military engagements, and the rather self-righteous view of their actions in the face of frequent and widespread denunciation from the global community. Again, this is an area where demagogues can exploit popular insecurities and the commonly held siege mentality to maintain foreign policy positions which would be untenable in most democratic societies.

This could not be better represented than in the surprise victory of Likud Bloc leader Benjamin Netanyahu in the May 1996 election for prime minister, who triumphed despite the great strides towards peace and security under the Labor government in the preceding years. Building on the reaction to terrorist attacks in Israeli cities earlier that year, Netanyahu was able to convince large numbers of Israelis that it was concessions to the Palestinians which had caused the terrorism, despite the consensus by most observers that it was just the opposite: the slowness and limited nature of Palestinian rights under the peace process. Yet such tactics have never been limited to the Likud: leaders of the Labor Zionist movement – including Shimon Peres, Yitzhak Rabin, Golda Meir, and others dating back to David Ben-Gurion – had also engaged in similar behavior to marginalize those on the Israeli left and peace movement seeking greater accommodation with the Palestinians and neighboring Arab states. Having for years demonized the Syrian and Palestinian leadership in an effort to win support for Israel's confrontational policies and refusal to accept territorial compromise, Rabin and Peres found themselves suddenly having to convince a still largely-skeptical public that these Arab leaders could actually be partners in making peace.[3]

Due to both the real and perceived strategic vulnerability of the Israeli state, more pluralistic models of foreign policy formulation are similarly challenged by the close and widely-accepted linkages between foreign policy and national security. In any society, when national security is seen to be at stake, democracy suffers. Thus, despite the existence of strong democratic institutions in Israel,[4] the level of involvement by the Israeli military in that country's foreign relations goes well beyond what would be considered acceptable in the United States and most Western democracies.[5] Indeed, in a recent critique of the foreign policy of Arab despots, American Middle East scholar and former presidential advisor William Quandt observed, "Israel, despite its democratic form of government, also had autocratic leaders who made decisions in secret that were disastrous for its people and for its neighbors."[6]

Perhaps no aspect of Israeli foreign policy has been more controversial in the international community than its history of territorial expansion in contravention to international legal norms supporting the inviolability of international boundaries and the prohibition against territorial acquisition by force. Traditional strategic thinking in Israel has been based on the assumption that due to its small size, quick decisive offensive strikes were the best defense and that a qualitative military edge was necessary to challenge the numerical superiority of combined Arab forces. Without much in the way of strategic depth, Israel's occupation of the territory of neighboring countries provided a buffer giving Israeli forces time to organize and strike back before the attacking armies could reach Israeli population centers. While this rationale has lost much of its credibility by Israel's commitment to move population centers into the supposed buffer zones through the establishment of settlements in the occupied lands, all Israeli governments have backed, to varying degrees, such colonization efforts.[7]   Such actions, however, have resulted in widespread opposition in the international community, particularly among Third World nations which saw such Israeli policies – made possible in part by the economic, military and diplomatic support of Western nations – as comparable to traditional Western colonialism and imperialism. Indeed, such transfers of one's civilian population onto lands seized by military force is itself a direct contravention of international law; on several occasions, the United Nations Security Council has called unanimously on Israel to end its settlement drive.[8]

As a result of such practices, Israeli foreign policy for much of the 1970s and 1980s was based on damage control, largely defensive actions designed to avoid complete isolation, as country after country broke diplomatic relations and the U.N. General Assembly passed anti-Israel resolutions in every session.[9] As both a cause and effect of this isolation, Israeli foreign policy during this period relied to a large degree on secret channels, covert actions (including paramilitary operations,) illicit arms transfers and other clandestine tactics. Israel's closest allies during this period included some of the most brutal and despotic regimes in the world, including the military-dominated juntas in Guatemala and El Salvador, the apartheid regime in South Africa, the dergue in Ethiopia, and such notorious dictators as Jean-Claude Duvalier in Haiti and Mobutu Sese Seko in Zaire; Israel even sent arms to the Islamic regime in Iran, the openly anti-Semitic junta in Argentina and right-wing terrorists like the Nicaraguan Contras.[10] An important manifestation of this isolation, combined with the aforementioned obsession with national security, was the eclipsing of the foreign ministry during this period to the prerogatives of the military. Indeed, the Israeli foreign ministry – while originally conceived to be equivalent and complementary to the military – became relegated to largely technical and supportive roles. Foreign policy was essentially subsumed by perceived military/security exigencies.

Changes in Israeli Foreign Policy

Several major changes in the international environment in the early 1990s have resulted in significant changes in Israeli foreign relations:

The collapse of the Soviet Union meant that the loss of large-scale Soviet military assistance to some of Israel's most intractable Arab adversaries created a more secure strategic environment for Israel. Syria, in particular, had maintained its military strength primarily through its close and heavily subsidized strategic relationship with the U.S.S.R. It was clear that the regime of Hafez al-Assad would now be essentially on its own and would need to seek at least some level of cooperation with the West and a less belligerent stance towards Israel.

Another factor was the Gulf War, which led to the defeat of the Israel's most powerful potential Arab adversary and the enhanced predominance of the United States and pro-Western Arab regimes. Israel also recognized that the ascendant oil-rich Arab monarchies of the Gulf, whose extensive military hardware and wealth could conceivably have been used against Israel, now had far more immediate concerns from radical secular nationalists like Saddam Hussein as well as with Iran and its allied extremist Islamist movements. These new challenges were real threats to the survivability of the family dictatorships of the Gulf. By contrast, Israel realized that these regimes not only knew that Israel was not such a threat, but now realized that they shared a stake in maintaining the status quo in the region. Furthermore, victories in both the Cold War and Gulf War placed the United States, a strong supporter of Israel, in a position to set up an effective Pax Americana for the Middle East, in which Israel would serve a key role. The Gulf War also led the Israelis to realize that in an era of medium-range missiles and long-range artillery, strategic buffers were not as crucial to Israeli security as they were in 1967. Another implication was that it would be better to make peace with its Muslim Arab neighbors before countries like Iraq and Iran developed a full nuclear capability. A related understanding by increasing numbers of Israeli officials was that technological superiority, more than acreage of land, would be the most decisive factor in maintaining Israel's security. With the United States, the world's leader in military technology, maintaining its close strategic relationship with Israel, ongoing and increasing cooperation in such matters was not difficult to assume. This also implied, as most clearly exemplified in the use of American servicemen manning anti-missile defenses in Israel during Gulf War, that greater dependence on the United States would be required, further eroding Israel's tradition of independence of action.[11]

Israel's inability to crush the Palestinian intifada, meanwhile, brought home the realization that Palestinian rights could no longer be ignored. In a similar vein, the failure of the 1982 invasion of Lebanon and its aftermath to advance Israel's strategic goals to its north further undermined support for military solutions to political problems. In addition, the rise of Islamist movements in Palestine, Lebanon and elsewhere in the Middle East helped raise awareness that some compromises might be necessary to avoid encouraging more radical anti-Israel elements and that strictly military solutions could actually exacerbate such threats to Israel's security interests.

Theodore Friedgut of Hebrew University argues that Israeli peace moves in 1993 reflected shifts in the Israeli public which recognized: the need for Israel to become a legitimate player in Middle Eastern politics rather than live in a constant state of war; the desire to remain both Jewish and democratic, rather than sacrifice either in absorbing large Palestinian populations in the occupied territories; and, a growing willingness to enter negotiations with any party which recognized their country's legitimacy and refrained from acts of terror. In addition, in a shift which mirrored the parallel evolution in the thinking of their Arab neighbors towards them, the failure to quell the intifada taught the Israelis that force could not necessarily lead the other side into submission.[12]

Still another important development was the Israeli recognition of the global trend towards regional economic blocs and multilateral action as cornerstones of contemporary international relations. Israeli economic power relative to its immediate neighbors is immense and could serve as both a carrot and a stick to bring these countries into peaceful cooperation. Israel's gross national product is higher than the combined GNP of Egypt, Lebanon, Syria, Jordan, the West Bank and Gaza. It is indeed a tempting prospect for an increasingly affluent Israel to put its economic and technological power towards expanding the economy through free trade with its neighbors rather than perpetually preparing for war. According to Gad Yaacobi, the recent Israeli permanent representative to the U.N., making peace with the Palestinians and neighboring Arab states would be advantageous in that

> In so doing we would remove the stigma of combatant in an intractable conflict, which would result in a significant improvement in Israel's international relations. The door to greater regional and international integration would open, leaving us to focus our considerable energies and resources previously devoted to war on the expansion of our economy.[13]

Israeli participation in the Middle Eastern economic summit in Morocco in October 1994 was seen by many Israelis as symbolizing the greatly expanded Middle Eastern economic cooperation in which Israel would play a major role. Subsequently, economic ties – many of them semi-clandestine but nevertheless real – began growing between Israel and various Arab countries, including wealthy Gulf states, though many of these were severed as the peace process began to bog down.

One result of the moves towards peace and the changing international climate has been a remarkable revitalization of Israeli foreign relations in recent years. The number of countries which formally recognize Israel has doubled to over 140, transforming the country from an international pariah whose very right to exist was questioned by a majority of the world community to a full participant in international affairs on a variety of levels.[14] Israel now has full diplomatic relations with Egypt and Jordan and incipient relations with as many as a half dozen other Arab states. Israel has also been developing close economic and diplomatic relations with the newly emerging states of Central Asia and has expanded its commercial links with China, Japan, and the newly industrialized nations of East and Southeast Asia.[15] This has led the foreign ministry to attain unprecedented status; indeed, the Oslo Accords was almost exclusively an initiative at the foreign ministry level, which largely bypassed the Israeli military.[16] The foreign ministry continues to play the major role in the peace process, even under the Likud government.

Increasing numbers of Israelis are recognizing that their survival really isn't threatened anymore. They have shaken much of the cultural baggage from the Holocaust and are questioning the costs of the racism and intolerance which the occupation of Arab lands has brought onto Israeli society. The younger generation, in emphasizing the state of Israel rather than the land of Israel, shows an increased pragmatism now reflected by some elements of the Israeli establishment.[17] In addition, there is a sense among the growing numbers of native-born Israelis in leadership that rather than seeing the Arab world as a mass bent on Israel's destruction, that these are individual nations with their own unique interests which can be approached separately. Related to this is the belated realization that the Palestinians are a distinct people with their own interests which could be recognized without threatening the survival of the Jewish state.[18] Furthermore, Israel's economic and military power, particularly with the backing of the United States, is sufficiently strong as to ensure that peace could be made on terms so overwhelmingly favorable that Israel could allow for a degree of territorial compromise.

However, there is a countervailing trend of religious extremism and right-wing politics in this same generation which grew up as occupiers. Their answer to the dilemma of Jewish identity versus democracy is to shelve any pretense of adherence to democratic principles and to reject the enlightened pragmatism of the new strategic thinking in order to rationalize the continued occupation of Palestinian land as some kind of religious obligation. The growth in such sentiment came out of a growing sense of the hypocrisy of the Labor Zionist leadership which dominated Israel for much of the country's history: These younger religious Israelis saw an elite which made lip service to democratic ideals and the rule of law yet engaged in widespread human rights violations of a subject population and openly defied basic principles of international law. The Labor Alignment, led by an elite Ashkenazi minority, would identify with social democratic and even socialist principles while discriminating against the poor Sephardic majority which, along with Israeli Arabs, were seen and treated like backward children needing to be uplifted and not as a part of the decision-making process. The Labor elites would extol the virtue of self-reliance while cementing close ties with Western nations and claim Israel's uniquely Jewish identity while emulating some of the worst of Western secular consumerism and its concomitant cultural values. This reaction to Labor's rule helped give rise to the religious right-wing populism which played a major role in the election of successive Likud governments, including that of Netanyahu.

It is now widely accepted in Israel that decades of often-brutal occupation policies has had a debilitating impact upon Israeli democratic culture and has led to an estrangement from many secular Labor Zionist values. Such alienated Israelis were easy targets for those whose messianic chauvinistic ideology, not unlike their extremist Muslim counterparts in other Middle Eastern states, provided a spiritual and ideological framework through which their country's abandonment of its ideals could be rationalized and a sense of community could be formed. Spearheading land grabs in Palestinian territories, made possible by generous financial support from the Israeli government and private contributors in Israel and the United States, these religious zealots have made alliance with security hawks to form an effective working majority in Israeli politics which belies the more moderate and pragmatic shift in attitude for much of the rest of Israeli society described above.

Still, the Likud leadership now seems to support what they consider to be a "realistic" peace between enemies in order to forestall the advance of the common and more serious enemies from Islamic extremism and radical nationalism. Their foreign policy goals appear to be essentially the same that was articulated by the previous Labor government, namely

(1) Legitimacy, recognition by, and normalized relations with all members of the international community; (2) Middle East peace – going far beyond "negative peace" – implying only non-belligerence – to an agreed, contractual settlement of the Arab-Israeli conflict, the exchange of ambassadors, genuine confidence-building and peaceful economic collaboration; (3) secure and recognized borders; (4) free trade, enabling the country's sustained industrialization through greater commercial integration within the global economy and ease of access to world markets.[19]

None of these goals can be fully realized, however, unless the peace process moves forward.

The Peace Process

The Israeli position has traditionally been that it has always wanted peace but only recently have the Palestinians and Arab governments reciprocated. Indeed, as late as the 1970s, the Palestine Liberation Organization and virtually all Arab states were on the record opposing peace, or even negotiations, with the state of Israel. Yet, at the same time, Israel seemed reluctant to accept the principle of land for peace or to even recognize the Palestinians as a people with distinct rights. Israel rejected the Rogers Plan in 1969, crafted by the US Secretary of State on the basis of U.N. Security Council resolution 242, perhaps emboldened by then-US National Security Advisor Henry Kissinger's quiet recommendation that they not take it seriously. When Egyptian President Anwar Sadat made peace overtures to Israel in 1971 based on principles similar to what would become the Camp David Agreement, the Israelis (again, with apparent advice of Kissinger) chose to ignore it, a decision which resulted in the October 1973 War. Subsequent peace plans brought forth by the Europeans, the United Nations or Arab states (such as the Fahd Plan) were also rejected by Israel with no apparent US encouragement that they accept. Israel did participate, however, in US-directed disengagement plans which consciously avoided any comprehensive peace and instead focused upon step-by-step bilateral negotiations through American mediators.

The Camp David Accord of 1978 returned the Sinai Peninsula, captured by Israel in the 1967 War, to Egypt in return for a peace treaty. This effectively neutralized the most militarily-powerful Arab state, enabling Israel to increase its repression in the occupied Palestinian territories and, with its southern flank no longer of concern, invade Lebanon soon after implementation of the treaty was finalized. The Camp David provisions for Palestinian autonomy were never implemented as promised and the United States – the guarantor of the treaty – never insisted that Israel follow through. In many respects, the agreement was more of a tripartite military pact than a peace treaty, in that it mandated $5 billion in additional arms transfers from the United States to the two countries and provided for expanded US military activity in the region.

Subsequent efforts to resolve the Palestinian question, long the heart of the conflict, were unsuccessful. The Israelis categorically rejected the Reagan Plan of 1982, which called for Jordanian administration of a demilitarized West Bank, and even ignored the US call for a freeze on construction of Israel's illegal settlements in the occupied territories, reiterating that Israel had the right to apply their full sovereignty over those lands captured in the 1967 war. The Reagan administration acknowledged that they would not apply any overt pressure to challenge Israeli intransigence, an indication that they were not actually serious about implementing their own proposal.[20] This came despite requests by leaders in the opposition Labor Alignment that the US cut non-military aid to the Begin government to pressure compromise on the Reagan initiative.[21]

For more than two decades, the international consensus for peace between Israel and its Arab neighbors has supported a settlement where there would be guarantees for Israeli security within its internationally-recognized pre-1967 borders, Israeli withdrawal from occupied Arab lands, compensation for and/or repatriation of Palestinians expelled from their homes in 1947-48 and subsequently, and the establishment of a Palestinian state in the West Bank and Gaza with some special status for Jerusalem.   While most Arab states and the PLO have gradually come to accept such a settlement, Israel – backed by the United States – has not, insisting that Palestinians do not have the right to statehood, neither repatriation or compensation was required and that total withdrawal from the occupied territories was unacceptable.

With Israel in control militarily of the situation on the ground and the United States controlling the peace process itself, the possibilities for such a peace settlement were dim. Indeed, the peace talks that begun in Madrid in 1991 were designed to avoid a multi-party peace process which could develop such a comprehensive formula. Instead, the US organizers accepted the Israeli desire for a largely bilateral approach, on the lines of Camp David, so to weaken the chances of Arab unity which might lead to Palestinian independence alongside Israel. In addition, the US placed conditions, supported by Israel, that forbade the Palestinians from sending their own delegation, instead having the Palestinians form a sub-set of the Jordanian delegation, and then only if none of their representatives had direct affiliation with the PLO or came from Jerusalem or the Palestinian diaspora.   The simultaneous multilateral talks focusing on regional issues were designed in large part to advance Israel's position in the Middle East prior to Israeli withdrawal from the occupied territories, thereby minimizing pressure which could be brought to bear for Israeli concessions.   It soon became clear that the right-wing Israeli government was effectively using the peace process as a stalling tactic to avoid any kind of agreement while greatly expanding settlement activities in the occupied territories to create a fait accompli on the ground, a strategy later openly acknowledged by Prime Minister Yitzhak Shamir soon after he left office.

The subsequent Labor and Likud governments have taken a somewhat more moderate perspective. For the essentially militarist Israeli political establishment, there became a realization that Carl von Clauswitz's dictum of war being diplomacy by other means could also work the other way.[22] They realized that the bargaining position of the Arab parties was weak. The PLO, in particular, had lost much of the diplomatic and financial backing necessary to maintain their legitimacy since the Gulf War and the intifada was languishing from both widespread Israeli repression and internal factionalism.

With Israel's newly-elected Labor government recognizing the need for progress with the Palestinians and the United States barring PLO participation in the peace talks, the Israelis decided in 1993 to meet secretly with PLO representatives in a third country. There was a growing realization by the Israelis that to not talk with the PLO would mean that they eventually might have to talk with the burgeoning radical Hamas movement, whose strength was gaining as the official US-monitored peace process faltered. In addition, the moderate Palestinian intellectuals in the official talks were actually holding out for more Israeli concessions than was PLO leader Yasir Arafat, and these official representatives did not have much of a following in the territories anyway.

In the Oslo Accords signed in September 1993, the Israelis, while continuing to refuse to recognize Palestinian statehood, for the first time appeared to recognize Palestinian nationhood. The terms for Palestinian autonomy proposed by Israel were actually more generous than the proposals made by the United States two months earlier in the official talks and involved formal Israeli recognition of the PLO, which the United States had opposed. Many in Israel, for better or worse, saw these Principles of Understanding as providing the first in a series of steps which would eventually lead to Palestinian statehood. Other Israelis, also for better or worse, saw it as simply a rehashing of the Likud's old formula of allowing autonomy for people but not for land, relinquishing Israeli responsibilities for occupation while still maintaining effective control by giving the Palestinians only limited autonomy in small enclaves comparable to American Indian reservations or the Bantustans of apartheid-era South Africa. The vagueness of the agreement, the asymmetrical power relationship between the two parties, and the US support of some of the more hard-lined elements in the Israeli government gave the Israelis an enormous latitude in interpretation.

Five years after the signing of the agreement, 70% of the West Bank and 30% of the much smaller Gaza Strip remained in exclusive Israeli hands, including most of the major roads and water resources. Israelis still determine who can come in and out of the territories and who can travel between the Palestinian zones. The Palestinian-controlled areas – approximately 17% of the West Bank – are chopped up into small enclaves surrounded by Israeli troops and heavily-armed settlers. Even where Palestinians are nominally in charge, Palestinian authorities have no right to arrest any Israeli, no matter how serious the crime. Israeli forces make periodic forays into the heart of such Palestinian cities as Nablus and Bethlehem (ostensibly to guarantee access to Jewish holy sites) and still control the center of the city of Hebron. Despite pulling back troops partially from 450 small towns and villages – consisting of an additional 20% of the territory – Israeli authority in these rural areas will also remain paramount. Most Palestinians are barred from entering Jerusalem, the West Bank's largest city and the Palestinians' traditional cultural, commercial, religious, health care and educational center. As transportation routes are currently designed, this also effectively cuts the West Bank in half.

Within Israel, there was vocal opposition by the extreme right of the Oslo Accords, particularly while the Labor government was in power; these Israeli rightists opposed any such compromise on behalf of the government. There was also some consternation in the Israeli peace movement, which feared that this agreement was unlikely to bring peace, a sentiment which grew as Prime Minister Netanyahu continued to stall in negotiations. Some members of the Israeli delegation to the Washington peace talks while Labor was in charge privately requested to American officials that the US put public pressure on their government to compromise further, so they could justify further concessions; the Clinton administration refused, however. Many Israelis, including some top military officers, believe that Israel would be far more secure with a demilitarized Palestinian state on their borders than to maintain its quasi-occupation with the logistical nightmare of providing security for the scores of Jewish settlements – many of them consisting of religious extremists who have engaged in provocative actions against the Palestinian population – scattered throughout the West Bank and Gaza.

Such a perspective remains a minority position, however, and there are few signs that Israeli policy will change. The Likud government of Netanyahu recognized the facts created by the Oslo Accords, largely because the re-occupation of heavily-populated Palestinian areas would likely be met with stiff resistance and would not be acceptable to Israeli public opinion, but they would not expand Palestinian self-rule much further. The Israeli government also claims it has full rights for military intervention anywhere, including the Palestinian-controlled areas.[23] Indeed, Israel had no compunction about bringing troops, tanks, armored personnel carriers and helicopter gunship into the supposedly autonomous areas during the September 1996 clashes.

Critics of the Oslo formula argue that current Israeli policy towards the Palestinians, and even the policies under Peres and Rabin, is not that major a departure from the policy of the past three decades. In many respects, it is argued, the Oslo Accords and their aftermath are simply a reformulation of old plans which circumvent and defer Palestinian self-determination and independence; Israel is simply reorganizing its occupation, not ending it. Indeed, with Israel redeploying its troops away from Palestinian population centers while still controlling most of the land and resources, expanding Jewish settlements and the infrastructure supporting them, and solidifying its hold over greater Jerusalem, there is little hope for authentic self-determination for the Palestinian people in any real sense beyond control over local administrative affairs. Quandt describes the Israeli-Palestinian talks as follows:

> Israelis determine how far they are prepared to go; the Palestinians protest and threaten to walk out; the United States urges both sides to be reasonable; and after many delays and much shouting, the Israelis get most of what they initially proposed. This is not surprising, given the disparities between the parties concerned and the lack of any real leverage on the Palestinian side, but it does suggest that the final-status negotiations. . . will be extraordinarily difficult.[24]

There is legitimate concern, then, that the interim agreements reached thus far will essentially become the final agreement. As a result, right-wing Jewish settlers and other Israeli hard-liners will feel emboldened, the Palestinians will feel betrayed and the extremists on both sides will gain.

The peace agreement between Jordan and Israel signed in October 1994 was less a long-overdue triumph of the forces of reason and reconciliation than simply a capitulation by the weaker party. From a strictly bilateral perspective, Jordan did not fare badly in the details of the final agreement. The major compromise by the Jordanians was not in regard to any of their own purely nationalistic interests, but in that this final treaty took place outside of a comprehensive Arab-Israeli peace agreement. The Clinton administration successfully pressured Jordan to abandon its longstanding promise to not pursue a separate peace and settle. And the United States had clout: US policies over recent years had so damaged the Jordanian economy that the king was essentially forced to agree to settle on US terms to get the needed assistance from the world's one remaining superpower in order to survive. With King Hussein's economy reeling and suffering from an enormous foreign debt, President Bill Clinton offered to bail out the troubled monarch if he made a separate peace with Israel.[25]

For the Israeli government, meeting Jordan's modest terms was fairly painless compared with the complexity of autonomy negotiations with the PLO, so it was something Israelis could celebrate without a lot of internal bickering. Since Jordan shared Israel's largest border, its opening could be a gateway to the broader Arab world. Indeed, even the right-wing opposition in the Knesset voted to approve the treaty with Jordan.[26] It put off still further the needed national debate regarding Palestinian statehood, attempting – In the words of journalist Gideon Sammet – to "put Arafat and the Palestinians in the freezer."[27] Indeed, this feel-good agreement on the part of the Israelis made it easier for them to further delay implementation of greater Palestinian autonomy. The Israelis and the United States clearly hope that Jordan could play an important role in the political direction of a non-sovereign Palestinian entity, for which they think the Jordanian government could be a moderating force. Indeed, the Israeli government believes that both they and the Hashemite monarchy share an interest in blocking the establishment of a Palestinian state.

Syria has long been considered the most intractable of Israel's front-line neighbors. However, a variety of factors –both international and domestic – have led this one-time rejectionist government into pursuing a peace agreement with its long-time enemy. However, the Israelis seem far less willing to take the necessary steps to make a negotiated settlement possible, and the United States likewise appears unwilling to push its ally to compromise. As a result, a final Syrian-Israeli peace accord may still be a long way off. While the Israeli public appears to be increasingly open to the possibility of a full withdrawal from the Gaza Strip and even the West Bank (outside of greater Jerusalem,) only a small minority support withdrawal from the region of southwestern Syria seized in the waning hours of the 1967 war.[28] Unlike the Gaza Strip and the West Bank, the vast majority of the Arab population in the Golan region was expelled following the Israeli conquest, thus relieving Israel of many of the burdens of occupation.[29] Despite an international outcry, the Israelis have effectively annexed the territory, announcing its direct administration under Israeli law as of 1981, contrasting with the ongoing military rule in the parts of the Gaza Strip and the West Bank still under Israeli control. The fertile farmland, generous water resources, and strategic topography of the Golan make it difficult, in the minds of many Israelis, to give up the territory.

The Syrians, however, will not concede any of their territory to the 1967 Israeli conquest, though they appear to be willing to make many other compromises. The Syrians insist that Israel will get the security it has been seeking if they withdraw, but can have no security if Israel continues to occupy any Syrian land.[30] While a growing number of Israelis realize that a full peace without the Golan is far more secure than no peace with the Golan, the Labor governments insisted on full diplomatic and economic relations prior to withdrawal. However, there is nothing in any U.N. Security Council resolution which calls for the establishment of full normal relations as demanded by the Israelis. Though it is perfectly reasonable for Israel to desire such relations with its Syrian neighbor (and Syria has expressed its willingness to eventually establish such relations,) Syria has no legal obligation to do so under U.N. Security Council resolutions 242 and 338 – which the US pledged to Syria in 1991 would be the basis of the negotiations – that only call for security guarantees. The Labor governments, however, believed that only through a full peace would the Israeli public accept over time the prospects of a withdrawal from the Golan. Yet it was these same leaders who helped build up the antipathy of the Israeli people to just such a peace treaty. After years of depicting Syria as an incorrigible enemy and insisting that returning the Golan to Syria would be putting Israel at great risk, it was difficult for the government to suddenly shift public opinion. Similarly, after decades of subsidizing Israeli settlements in the Golan with the assumption that they would be permanent, these settlers evolved into a powerful lobby. By 1994, it was clear that the Labor government could have secured a peace, but fearing it would hurt their electoral prospects, Peres delayed the agreement – even breaking off talks altogether two months before the election – but then lost the election anyway. The Likud government which succeeded him opposed giving up the Golan under any circumstances. While there are some doubts as to whether a Labor government could make peace anyway, relations with Syria, perhaps more than any other issue, provides the most distinct foreign policy divergence between the two major Israeli political blocs.

Whatever happens in terms of a final peace settlement, Syria and Israel will likely remain regional rivals as the two most powerful militaries in the Levant. Indeed, virtually the entire Levant is considered by Damascus to be "Greater Syria," and while the Syrian government appears to have no actual territorial designs beyond its internationally-recognized borders, they are determined not to surrender to Israel the consolidation of its strategic, political and economic agenda in the Middle East. As a result, relations with Syria will continue to be a major priority for Israeli policy makers whatever the fate of the Golan.

Lebanon was never a major player in the Arab-Israeli wars, yet became a target of Israeli attacks in the 1970s when, taking advantage of the weak central government, Palestinian guerrilla groups set up bases in the country from which they launched attacks against Israel. Israel has occupied a broad swath of land in southern Lebanon, approximately 10% of the country's land area, since 1978, with the assistance of a right-wing Lebanese militia which has essentially evolved into a foreign regiment of the Israeli army. Only a minority of Israelis raised the profound moral and legal implications of the 1982 invasion of Lebanon, in which Israel temporarily occupied nearly half the country – including, for a brief period, the capital city of Beirut – at a cost of over 20,000 Arab lives, mostly civilians. However, most Israeli policy makers now recognize that the invasion – largely supported by the United States, which blocked the United Nations from taking any decisive action to stop it – was a disaster politically. A 1983 peace treaty with the right-wing minority government of Amin Gemayal, installed under Israeli guns in 1982, was soon abrogated. While driving out the PLO and destroying the leftist Lebanese National Movement, the Israelis left a vacuum filled by the far more threatening Hizbullah, which had not been a factor in Lebanese politics prior to the invasion. In addition, the attempt to install a pro-Israeli regime in Beirut resulted in a chain of events which led to a Lebanese government whose foreign policy is effectively controlled by Israel's arch-enemy Syria.

Most of Hizbullah's fighters are composed of Shiite Muslims native to the Lebanese farming villages in or adjacent to the Israeli zones of control. Hizbullah receives the core of its political support from the hundreds of thousands of Lebanese Shiites who fled north from Israeli attacks into the slums of greater Beirut, and has come from almost nowhere to become one of Lebanon's most powerful political groupings. Israel's northern border regions are less secure now than they were immediately before the 1982 invasion. Israel is justifiably concerned that Hizbullah is not just anti-occupation, but anti-Israel. However, Israeli peace activists and others note that there is little question that the popular support for these radical Islamists would lessen considerably if Israel ended its occupation. Both the Lebanese and Syrian governments have agreed to disarm Hizbullah (as they have done with other militias) as well as to guarantee Israel's security, but only if Israel withdraws. Indeed, U.N. Security Council Resolution 425 and nine subsequent unanimous votes have called on Israel to withdraw from all Lebanese territory unconditionally. As with many other such decisions by the world body, however, Israel has chosen to ignore it and the United States has blocked the U.N. from applying any pressure to encourage compliance.

With rare exceptions, almost all of the Hizbullah attacks against Israelis have been against Israeli soldiers in occupied Lebanon, not civilians in Israel itself. It is thus the so-called "security zone" in which Israelis are most vulnerable. As casualties mount, increasing numbers of Israelis have called on their government to negotiate a total withdrawal replaced by an enhanced United Nations presence and a sizable demilitarized zone. The United Nations peace keeping force currently in place, which is supposed to separate the sides, has been only minimally effective. These U.N. forces say they could do a better job in preventing possible Hizbullah attacks against Israel if they would be allowed to fulfill their mandate to patrol all the way up to the Israeli border, but Israel has refused to cooperate.[31]

In many respects, Lebanon would be the easiest of the various tracts of the peace process to resolve, since Israel does not claim to have any long-term territorial ambitions. The differences are in the priority, phasing and feasibility of the specific proposals.

The Israelis have periodically pressured the Lebanese to make a separate peace, which have included blockades of the southern

Lebanese coast and periodic bombing and shelling. One of the most intense of these episodes was in April 1996 when Israel launched a sixteen-day barrage against Lebanon while Hizbollah fired rockets into parts of northern Israel. When the Lebanese refused to make a separate peace despite devastating attacks on dams, power stations, roads and other parts of the country's infrastructure, Israel and the United States then sought to pressure Syria to enforce an agreement which would end Hizbullah's attacks against Israeli occupation forces. All the Israelis could get, however, was a written confirmation of a July 1993 agreement, which followed a similarly bloody Israeli assault, that forbade attacks against each others' civilian populations. The new agreement also provided for outside monitoring, but without any enforcement mechanisms. Lebanon and Syria had demonstrated their openness for just such a deal throughout the fighting. The only other new component of the 1996 agreement was the understanding that Hizbullah would not assault Israeli occupation forces from civilian areas, which – despite Israeli claims to the contrary – they had generally avoided doing anyway. The result of this ongoing battle has been to enhance the prestige and influence of Hizbullah, whose resistance in the face of enormous military pressure has won the admiration of Lebanese from across the political spectrum disillusioned by the lack of progress on the diplomatic front.

Israel's Lebanese policy has essentially paralleled that of its Hizbullah enemy: terrorize innocent civilians in order to influence government policy. Yet just as the shelling of Israel by the Islamic extremists of Lebanon only hardened the attitude of the Israeli government, however, so have Israeli attacks make it even more difficult for Lebanon and Syria to compromise further with the Israel. In addition, just as Hamas attacks against Israeli civilians turned many Israelis against the peace process, so have Israeli attacks against Lebanese civilians turned many Lebanese and other Arabs against the peace process.

For many years, the Israeli refusal to recognize Palestinian rights or even negotiate with its leaders was the primary reason (or excuse) for Arab, Islamic and other Third World governments to reject normal economic and political relations with Israel. As a result, whatever the inadequacies of the Oslo Agreement, Arafat's handshake with Rabin did allow neighboring Arab states to more vigorously pursue peace negotiations with Israel and for others to open up trade and diplomatic relations with the once-isolated Jewish state. However, the election of

Netanyahu as prime minister and the subsequent stalling of the peace process put much of the progress elsewhere on hold. While the Rabin and Peres governments certainly took a number of actions which disappointed Arab governments – attacks against civilian targets in Lebanon, expansion of existing settlements in the West Bank and limiting the geographical and administrative authority of the Palestinian National Authority – there was still hope in many circles that the peace process would move forward and eventually result in Palestinian independence. Such a scenario may have been overly-optimistic even under a Labor government, but it seemed virtually impossible under a Likud government. This has led to Arab states to freeze the progress towards more normal relations which, in turn, has strengthened hard-line elements in Israel. In response, Israeli supporters of greater compromises on the part of their government have been emboldened to challenge this retrenchment. In addition to the traditional pro-peace forces of the Israeli left, the Netanyahu government also began feeling pressure from segments of the business community who saw their potentially lucrative ties with other Middle Eastern states in jeopardy. Still, much of the Israeli right continues to hold onto many of Israel's foreign policy perceptions of an earlier era, in some cases reinforced by deeply-felt religious beliefs, and are content to risk continuing diplomatic isolation and limiting economic growth in order to maintain the status quo on the ground. This failure to compromise on the part of the Israeli government is further enhanced by the assurance of continued support of the United States.

The Role of the US

It was Ben-Gurion who emphasized that due to the existential threat against Israel by its Arab neighbors that it was incumbent upon Israel to trust "first and foremost in itself as a power of growing greatness," which was understood to mean the freedom to engage in unilateral action and the military means to do so in a decisive and effective manner.[32] Yet, due to its small industrial base, Israel needed to find outside sources of financial and military support in order to maintain this effective military muscle. In the first twenty years of the country's existence, Israel relied primarily on France, and, to a lesser extent, Great Britain as its primary source of arms and support. Since 1967, it has been the United States that has fulfilled this role and has taken this relationship to a new and unprecedented degree. Indeed, at this point it is hard to understand Israeli foreign policy outside of its relationship with the United States. Israel is certainly not a puppet of the United States and it is not uncommon for the interests of the two nations to occasionally diverge. At the same time, however, the foreign policy interests of the two are now so intertwined, and the role of the United States in the international relations of the contemporary Middle East is so critical, that, in the final analysis, there can be no serious discussion of Israeli foreign policy outside the context of its relationship with the United States.

First is the matter of foreign aid. US aid to Israel began in the early 1950s with small grants and expanded modestly over the next decade to include Export-Import Bank loans, Food for Peace aid and general economic loans. Military loans began only after the 1967 war. These were replaced by grants exclusively in 1985. US economic aid increased greatly in subsequent years and grants replaced loans for economic assistance in 1981. In recent years, the annual US subsidy for Israel has remained at approximately $3 billion in military and economic grants, in addition to more than $500 million from other parts of the budget or off budget.[33] Unlike most US recipients of economic aid, which are required to use the bulk of the money for specific projects, such as buying certain US agricultural surpluses or finished goods, most US aid to Israel goes directly into the government's treasury to use as they will. In most other countries, officials of the US Agency for International Development oversee the actual programs, either administered directly, through non-governmental organizations, or under co-sponsorship with a government agency. Since 1971, however, Israel has been the exception: the US government sets the funding level and these become simply cash transfers to the Israeli government.[34]

Between 1992 and 1996, the US guaranteed an additional $2 billion in loans annually, originally designated for the construction of housing for Jewish immigrants from the former Soviet Union, though this too has essentially gone into the Israeli treasury to be used as the government sees fit. In addition, Congressional researchers have disclosed that between 1974 and 1989, $16.4 billion in US military loans were converted to grants and that this was the understanding from the beginning. Indeed, all past US loans to Israel have eventually been forgiven by Congress, which has undoubtedly helped Israel's often-touted claim that they have never defaulted on a US government loan. US policy since 1984 has been that economic assistance to Israel must equal or exceed Israel's annual debt repayment to the United States. In addition, there is the more than $1.5 billion in private US funds which go to Israel annually, in the form of $1 billion in private tax deductible donations and $500 million in Israeli bonds.[35] The ability of Americans to make what amounts to tax-deductible contributions to a foreign government, made possible through a number of Jewish charities, does not exist with any other country. Nor do these figures include short and long-term commercial loans from US banks, which have been as high as $1 billion annually in recent years.[36]

The large amounts of US aid to the Israeli government has not been as beneficial to Israel as many would suspect. Most of the economic assistance has gone primarily to finance non-productive sectors, such as the settlements in the occupied territories and the military, as well as to finance loan repayments to American banks. Indeed, each fiscal year since 1974, approximately $1 billion of Israel's $1.2 billion in Economic Support Funds has been used to cover the interest and principle due from previous US loans, which were borrowed primarily to finance arms purchases from the US.[37] In addition, the $1.8 billion in annual military aid is in fact simply a credit line to American arms manufacturers, and actually ends up costing Israel two to three times that amount to train operators, to staff and maintain, to procure spare parts, and other related costs.[38] The overall impact is to increase Israeli economic and military dependency on the United States and to drain Israel's fragile economy,[39] taking money away from Israel's once-generous social welfare system. Ezra Sohar has observed how, unlike borrowing money to build a factory, borrowing money for armaments does not produce profits or create the ripple effect or ancillary industries that strengthens the overall economy.[40] Until the 1967 War, when Israeli military spending averaged a little over 8% of the GNP, Israel's annual growth rate posted a healthy 9%. When military spending dramatically escalated with an enormous increase in procurement of US weapons, at times reaching as much as 35% of GNP, the economy faltered. Currently, military spending is slightly under 20% of the GNP, and the economy is still struggling.[41] Thus, what many consider one of Israel's greatest foreign policy achievements – to be on the receiving end of a level of economic and military aid unprecedented in world history – has also created an enormous burden on the society.

On the diplomatic front, the United States has repeatedly utilized its veto power to prevent the United Nations from taking effective action against ongoing Israeli violations of international law and United Nations Security Council resolutions. Indeed, during the past thirty years, the United States has used its veto to protect Israel from sanctions and censure more than all other members of the Security Council have used their veto power on all other issues combined. In addition, the US has blocked enforcement of those resolutions of censure which it did support. Upon coming to office, the Clinton administration promised to block any UN resolution which referred to the West Bank and Gaza as "Palestinian" and to similarly oppose any United Nations resolution critical of Israel that did not condemn Arabs as well. In addition, in a June 1993 paper to the delegations in the Washington peace talks, the US for the first time would not recommit to UN Security Council Resolutions 242 and 338, long considered the basis of Arab-Israeli peace. The US also abstained on a paragraph in a 1994 UN Security Council resolution because it referred to the West Bank and Gaza as "occupied territories;" the US now insists that they should instead be considered "disputed territories," implying that both the conquered and the conqueror have equal claim to the lands seized by Israel in 1967.

The Clinton administration also insists that the United Nations no longer has any standing regarding the legality of Israeli settlements, the status of Jerusalem, the fate of Palestinian refugees, or Palestinian sovereignty. All previous resolutions by both the General Assembly and Security Council are no longer relevant, so goes the American argument, since these issues should instead be resolved in the "final status" negotiations outlined in the Oslo Accords, the talks in which Israel's Likud government pledged it will not compromise at all on those very issues. Legally, no bilateral agreement between two parties can supersede the authority of the United Nations Security Council, particularly since one of the two parties (the Palestine National Authority) has made it clear that such resolutions are still very relevant and no other member of the Security Council agrees with such an interpretation.[42] However, the United States – virtually the only country outside Israel itself opposing Palestinian statehood and largely supportive of current Israeli positions – has the power to block any U.N. action and still controls the peace process.

In effect, the United States appears intent on maintaining this control in a manner which prevents Israel from living up to its international obligations or compromising more than it desires. The Israeli leadership is generally quite pleased with this situation; indeed,

Israel has a degree of leverage in the international arena which is perhaps greater than any small country in history, essentially able to pursue its foreign policy agenda with impunity regardless of international law, the United Nations and world opinion.

Ramifications of Policies

In previously-published articles, I have examined how US support for Israel has come primarily not from a moral commitment to the survival of the Jewish state nor as a result of domestic pressures in the US, but from how Israel supports American strategic interests in the Middle East and beyond.[43] Israel has helped suppress victories by radical nationalist movements in Lebanon, Jordan, and Yemen, as well as in Palestine. They have kept Syria, for many years an ally of the Soviet Union, in check. Their air force is predominant throughout the region. Israel's frequent wars have provided battlefield testing for American arms, often against Soviet weapons. They have been a conduit for US arms to regimes and movements too unpopular in the United States for openly granting direct military assistance, such as South Africa, Iran, Guatemala, and the Nicaraguan Contras. Israeli military advisors have assisted the Contras, the Salvadoran junta and other governments allied with the United States. Their secret service has assisted the US in intelligence gathering and covert operations. Israel has missiles capable of reaching the former Soviet Union and has cooperated with the US military-industrial complex with research and development for new jet fighters, anti-missile defense systems, and even the Strategic Defense Initiative.

One of the more unsettling aspects of US policy in relation to Israel is how closely it corresponds with historic anti-Jewish oppression. Throughout Europe in past centuries, the ruling class of a given country would, in return for granting limited religious and cultural autonomy, set up certain individuals in the Jewish community to become the visible agents of the oppressive social order, such as tax collectors, money lenders and middle-level managers. When the population would threaten to rise up against the ruling class, the rulers could then blame the Jews, sending the wrath of an exploited people against convenient scape goats, resulting in the pogroms and other notorious waves of repression which have taken place in most of the Jewish Diaspora throughout history.

The idea behind Zionism was to break this cycle through the creation of a Jewish nation-state, where Jews would no longer be dependent on the ruling class of a given country. The tragic irony is that, as a result of Israel's inability or unwillingness to make peace with its Arab neighbors, the creation of Israel has perpetuated this cycle on a global scale, with Israel being used by certain major Western powers – initially Great Britain and France and more recently the United States – to maintain their interests in the Middle East.[44]   Therefore, one finds autocratic Arab governments and other Third World regimes blaming "Zionism" for their problems rather than the broader exploitative global economic system and their own elites who benefit from and help perpetuate such a system.

Critics of US Middle East policy have generally emphasized its impact on the suffering of Palestinians, Lebanese, and other Arabs. But it also has a negative impact on Israel. The late respected Israeli intellectual Ishawa Leibowitz once noted

> The existence of the Jewish people of 60 to 80 generations . . .was a heroic situation. We never got from the goyish world a cent. We supported ourselves. We maintained our own institutions. Now we have taken three million Jews, gathered them here and turned them over to be parasites – parasites of America. And in some sense we are even the mercenaries of America to fight the wars of . . .what the ruling persons in America consider to be American interests.[45]

The unconditional support by the US government of Israeli foreign policy is increasingly seen as effectively sabotaging the efforts of peace activists in Israel to change Israeli policy, which the late Major General and Knesset member Mattityahu Peled referred to as pushing Israel "toward a posture of callused intransigence."[46]   In the Israeli press, one can find comments like those in Yediot Ahronot which describes their country as "the Godfather's messenger," since Israel undertakes the "dirty work" of the Godfather, who "always tries to appear to be the owner of some large respectable business."[47]   Israeli satirist B. Michael describes US aid to Israel as a situation where "My master gives me food to eat and I bite those whom he tells me to bite. It's called strategic cooperation."[48]

A number of Israelis and other left-wing Zionists argue that, like any other nationalist movement, Zionism has pluralist, democratic and inclusivist elements alongside reactionary, chauvinistic and militarist elements. The primary reason the latter has dominated, they argue, is not anything inherent within Zionism per se, but the blank check offered by the US, which encourages Israeli oppression of its Middle Eastern neighbors and close ties with the West and undermines the last vestiges of Labor Zionism's commitment to socialism, non-alignment, and cooperation with the Third World.[49] As former Secretary of State Henry Kissinger put it, "Israel's obstinacy. . . serves the purposes of both our countries best."[50] The rise of the Likud Bloc in Israel from a minority faction to the dominant party, as well as the rightward drift of the Labor Party, is in large part due to this large-scale American support. No government with those kinds of policies could last very long in office, given the self-defeating effect of such militarization on economic grounds or in terms of international isolation, were they not supported to such a degree that they did not have to worry about the consequences of their policies on their own population. The US has protected successive Israeli governments from international sanctions resulting from their violations of international law as well as from economic ruin resulting from the huge costs of militarization and occupation. Not having to pay for their mistakes, there is no motivation to compromise. There is nothing inherent in Zionism that makes it more repressive or expansionist than other nationalist movements; any country located in a hostile region given such a superpower umbrella would likely engage in similar activities.

What has resulted, then, is a new kind of dependency between two advanced technological societies in which the smaller dependent country is widely perceived to be the exploiter in the bilateral relationship. This is particularly ironic since Israel was founded on the principles of self-determination and non-alignment largely to avoid once again finding itself in the role of scape goat. Increasingly, American critics of US support of Israel are portraying a tail-wagging-the-dog situation which presents an erroneous analysis that tiny Israel – through its agents in the American Jewish community – is manipulating US foreign policy. Such scape goating of Jews is not only disturbingly familiar, but it also serves a purpose. As A.F.K. Organski observed, in his comprehensive study of US-Israeli relations,

> The belief that the Jewish lobby . . .is very powerful has permitted top US policy makers to use "Jewish influence" or "domestic politics" to explain the policies . . .that US leaders see as working to US advantage, policies they would pursue regardless of Jewish opinion on the matter. When Arab leaders or officials of allies protest, US officials need give only a helpless shrug, a regretful sigh, and explain how it is not the

administration's fault, but that policy makers must operate within the constraints imposed by powerful domestic pressures molding congressional decisions. Presidents, and those who speak in their names, have followed this strategy time and time again. Congressmen employ this same device . . . .[51]

The reality is very different. As Organski puts it,

. . .the United States has used its relationship with Israel as a means to control its client. When American leaders crack the whip, Israel responds and the Israeli show of resistance is just that – a show. The real constraint on American leaders has been their fear of weakening an important ally . . . [T]here has been no question in either the patron's or the client's mind who is in control. When it comes to important questions, Israel does as she is told.[52]

My own prior research upholds this analysis: US foreign policy has never been the kind of pluralistic enterprise where a small minority group or a small foreign country can wield such influence. The governments of Morocco, Turkey and Indonesia – like Israel – are granted US diplomatic and military support for their illegal occupations of neighboring states without critics crediting a domestic lobby for US backing. The US has always shielded its allies from the enforcement of international law when it was deemed to be in US interests. The US supports Israel and opposes the Syrians and Palestinians for the same reason it has supported any pro-Western ally against any radical nationalist government or popular national liberation struggle. Yet due to centuries-old anti-Semitic stereotypes which are still used to exaggerate the power of Jews in the United States – often encouraged by US diplomats and members of Congress as a means of making themselves appear not responsible for controversial US policies – the real motivations behind US policy remain obscured.[53]

Facing the Future

US support of Israeli foreign policy will likely remain strong for the foreseeable future. Strategic issues will continue to dominate the thinking and priorities of the American government and, despite the changing world and regional environment, there is reason to believe that US support for Israel will remain high.

Many analysts predicted that American military and economic support for Israel in the 1990s would decline. This was based on three factors:

First of all, it was argued that Israel was no longer needed as a surrogate for US interests. The end of the Cold War also ended Israel's role as a counterweight to Soviet influence in the Middle East. In addition, the dramatic increase in military cooperation and arms transfers to the states of the Gulf Cooperation Council during and after the Gulf War demonstrated that Israel was not the only Middle Eastern country on which the United States relies to maintain its interests in the region.[54]

However, it should be noted that Israel's role as a surrogate for US strategic interests has never been limited to concerns over Soviet influence. As in many other parts of the Third World, the Cold War was often as much an excuse than the actual reasons for US concerns over instability and challenges to US economic and political hegemony. Indeed, radical nationalism and – more recently – extremist Islamic forces have been seen by American policy makers to be at least as threatening to American interests in the region as was Communism, and Israeli support in challenging such perceived threats to American hegemony has always been, and will continue to be, quite welcome.[55]

In addition, the potentially unstable Gulf monarchies, still suspicious of US intentions and lacking the advantages of Israel in terms of well-trained armed forces, technological sophistication, and ability to mobilize their human and material resources, can never be a substitute for the US alliance with Israel. Given that continued support of Israel did not interfere with an unprecedented degree of cooperation with Egypt and the Gulf monarchies or with rapprochement with Syria, there appears to be few risks involved with the US continuing such an alliance with Israel even as the US cultivates closer strategic relationships with authoritarian Arab regimes.[56]

It is not coincidental that Israel's potential as an ally against Iran has been recently stressed by the Israeli government and its American supporters. Indeed, Iran has played an increasingly prominent role in Israeli foreign policy planning in recent years. The Iranian government's strongly chauvinistic interpretation of Islam, as well as its support of radical Islamic groups challenging Israel in Lebanon and Palestine, is a cause of concern among both American and Israeli policy makers. However, given Iran's great geographic distance from Israel and its absence of long-range military power projection capabilities, Iran cannot be fairly portrayed as a realistic threat to Israel's security. Furthermore, the election of a moderate president in 1997 and the country's domestic problems which has distracted it from its once grandiose designs of encouraging Islamic revolution beyond its borders. It has even cut back on its support of Hizbullah guerrillas in southern Lebanon fighting Israeli occupation forces and Israel itself has acknowledged that Iranian support for international terrorism has declined. In a further irony, Israel and the United States collaborated in arming Iran during the early to mid-1980s, the most radical and expansionist phase of its revolutionary government. Why, then, has there been this more recent fixation on Iran? Part of the reason may be that Israeli national security managers, like national security managers elsewhere, are trained and owe their positions to finding potential threats; as threats to Israel on its immediate borders decline, they are forced to look further afield. Ultimately, however, the answer may lie in the Israeli role of surrogate in the American policy to isolate and undermine Iran's Islamic regime.

The second factor which led to predictions of reduced Israeli-US cooperation was the enormous costs to the American taxpayer for its ongoing economic and military support of Israel. At a time of huge budget deficits, cutbacks on valued domestic programs, and strong popular resistance to raising taxes, foreign aid is particularly vulnerable to cutbacks. Given the high level of economic assistance to Israel, such aid would appear to be susceptible to major reductions by policy makers eager to place priority on programs benefiting the United States and deficit reduction rather than contributing to the treasury of a relatively affluent foreign country. What such arguments ignore, however, is that most US aid to the Israeli government comes back to the United States in the form of arms purchases and interest on previous loans, as described above.

Thirdly, there has been an assumption that with Israel making peace with its neighbors and dramatically reducing its international isolation, US aid and cooperation would become less important. However, despite claims to the contrary, US aid was never related to Israel's actual security needs. Major General Peled (Ret.) reported that as far as he could tell, the annual $1.8 billion figure of arms transfers to Israel was arrived at "out of thin air."[57] Such an amount, according to Peled and others, is far more than Israel has needed to replenish stocks, is not apparently related directly to any specific security requirements, and has remained relatively constant in recent years, thereby reenforcing the impression that it is little more than a US government subsidy for American arms manufacturers. This benefit to American defense contractors is multiplied by the fact that many of the major arms transfers to Israel creates a new demand by some Arab states – most of which can pay hard currency through petrodollars – for additional American weapons to challenge the Israeli buildup. The resulting arms race is a bonanza for US arms manufacturers. In addition, 99% of all arms transfers to Israel have taken place since 1967, when Israel proved itself more powerful than any combination of Arab forces and became the occupiers of large Arab populations. If the US was really concerned about Israel's survival, most aid would have come during Israel early years, when it was most vulnerable strategically. In one of my analyses of US foreign aid patterns, I argue that the stronger, more aggressive, and more willing to cooperate with US interests that Israel has been, the stronger the support.[58] As a result, the prospects for peace will not reduce the close military relationship between Israel and the United States because US military support for Israel was never based on any actual concerns for Israel's security. Indeed, strategic cooperation between the US and Israel has increased as the Cold War ended, Iraq was defeated, and Israel started to make peace with its historic enemies. Meanwhile, the US continues selling tens of billions of dollars worth of arms annually to autocratic Arab regimes which are yet to even formally recognize Israel's right to exist.

The inescapable fact remains, however, that unless there are some dramatic changes in Israeli policy, peace will not be forthcoming. Given that the PLO has essentially played all its cards diplomatically and Israel has unchallenged supremacy militarily, Israel has the power to stall the peace process. Little pressure can be expected from the United States for Israel to compromise further. There is little incentive in the short run for the Israeli government to not move Palestinian autonomy beyond its current circumscribed parameters, to not maintain and expand its illegal settlements in the occupied territories, and to not continue its occupation of East Jerusalem, the Golan, southern Lebanon and most of the West Bank. Should Israel take such a position, the result is that most Arab states will not likely move beyond a kind of "Cold Peace" and others will remain actively hostile. Extremist Islamic groups and nationalist demagogues will continue to pose a threat to Israeli and Western security. A high level militarization will continue to stricken the Israeli economy and the crippling dependence on the United States will endure.

A second scenario would involve peace, demilitarization, compliance with international law, and a normalization of relations. This would mandate granting Palestinians full independence on the West Bank and Gaza, presumably as a largely demilitarized state with listening posts and other security mechanisms for Israel, and with some special status for Jerusalem which recognizes the city's central role for both peoples. Israel would withdraw from all Syrian and Lebanese territory in return for strict security guarantees. Jewish settlers would either be withdrawn from territories seized in the 1967 war or would remain as law-abiding residents of the state of Palestine with the freely-granted permission of the Arab administrative authorities. Palestinian refugees would be granted the right to repatriate to their homeland or be given generous financial compensation. In return, there would be full, normal, and peaceful relations with Israel's Arab neighbors, and comprehensive arms control provisions would be negotiated. In short, Israel would finally become part of the Middle East and its economy would prosper without dependence on foreign aid.

Despite the shortcomings in the Oslo Accords, the dictatorial nature of the Syrian regime and the extremist ideology of the Lebanese fighting the Israeli occupation, those supporting a settlement based on the formula of land for peace and statehood for both Palestinians and Israelis once had reason to hope. The idea was that greater cooperation over time would build a sense of security, break down stereotypes and fears, and a positive feedback loop would result where Israeli concessions would be met by greater interaction with Arabs and less hostility which could then lead to greater concessions and onward. The belief was that the attitudinal prism of the Israelis, what social scientists call weltanschauung, would evolve to one of accommodation. The assumption was that the US, while maintaining basic guarantees for Israeli security, would encourage this process through its role as chief sponsor of the peace process and facilitate arms control and a gradual demilitarization of the region. However, as demonstrated above, the US government has taken positions at least as recalcitrant as the Israeli government towards the Palestinians, Syrians and Lebanese and has strong economic interests in maintaining the regional arms race.

Thus, the more negative scenario appears more likely: Israel will continue to dominate the Palestinians and will resist Syrian and Lebanese security commitments in return for withdrawal, resulting in terrorism and extremist reaction, which would in turn further harden Israeli attitudes, creating instead a negative feedback loop. What progress for peace which will occur would be with autocratic Middle Eastern regimes interested primarily in taking advantage of closer economic relations or with pleasing the US government. Indeed, already Israel appears to have taken advantage of the exaggerated view by some foreign governments of the power of American Jews in the United States, with some countries hoping that by establishing good relations with Israel, foreign trade and investment from the US would soon follow; failure for this to come through could backfire against Israel. Another danger is that Israeli technical and economic capabilities are so vastly superior to that of many of these countries, that closer economic ties without peace could stir up resistance by an overbearing Israeli presence insensitive to local needs.[59]

Only when Israel sees its future with the Third World – made necessary by its geography, its Semitic language and culture, its majority Sephardic population, and the Jews' history of exploitation by the Europeans – will Israel end its isolation and find the real security that it has been missing. To be part of the Third World does not mean that Israel would become poorer or less committed to democracy and progressive Western values than it is currently; it simply means that Israel would ally its interests with its region and with other historically-oppressed peoples rather than with that of Western powers whose priorities are not consistent with the long-term security and development of Israel and the rest of the Middle East. Many of the so-called "supporters of Israel" in American politics are actually making Israel vulnerable by tying its future to an increasingly unpopular Western neo-liberal economic order and blocking its more natural alliance with the world's Afro-Asian majority.[60] The combination of Israeli technology, Palestinian industriousness, and Arabian oil wealth could result in an economic, political, and social transformation of the Middle East which would be highly beneficial to the region's inhabitants, (though not necessarily to certain elites in the United States and other Western nations who profit enormously from the continued divisions between these Semitic peoples.)[61]

There are two forces within domestic Israeli politics which might make this more positive scenario possible. Firstly, there are some signs of a resurgence of the traditional Labor Zionist principles of non-alignment and self-sufficiency. The kind of dependency on the United States which has evolved in recent decades is an anathema to the visions of the early Zionist pioneers from whom the Labor movement claims its ideological roots. Secondly, there is the pragmatic recognition that Israeli security would actually be enhanced by withdrawal and Palestinian statehood, a position most forcefully articulated, not by the peace movement and the traditional Israeli left, but by once hard-lined security-conscious authorities as the late Yeshovat Harkabi.[62] Furthermore, there is a palpable fear among many Israelis that Israel's close ties with what many countries perceive as an imperialist power like the United States alienates Israel's potential allies in the Third World and leaves Israel vulnerable to the whims of US foreign policy. Like the Jews of medieval Europe, they fear Israel could be suddenly abandoned by the West after being set up to become the visible agent of an oppressive world order.[63]

In essence, then, an increasing number of Israelis are recognizing that they, like the Palestinians and other Arabs, are also victims of US policy. Like El Salvador and South Vietnam, Israel has become a client state whose leadership has made common cause with US global designs that could ultimately lead to the country's self-destruction. Israeli leaders and their counterparts in many American Zionist organizations have been repeating the historic error of trading short-term benefits for their people at the risk of long-term security. This cycle can only be fully broken, however, when Israeli foreign policy can become independent of US strategic prerogatives. Only then will Israelis, Palestinians and other Arabs finally be allowed to settle their differences among themselves and join together in liberating the Middle East from both undue influence by Western powers and the misrule of their own leaders.

Notes

1. It is equally unlikely, Arab claims not withstanding, that a conquered Jewish population would be treated any better than Arab populations which have experienced Israeli occupation.

2. Indeed, if Joseph McCarthy, Ronald Reagan and other American politicians could convince large sectors of the US electorate over the past few decades that the United States faced a clear and present danger of takeover by the Soviet Union requiring enormous sacrifices at the expense of the nation's financial resources, obligations under international law and even domestic civil liberties, it is not surprising that Israeli politicians – faced with more credible threats and a population more psychologically vulnerable to such manipulation – could do the same.

3. It was Peres' attempt to cater to Israel's right wing on foreign policy issues which ended up costing him the election: his breaking of the unofficial cease fire with Hamas by ordering the assassination of one of their leaders in January 1996 led to the wave of retaliatory terrorist bombings that followed, allowing for Netanyahu's cynical manipulation of the public fears during the campaign. In addition, the Israeli attacks against Lebanon during April of that year led tens of thousands of Israeli Arabs and Israeli peace activists to abstain from voting in the election that following month, providing the narrow margin of victory for Netanyahu.

4. These democratic institutions have generally served Israel's Jewish population well, though the country's Arab minority has always suffered discrimination on a variety of levels which has prevented them from fully benefitting from Israeli democracy. The situation of those under Israeli occupation is worse still.

5. See Yehuda Ben Meir, Civil-Military Relations in Israel (New York: Columbia University Press, 1995).

6. William Quandt, "The Middle East on the Brink: Prospects for Change in the 21st Century," Middle East Journal, Vol. 50; No. 1, Winter 1996

7. Many of these settlements have been rationalized on security grounds. However, such settlements actually proved to be an obstacle in 1973, when the Israeli counter-attack against advancing Syrian troops in the Golan was delayed due to the need to first evacuate Israeli civilians from the settlements.

8. See article 49 of the Geneva Convention on the Protection of Victims of War, as well as U.N. Security Council resolutions 446 and 465.

9. Aharon Klieman, "New Directions in Israel's Foreign Policy," Israel Affairs, Vol I, #1.

10. See Jane Hunter, Israeli Foreign Policy: South Africa and Central America, (Boston: South End Press, 1987); Hunter also edited the newsletter Israeli Foreign Policy, during 1980s, which examined some of these episodes in detail.

11. Efraim Inbar, "Contours of Israel's New Strategic Thinking," in Political Science Quarterly, Vol. 111, No. 1, 1996.

12. Theodore H. Friedgut, "Israel's Turn Toward Peace," in Robert O. Freedman, Israel Under Rabin, (Boulder: Westview Press, 1995).

13. Gad Yacobi, "Normalization or Perpetual Isolation?," Commentary, Vol. 59; No. 20, August 1993, pp. 612-613.

14. This was most apparent in the 1975 resolution equating Zionism as racism, which many interpreted as delegitimizing the raison d'etre of Israel's existence.

15. Klieman, op. cit.

16. Ibid.

17. Inbar, op. cit., p. 51.

18. Friedgut, op. cit., p. 78.

19. Klieman, op. cit., p. 109.

20. Ron Young, Missed Opportunity for Peace: US Middle East Policy, 1981-1986, (Philadelphia: American Friends Service committee, 1987), p. 89
   It is noteworthy that the bulk of US media coverage during this period appeared to blame the Jordanians and the Palestinians for the impasse because they had not fully accepted the Reagan Plan as presented, ignoring the fact that the Israelis had rejected it altogether.

21. Articles by Max Frankel in the New York Times, Nov. 15-16, 1982.

22. Friedgut, p. 79.

23. Jerusalem Post, April 26, 1996.

24. Quandt, op. cit., p. 15.

25. See my article, "The Jordanian-Israeli Peace Agreement: Peace or Pax Americana?" Middle East Policy, Vol. III, No 4; Spring 1995, especially pp. 60-61.

26. The exception was a handful of members of the extreme right wing, who still insist that the East Bank is part of Eretz Israel.

27. Quoted from Ha'aretz by Peretz Kidron, Middle East International, November 4, 1994.

28. Cited by prominent Israeli peace activists in interview by author, Jerusalem, May 1993.

29. There are still a number of Druze villages in the occupied Golan, most of which have engaged in periodic campaigns against the Israeli occupation. See, for example, R. Scott Kennedy, "The Druze of the Golan: A Case of Nonviolent Resistance," in Journal of Palestine Studies, Vol XIII, No. 2 (Winter 1984).

30. Interviews with Syrian foreign ministry officials, Damascus, May 1993.

31. Interviews with UNIFIL personnel, February 1981.

32. Cited in Inbar, op. cit., p. 42.

33. The breakdown of grant aid over the official $3 billion includes bank charges incurred by US government for lump sum withdrawal ($60 million); interest earned by Israel on ESF aid money reinvested in US treasury notes ($90 million); supplemental State Department funded aid ($93.5 million); supplemental Defense Department items ($242.3 million); a contract with the Immigration and Naturalization Service ($17 million); and, assistance from the Commerce Department ($2.5 million).   ["House Appropriations Committee Funds US-Israeli Cooperation," Near East Report, Vol. XXXIX, No. 18, Aug. 14, 1995, p. 99 and Shawn Twing, "A Comprehensive Guide to US Aid to Israel," Washington Report on Middle East Affairs, April 1996, p. 7].

34. In other countries which receive US economic aid, there is a mission of the Agency for International Development as part of the US Embassy which audits all the relevant expenditures. Without such a presence in Israel, there have been a number of scandals involving US funds, such as when General Electric's manager for Israel was caught paying kickbacks to Israeli authorities responsible for procurement, or when General Rami Dotan was found to be siphoning off US funds for his personal use.

35. Martha Wenger, "The Money Tree: US Aid to Israel", Middle East Report, May-Aug. 1990, p. 12.

36. Ibid.

37. Twing, op. cit., p. 7.

38. Interview with Major General Mattityahu Peled (Ret.), May 12, 1992, Seattle, Washington.

39. It is noteworthy that in the development of a new anti-missile defense system for Israel, the US initially insisted that it be mobile, despite the Israeli preference for a cheaper and simpler fixed system, which would have been quite adequate for their small territory.

40. Joel Bainerman, "Looking the Gift Horse in the Mouth: Israelis Ask if US Generosity Might Actually Be Hurting their Country," Washington Post, Oct. 29, 1995, p. C4.

41. Simcha Bahiri, "A Peace Economy for Israel, The New Economy, Spring 1995, cited in Joel Bainerman, "Looking the Gift Horse in the Mouth: Israelis Ask if US Generosity Might Actually Be Hurting their Country," Washington Post, Oct. 29, 1995, p. C4.

42. Indeed, given the PLO's relative weakness towards Israel, the collapse of Arab unity since the Gulf War and the United States' bias in support of the Israeli occupation, these international legal standards upheld by the United Nations are among the few tools the Palestinians have left to support their rights.

43. See my article, "The Roots of the US-Israeli Relationship," Nos. 21-22, New Political Science, Spring-Summer 1992.

44. In addition to the examples of how Israel has supported US interests above, Israel was used by Great Britain and France to advance their goals in the Middle East as well, most notably when they utilized Israeli forces in their attempt to regain control of the Suez Canal in 1956.

45. Interview, PBS documentary, 1987.

46. Matti Peled, New Outlook, May/June 1975.

47. Nathan Shaham, Yediot Ahronot, Nov. 28, 1996, cited in Noam Chomsky, World Orders Old and New, (New York: Columbia University Press, 1994), p. 206.

48. B. Michael, Ha'aretz, Nov. 11, 1983, cited in Ibid.

49. For example, see Cherie Brown, et al, "A Draft Policy on Jewish Liberation," Ruah Hadashah, #4 (1981); particularly, pp. 11-13.

50. Henry Kissinger, Years of Upheaval, (Boston: Little, Brown, Company, 1982), p. 621.

51. Organski, op. cit., p. 28.

52. Ibid., pp. 198-199.
   Even in cases where there has been a standoff, the reasons are not as clear-cut as they may appear. For example, there were a number of reports in the Israeli press that the initial decision to deny the $10 billion loan guarantee was not actually based on Israeli settlement policy as publicly announced, but out of an American desire to restructure the Israeli economy along a stronger "free-market" orientation. Pioneered by one-time University of Chicago economist and former Secretary of State George Schultz, the reported US plan would be for the Israeli government to severely weaken the Histradut (Israel's powerful trade union federation), abolish the minimum wage, privatize state-controlled enterprises, and lower taxes. Such economic restructuring has been a requirement for US-backed loans to a number of countries as a means of creating a more favorable climate for US investment, so it should not be surprising that Israel should be held to such standards as well. The use of the settlements controversy as a cover was done apparently to assuage allied Arab states into thinking that the United States was sincere about supporting the peace process.

53. Again, see my article in New Political Science, op. cit.

54. See my article, "The US-G.C.C. Relationship: Its Rise and Potential Fall," Middle East Policy, Vol. 2, #1; Summer 1993.

55. See my article, "The Roots of Political Islam," in Peace Review, Summer 1995, Vol. 7, No. 1.

56.   Take, for example, the Israeli role in the Gulf War.   Rather than being a liability, as was often depicted in the American media, the Gulf War proved Israel once again to be a strategic asset: Israeli developments in air-to-ground warfare were integrated into allied bombing against Iraqi missile sites and other targets; Israeli-designed conformal fuel tanks for F-15 fighter-bombers greatly enhanced their range; the Israeli-provided mine plows were utilized during the final assaults on Iraqi positions; Israeli mobile bridges were used by US Marines; Israeli targeting systems and low-altitude warning devises were utilized by American helicopters; and, Israel developed key components for the widely-used Tomahawk missiles.

57. Interview, May 12, 1992, Seattle, Washington.

58. See my article in New Political Science, op. cit.

59. Klieman, op. cit., p. 116.

60. Even the Gulf War and subsequent attacks against Iraq may have been, in the long term, a strategic setback for Israel, as it has more firmly allied Israel – in the minds of millions of Arabs – with the Western powers and unpopular Arab monarchies.

61. It would be overly-simplistic to imply this is part of some grand conspiracy by Western capitalists to divide and rule the Middle East.   However, the policies of the United States and some European powers has directly resulted in a regional system which greatly benefits Western oil companies, arms manufacturers, and national security elites at the expense of the region's population, including Israelis.   Though it is doubtful that US foreign policy toward the region is calculated with such a sinister goal in mind, given the forces that benefit from such policies in the Middle East and elsewhere, it might also be more than just coincidence.

62. See, for example, Israel's Fateful Hour, (New York: Harper &
Row, 1988).

63. For example, see Cherie Brown, op. cit. I elaborate on this thesis in my
article, "Zionism, Anti-Semitism and Imperialism," in Peace Review, Vol. 6,
No. 1 (Spring 1994).

Chapter 6

Women and the Changing Political Dynamics in the Middle East and North Africa

Valentine M. Moghadam

Introduction

Many of the world's regions are in the midst of significant change, and some are in transition from one socio-economic and political order to another, but the changes in the Middle East and North Africa have not received sufficient attention. Economically, the region is undergoing a shift, and the wealthy oil-based regional economy awash in petrodollars is now a phenomenon of the past. Today, in the post-oil boom era, Middle Eastern states are struggling to balance budgets, deal with soaring unemployment, alleviate poverty, and build competitive, export-oriented industries. Policies of structural adjustment, designed by the World Bank and the International Monetary Fund, are being implemented to open up the economies, reduce the public sector, expand the private sector, and invite foreign investment. Reduced oil income and the need for integration into the global economy are forcing Middle Eastern states to compete with fast-growing east and southeast Asian states – and this is not an easy task.

The changes in the economic sphere are paralleled by developments in the realm of politics, at the levels of both the state and civil society. A number of Middle Eastern states began to liberalize their hold over society in the 1980s and to permit political parties and elections.[1] Political liberalization and heightened activity within civil society are linked to the worldwide expansion of discourses of democratization, participation, good governance, and human rights. In the region, "democratization from above" (such as the introduction of elections) and initiatives from below (such as the formation of non-governmental organizations) are challenging entrenched systems of rule and allowing new forms of political activity and participation. It should be noted, though, that the spread of political liberalization in the region has occurred against the backdrop of Islamic fundamentalist movements. Moreover, although intellectual discussions about democratization, human rights, and civil society are quite spirited in the region, no Middle Eastern state can be called democratic; personal and group freedoms are limited; and authoritarianism remains the rule.

In tandem with the economic and political changes that the region has been undergoing, there has been a proliferation of non-governmental organizations (NGOs) and private voluntary organizations (PVOs) dealing with development-related issues, provision of social services, human rights, and women's concerns. The expansion of NGOs in the region is also a function of a global trend that gained momentum in the 1980s, when donor governments and multilateral funding agencies embraced non-governmental organizations as partners in development, and began to urge attention to the environment, human rights, good governance, and women in development.

In this context I will discuss an important aspect of the changing political dynamics of the region, namely the rise and expansion of women's organizations in the Middle East and North Africa. Attention will be placed on feminist organizations, that is, those with a focus on human rights and women's rights. This article examines the international and region-specific factors behind the rise of women's organizations, the different types of non-governmental organizations (NGOs) that have emerged, the challenges that they face, and their political implications. By non-governmental, I am referring to those women's organizations that are not part of governmental structures or auxiliaries of ruling parties – even though some of the discussion below could apply to government-sponsored women's groups in some countries.

Women's Organizations: A New Political Voice

The International Conference on Population and Development (ICPD) held in Cairo in September 1994, drew attention to the large numbers of Arab and especially Egyptian NGOs. One especially interesting document, prepared by Palestinian NGOs for the OCPD NGO forum, was entitled "Palestinian Population Policies and Sustainable Development"; it emphasized the link between population policies and the role of NGOs, especially women's NGOs, and stressed the contribution of the Palestinian women's movement.[2]   In early November 1994 Amman, Jordan was the venue of a regional conference of Arab women's non-governmental organizations. The two-week deliberations resulted in a document entitled "Work Programme for the Non-Government Organizations in the Arab Region". This document expressed the priority issues of Arab women's NGOs, and these included political, legal, and economic issues.[3] The NGO document characterized Arab women's situation as follows: absence of real equality; absence of effective participation in development; absence of a just and comprehensive peace (a reference to Palestine); increasing violence against women; lack of socio-economic security for women. The document noted that as of 1994, only eight Arab countries (Egypt, Iraq, Jordan, Kuwait, Libya, Morocco, Tunisia, and Morocco) had signed the UN Convention on the Elimination of All Forms of Discrimination Against Women, but even they had done so with reservations that impeded implementation. Women were still not involved in political decision-making, and there remained "concepts and traditions which prevent women from assuming high positions in the legislative and judicial fields". The poor state of statistics and data on women and gender was also noted, and the NGO document asserted several times that women's multiple roles, especially their care-giving responsibilities, are onerous. At the final preparatory conference in New York in March 1995, the following priorities were delineated:

> To strengthen the basis of the democratic process in both the political and social realms; to ensure the sanctity of human rights and the amendments of legislation that target the elimination of all forms of discrimination and violence against women, in particular, family laws.

To urge all governments to sign and ratify the International
Conventions for [sic] the Elimination of All Forms of Discrimination
Against Women without any reservations, and subsequently to
incorporate these elements within their respective national civil laws to
eradicate all forms of oppression against women.

To condemn fundamentalism and cultural extremism, which can lead to
terrorism and violence against women.

To promote social development to counteract the negative impact of
applied structural adjustment programs and to ensure the basic human
needs of women.[4]

In June 1995, the Arab Women's Tribunal, the first of its kind, was
held in Beirut, organized by the NGO El-Taller in cooperation with
Secours Populaire Libanais. Women from various Arab countries
testified before the court, sharing with the jury and audience a personal
experience of violence and humiliation, whether domestic, social, or
political. The tribunal heard from an Algerian lawyer who told of
innocent women being mowed down by gunfire in the streets for the
crime of not wearing Islamic attire, from women who had quietly
endured years of violence and humiliation at the hands of abusive
husbands, fathers or brothers, and from a Palestinian women from a
refugee camp in Lebanon who survived rape, the slaughter of her
family, and serious injuries.[5] The Tribunal was presided over by Asma
Khader, a lawyer, president of the Jordanian Women's Union, and a
member of the International Human Rights Committee.

At the Fourth World Conference on Women in Beijing (September
1995), Collectif 95 Maghreb Egalité, an NGO of women's
organizations from Algeria, Morocco, and Tunisia, was the major
organizer behind a "Muslim Women's Parliament" at the NGO Forum
which decried discrimination against women in the Arab world and in
Muslim countries in other regions. The Collectif distributed three
documents, *Women in the Maghreb: Change and Resistance, One
Hundred Measures and Provisions for a Maghrebian Egalitarian
Codification of the Personal Statute and Family Law,* and *Maghreb
Women "With All Reserves".* The last compared the national
legislation in the three Maghreb countries with international
conventions, especially the Convention on the Elimination of All
Forms of Discrimination Against Women.[6]

On 14 September 1995, near the end of the Fourth World
Conference on Women in Beijing, the Arab women's NGOs held a
press conference to express their disagreement with those government
delegations from Muslim countries that had claimed the existence of a
contradiction between Islamic values and international standards of
human rights. The Arab women's NGOs prepared a press release that
spelled out their views on equality, development, peace, and
reproductive health.[7] On equality, the women's NGOs stated: "We
believe that equality as well as political, economic and social justice at
all levels are prime objectives for Arab women. We also believe that
the elimination of all forms of discrimination against Arab women is a
pre-requisite for the development of women and their societies." On
peace, they declared:

> We do not think that Arab women can enjoy peace under the Israeli
> occupation of the Arab lands in Palestine, Lebanon and Syria. … We
> also denounce the prolonged economic embargo on Libya and Iraq to
> which women and children have been the major victims. We believe
> that restrictions on public liberties and the violations of human rights in
> some Arab states represent a serious threat to social peace. Meanwhile,
> the violations of women's rights perpetuated by the religious extremism
> of the militant political Islamist movement, especially in Algeria and
> Sudan, represent another threat to women's rights. We condemn all
> forms of violence that constitute a setback for the rights of women.

On reproductive health, the press release stated the following:

> Reproductive health of women should be viewed within the
> comprehensive framework of women's health, throughout the different
> cycles of women's lives, and not in the limited scope of maternal health
> and family planning services. This implies providing primary health
> care services for all women especially the poor and unprivileged. We
> also believe that providing correct and accurate information on
> women's reproductive and sexual health is vital for the development of
> women's health and the elimination of all harmful practices against the
> girl child.

In Jordan in the fall of 1997, some 100 Jordanian women met in
Amman for a two-day meeting on women's concerns and the political
process. The national agenda they agreed to – and which they wanted to
see addressed by parliamentary candidates and the members of
parliament – included modernization of the family law, health

insurance for all, a new child protection law, a law to protect women from abusive husbands, a quota for women in parliament and in diplomatic posts, improvements in school curricula, electoral reform, equal rights for women and men in employment.[8]

Clearly, Middle Eastern women have come a long way since the mid-1980s, when a comparative and historical study of women's movement worldwide, written by two US sociologists, stated that "independent women's movements are totally absent in the Middle East and North Africa."[9] Even at the time, this assessment of women's movements in the region was surprising, for at least two reasons. First, the authors ignored the continuity of women's organizations in Egypt, as well as the interesting fact that the very first protest against the new revolutionary Islamic regime in Iran was carried out in March 1979 by women reacting to efforts to impose veiling.[10] Second, the authors' explanation for the rise of women's movements centered on the expansion of female education – a process that was in full swing in the Middle East during the 1970s and 1980s. Stereotypical thinking about women in the Middle East and North Africa and assumptions about their status remain fairly common, and perhaps for this reason, the authors missed the opportunity to notice the dramatic rise of audacious and decidedly independent feminist groups in Algeria, who were protesting the first draft of a very conservative Family Code in 1981.

In fact, during the 1980s women's organizations – whether tied to political parties or independent feminist – were emerging in many countries of the region. Proposed changes to Egypt's Family Law in 1979 brought about considerable activity. Moroccan, Tunisian, and Egyptian women activists and intellectuals were traveling to meet each other. In Tunisia, the feminist magazine *Nissa* was formed, the product of several years' efforts. In 1985 a broadly-based Arab Women's Solidarity Association (AWSA) was formed, headed by the well-known Egyptian writer and gynecologist Nawal El-Saadawi, in part to protect and improve Egypt's Family Law, and in part to articulate women's other problems.

At the same time, the region is home to numerous women's associations and societies that are essentially charitable in nature, providing relief, some training, and welfare to poor and rural women. Philanthropic and charitable activity by middle-class and elite women (and men) has a long history, in the Middle East and throughout the world. These associations have existed since at least the 1920s, and they may be seen as having legitimized a social role for women and thus prepared the way for the more radical women's groups that emerged in the 1980s. More recently, the women's organizations have directed their attention to such issues as fundamentalist movements, family laws, structural adjustment policies, and women's empowerment. The expansion of the international development discourse to include human rights, participation, and women's integration has emboldened Middle Eastern women activists and provided them with rhetorical legitimization.

Women's Mobilization: An Explanation and Typology

What explains the proliferation of women's non-governmental organizations, and in particular, the mobilization of women and the articulation of such concerns and demands as those expressed in the passages above? In the section that follows we identify demographic, economic, political, and international factors.

Demographic factors include urbanization, the growth of an educated female population in urban areas, and the entry of women into paid labor. Increasingly large populations are now concentrated in cities, and this creates pressures for social services as well as opportunities for action. The age of first marriage for women is rising, and family size is decreasing for educated and employed women. Such demographic changes are giving these "modernizing women" more time for other public activities, and allowing them to make demands on governments for equality, autonomy, and empowerment. In the past elite Middle Eastern women were involved in charitable work, but their numbers were small and the range of their activities limited. Today's activism by young middle-class and lower-middle women includes involvement in NGOs that deliver services, financing, technical assistance, or research.

Economic factors include the reduction of public spending in the areas of health, education, and social welfare, and state failures in areas such as female illiteracy, reproductive health, and legal reforms, which have spurred non-governmental organizations into action and focused women's attentions on the links between development and status-of-women issues. Structural adjustment policies usually call for the introduction of "user fees" in education and healthcare, with the result that poor families that would have been inclined to keep their daughters in school withdraw them due to rising costs. This outcome along with rising prices due to economic liberalization, necessitates non-governmental public action. NGOs provide health, educational, and social services and are catering to the basic needs of local communities, thereby filling the gaps created by recent state economic policies.

Political factors. The proliferation of NGOs in the MENA region, especially those focused on issues of human rights and women's advancement, reflect two parallel political developments in the MENA region: the rise and spread of fundamentalism, and the growth of a movement for democratization. NGOs in general, and women's organizations in particular, reflect shifting relations between the state and civil society and contribute to the broad democratization process. Women's NGOs are especially significant because of the historic exclusion of women from public forms of power, and because of the challenges they represent to Islamist political movements and to the cultural conservatism of the state.

International factors include opportunities afforded by the UN Decade for Women (1976-85) and the Nairobi Conference (1985); the increasing recognition of the importance of a grassroots, participatory, and bottom-up approach to development through non-governmental organizations; and the international conferences of the 1990s under the auspices of the United Nations. The International Conference on Population and Development (Cairo, 1994), the International Conference on Human Rights, and especially the Women's Tribunal (Vienna, 1994), the World Summit on Social Development (Copenhagen, March 1995), and the Fourth World Conference on Women (Beijing, 1995) did much to foster NGOs and women's organizations in the region. Not only did UN agencies operating in the region assist NGOs and women's organizations in preparations for the conferences and facilitated their participation, but the UN represents a kind of "role model" in that its involvement in women's issues and commitment to women's integration and advancement exemplify the kind of organizational and institutional change that governments can emulate.

Another important international factor behind the rise of women's organizations in the region is the spread of global feminism. Embodied in transnational feminist networks such as Women Living Under Muslim Laws (WLUML), Development Alternatives with Women for a New Era (DAWN), Women in Development Europe (WIDE), the Sisterhood is Global Institute (SIGI), Women, Law and Development International (WLDI), the International Association for Feminist Economics (IAFE), and the Asia-Pacific Research and Resource

Organization for Women (ARROW), among others – global feminism has created a much-needed space for the nurturing of women's organizations. The internationalization of discourses of equality, empowerment, autonomy, democratization, participation, and human rights, has been captured and indeed extended by women's organizations around the world.

In a recent paper I have defined global feminism as "the discourse and movement of women aimed at advancing the status of women (through greater access to resources, through legal measures to effect gender equality, and through the self-empowerment of women) within national boundaries but through transnational forms of organizing and mobilizing".[11] Global feminism is predicated upon the notion that notwithstanding cultural, class, and ideological differences among the women of the world, there is a commonality in the forms of women's disadvantage and in the forms of women's organizations worldwide. These organizations are increasingly networking and coordinating their activities, engaging in dialogue and forms of cooperation and mutual support, sending representatives to meetings in other countries and regions, and utilizing a similar vocabulary to describe women's disadvantage and the desired alternatives. A vivid demonstration of "global feminism on the ground" was the myriad preparatory activities around the world for the Fourth World Conference on Women, and of course the participation of numerous women's non-governmental organizations at the conference itself. Indeed, the Beijing Declaration and Platform for Action may be regarded as the "manifesto" of global feminism.

Having reviewed the demographic, economic, political, and international factors behind the expansion of non-governmental organizations and women's groups in particular, we now turn our attention to the types of women's non-governmental organizations that have emerged in the region. An analysis of the many organizations that have emerged reveals that they have varying orientations and strategies and suggests a seven-fold typology: service organizations, professional associations, development research centers and women's studies institutes, development and women-in-development NGOs, worker-based organizations, women's organizations affiliated to political parties, and human rights/women's rights organizations. We shall discuss each in turn.

Service organizations are the oldest type; they include charitable organizations and they have a largely "welfare" approach. Women's

NGOs that are service-oriented are the most numerous and the most traditional of the women's organizations. Nevertheless, they perform valuable functions in the areas of women's education, health (including reproductive health and family planning), and related services. Some of the more feminist social work organizations provide legal services and counseling for battered women, such as the Women's Center for Legal Aid and Counseling, a Palestinian organization based in Jerusalem. Other service-oriented women's NGOs include the Palestinian In'ash al-Usrah Society in al-Bireh, founded in the mid-1960s, the Women's Health Program of the Union of Palestinian Medical Relief Committees, based in Jerusalem, the Friends of the People Society for Social Work, based in Egypt, and the Turkish Mothers Association. This category also includes charitable societies such as the Queen Alia Fund for Social Development in Jordan; Syria's Association of St. Lian for Women, the Red Crescent associations, the YWCAs, mother-and-child welfare societies, organizations to combat illiteracy, and many family planning associations.

Professional associations seek equity for their members within the profession and the society; some also promote women-owned businesses and prepare women for jobs in the private sector. Although these are elite associations, they provide a role model for young women and girls and challenge patriarchal images of women. Examples of this category of women's NGOs are the Professional and Business Women's Association of Jordan; the Women's Committee of the Egyptian Chamber of Commerce; the Egyptian Women Writers' Association; Egyptian Women in Film; Egyptian Medical Women's Association; Egyptian Women's Scientists' Society; the Women's Rights Committee of the Arab Lawyers' Union (based in Cairo); the Bahrain Society of Sociologists; the Women's Committee of the Association of Iraqi Engineers; the Women's Committee of the Iraqi Bar Association; the Association of Turkish Women Lawyers; l'Association des Journalistes Tunisiennes. Also in Tunisia, two organizations formed in 1990 to assist women's economic endeavors are the National Chamber of Women Heads of Businesses (CNFCE); the National Federation of Tunisian Women Farmers (FNAT), and the Association for the Promotion of Women's Economic Projects (APROFE). In Algeria, the social-professional association SEVE seeks to promote and assist women in business.[12]

The principal objective of these associations is to seek equity for their members within the profession and in the society; some of them also engage in charitable and welfare activities, and some include advocacy for women's rights. For example, the Women's Rights Committee of the Arab Lawyers Union (with chapters in most Arab countries) provides legal advice and juridical aid for women; carries out research on women's legal status in the Arab world; and seeks the abrogation of existing laws that constrain women and the expansion of Arab women's political, civil, economic, social, and cultural rights.[13] The women's chapter of the Egyptian Association for Industry and Environment held a national workshop in June 1995 on "the role of women in protection of environment and natural resource conservation".[14]

Development research centers and women's studies institutes are usually national-based but are increasingly conducting transnational research activities, especially in North Africa. They may engage in "pure" research of an academic nature, or combine it with advocacy for gender equity, women's empowerment, socio-economic development, and social justice. In any case, they provide useful research for other organizations involved in action. The Institute for Women's Studies in the Arab World, of the Lebanese American University (formerly Beirut University College), publishes a quarterly magazine called *Al-Raida*, which tackles such taboo subjects as violence within the family as well as trends in women's education, and pays close attention to literature and scholarly publications by women.

Morocco's Collectif Etudes Recherche Action pour le Développement and Tunisia's the Centre de Recherche de Documentation et d'Information sur la Femme (CREDIF) are both respected institutes. The Association des Femmes Tunisiennes pour la Recherche et le Développement (AFTURD) was set up in 1989 as an offshoot of the Association of African Women for Research and Development. Its aim is to carry out studies on women's integration in the development process with a view to enhancing women's contributions to economic and social development and calling for women's participation in decision-making.[15] Among the Palestinians there is the Women's Studies Program of Birzeit University and the Women's Training and Research Society (Women's Studies Centre) in Jerusalem.

Examples from Egypt are the New Woman Research and Study Centre in Cairo (research to help create "a powerful Egyptian women's movement"), and the Ibn Khaldoun Centre for Development Studies, which includes a gender focus and which publishes a monthly magazine called *Civil Society: Democratic Transition in the Arab World.*[16] Also in Egypt, the Al-Mishkat Centre for Research and Training conducts research activities, documentation, and training. The organization Nour, located in Cairo, promotes Arab women's writings, by *inter alia*, publishing good quality low-cost paperback editions, producing a newsletter, building links with publishing houses, etc.[17] In November 1995 Nour organized the First Arab Women's Book Fair.

In Turkey, the Women's Research and Education Center, based at Istanbul University, the Women's Library and Information Center, also in Istanbul, and the Turkish Association for Research and Analysis on Women's Social Life have been active for some years. In the early 1990s women's studies centers and programs were established at Ankara University and at Middle East Technical University (also in Ankara). These centers and institutes tend to be feminist in nature.

In the Islamic Republic of Iran, where most women's organizations are in the field of service, welfare, and charity, several groups of women are producing magazines, journals, and research papers that provide valuable information and provocative debate. The main women's magazines, *Zanan, Payam-e Hajjar,* and *Zan-e Rouz,* vary in their approach to the official Islamic discourse, but they all take up issues of discrimination against women. *Farzaneh: Journal of Women's Studies and Research,* is more academic in its approach, and is published by the Centre for Women's Studies and Research, in Tehran. The extent to which these publishing collectives are feminist or contributing to women's empowerment is in dispute among Iranian feminists abroad. There is some consensus, however, that *Zanan* is especially worth following.[18]

Development and women-in-development NGOs provide technical assistance and expertise on issues related to sustainable development, and implement projects on income-generation and micro-enterprises for poverty-alleviation, literacy and education, health, family planning, and community development. In Egypt, many NGOs are cooperating with the Ministry of Social Affairs in implementing the "Productive Families Project", which seeks to capitalize household resources by converting the home into a unit of production. An umbrella organization, the General Association for Vocational Training and Productive Families, coordinates NGO assistance in the provision of credits and loans, equipment, training, and marketing. Tunisia also has in place a "productive families" program in which NGOs are involved in poverty-alleviation and income-generating projects. In Jordan, the

National Project for the Development of Traditional Handicrafts was sponsored by the Queen Noor Institution. Since 1985 it has provided income-generating opportunities for poor women and aims also to revive Jordan's traditional handicrafts. The Institution undertakes the marketing of production at home and abroad. The number of beneficiaries of the project in 1991 was estimated at 2,000, including 740 women.[19] Other NGOs without royal sponsorship have evolved as the vehicle of donor funding and are regarded as "closer to the grassroots" or more efficient than government agencies. This category includes ENDA Inter-Arab, based in Tunis; Lebanon's Association for Popular Action, la Fondation René Moawad, and the Lebanese Women's Council. Tunisia's Association de Promotion des Projects de Femmes dans l'Economie (APROFE) was set up in 1990 and works to improve the integration of women in investment and employment, and is particularly interested in helping women to start up new projects.[20]

In Egypt, the Association for Development and Enhancement of Women (ADEW) has projects geared to low-income women maintaining households alone, providing credit, legal assistance, and awareness of "their importance and potential in the development process".[21] With funding from international donors, donations from Egyptians, and membership fees, ADEW assists in developing and implementing action-oriented programs that: generate employment for women who maintain households alone; improve the leadership skills for community women; create awareness of the needs and problems of female-headed households and elicit the support of government officials and private and institutional donors; establish links between women's NGOs, local women, donor agencies, private individuals, and banks; assist local organizations in setting up similar programs. Technical assistance provided by ADEW includes: introducing options for diversification of product lines to meet demand and increase profit; assisting local women in identifying new wholesale and retail market opportunities; training local women on basic budgeting principles.[22]

In addition to country-based development NGOs, there are a number of regional networks or regional bodies. The Center of Arab Women for Training and Research (CAWTAR), based in Tunis but acting as a regional body, receives funding from the Tunisian government, Saudi Arabia, and other Arab sources. It provides training on gender issues, produces gender-disaggregated statistics, and undertakes studies on economic and social policy issues.

Worker-based and grassroots women's organizations are concerned with the welfare and equity of women workers. This category includes such organizations as Egypt's Central Agricultural Cooperative Union, which has women members; and the Women's Committee of the General Federation of Agricultural Workers' Cooperatives, in Iraq. In Tunisia, the National Commission on Working Women was created in July 1991 within the Tunisian General Federation of Workers (UGTT). The Commission has 27 branches throughout Tunisia, and carries out surveys and studies pertaining to women and the workplace. Among the Palestinians, women's grassroots organizations are especially active, and many became prominent during the Intifada, when they worked to realize the dual objectives of promoting women's productive, professional, and political activities *and* providing products and services for Palestinian families and communities to sustain the Intifada.

The extent of worker-based and grassroots organizations in the MENA region in which women participate or which are led by women needs further study. Women's trade union participation is very weak in the region, partly a reflection of their limited participation in the formal work force, and partly a reflection of the masculinist nature of the trade unions. Nevertheless, women's committees of trade unions do exist, and women sometimes attain leadership positions within some unions and other worker-based organizations. The Egyptian Trade Union Federation has a women workers' department. Women have been elected officers in all 23 unions of the ETUF, although in 1990/91 they represented only 621 out of a total of 18,062 union officers.[23] In Turkey in 1996, a woman was the chairperson of the All Social Unions, an affiliate of the Confederation of Public Workers' Union. As women's employment expands in the region, especially in the context of export-led development, it will be increasingly important to monitor the way that women workers organize and mobilize in response to employment conditions and management strategies.

Women's organizations affiliated to political parties are the women's affiliates of non-ruling political parties, whether left-wing, Islamist, or other. Of course, many of the General Federations of Women and National Unions of Women are affiliated with the ruling parties. For example, the Union Nationale des Femmes Tunisiennes is affiliated with the PSD, the General Federation of Iraqi Women with the Iraqi Baath Party, and the Syrian Women's Federation with the Syrian Baath Party. In Turkey the main political parties all have women's commissions, and several are responding to feminist calls for an increase in the number of women candidates on their electoral lists. Other, non-governmental and non-official women's organizations may be affiliated with left-wing parties or may have grown out of existing political parties and organizations. For example, at least three of the prominent feminist organizations in Algeria emerged from left-wing (Trotskyist and socialist) political organizations.

Historically, women's organizations tied to political parties have subsumed "the woman question" to larger political, party, and nationalist objectives. There is a vast feminist literature concerning this in the Iranian case. The sidelining of women's equity and empowerment issues in the interests of nationalist goals has also been characteristic of the Palestinian women's organizations.[24] By contrast, independent feminist groups emphasize women's rights and human rights issues.

Human rights/women's rights organizations are perhaps the ones with the most transformative potential and the ones most likely to experience state harassment. Human rights NGOs were encouraged by the International Conference on Human Rights and by the new development agenda that emphasizes non-economic issues such as good governance, democratic participation, human rights observance, and the status of women. The women's rights organizations are explicitly oriented towards women's empowerment. Examples from Turkey are the Rainbow Istanbul Women's Platform, and the Purple Roof Women's Shelter Foundation. The latter, in particular, represents an attempt to "institutionalize feminist activism" through campaigns centered on violence against women and the establishment of battered women's shelters in various municipalities.[25]

Active and vocal groups in Egypt are the New Civic Forum (in which Mona Zulficar, a prominent women's rights lawyer, is actively involved), the Women's Rights Committee of the Egyptian Organization for Human Rights, and the Reproductive Rights Group. The Palestinian Organization for Human Rights (Al-Haq), the first Palestinian human rights organization, has had a section on women's rights for a number of years. Al-Haq convened a major conference on women and the law in September 1994. The Jordanian Women's Union, led by lawyer Asma Khader, is actively engaged in campaigns to end restrictions on women's mobility and travel, to protect women from domestic violence, rape, and "honor crimes" and to amend the law on nationality so that women may pass on their nationality to their non-Jordanian husbands and children.[26]

North Africa is home to la Commission Femmes de la Ligue Tunisienne des Droits de l'Homme (LTDH) and l'Association Tunisienne des Femmes Démocrates; Morocco's l'Organisation Marocaine des Droits des Femmes, l'Association Démocratique des Femmes du Maroc, and l'Union de l'Action Féminine (many of whose members are involved with the publication *8 Mars*). An interesting case study of mushrooming democratic, human rights, and feminist organizations is Algeria. Its Association pour l'Egalité entre les Hommes et les Femmes Devant la Loi (known as Egalité) was established in May 1985 around the Family Code struggle. The period 1989-1994 saw the formation of the following feminist organizations: l'Association Indépendante pour le Triomphe des Droits de la Femme (known as Triomphe), Emancipation, Defense et Promotion (known as Emancipation), Voix des Femmes, El Aurassia, and Rassemblement des Femmes Democratiques.[27] The objectives of the Algerian women's rights organizations include some that are fairly representative and others that are specific to the Algerian case: the abolition of the Family Code; full citizenship for women, enactment of civil laws guaranteeing equality between men and women, in areas such as employment and marriage and divorce (abolition of polygamy and unilateral male divorce, equality in division of marital property). When Egalité was formed, its secretariat consisted almost entirely of members of the Socialist Organization of Workers (OST, Trotskyist tendency), which became the Workers' Party (PT) in 1990. According to Cherifa Bouatta, the members of Emancipation belonged to the PST (Socialist Workers Party), and those of Defense et Promotion belonged largely to the PAGS (Parti de l'Avant-Garde Socialiste, or the Communist Party). In Algeria these are referred to as democratic women's organizations, to distinguish them from both the state-affiliated women's groups and the pro-Islamist women's groups.

Women's Organizations:
Constraints and Opportunities for Growth

In a previous section, we discussed the demographic, economic, political, and international factors behind the expansion of women's organizations in the region. The international factors in particular constitute an enabling environment for the nurturing and fostering of

women's groups.   Many international organizations – including some
of the feminist networks mentioned earlier, as well as international
NGOs – have provided technical assistance, funding, and moral and
political support for women's organizations in the Middle East and
North Africa.   In addition to opportunities for growth, however, the
women's organizations face a number of constraints, some more
serious than others.

Given the importance of international factors in the rise and
expansion of NGOs in general and women's organizations in particular,
it would be expected that external support, including funding, would be
a major component of the NGOs' operations.   Indeed, many NGOs,
including the women's NGOs, receive funding from international
NGOs, UN bodies, or the Dutch, Canadian, Danish, German, Swedish,
and American development agencies.   In Egypt, USAID is one of the
principal funding sources, funding many community development and
family planning projects, as well as certain women's groups.   United
Nations agencies are increasingly establishing relations with NGOs in
the MENA region.   Until recently, cooperation between the UNDP and
Arab countries was channeled through governmental machinery.
Today, the UNDP cooperates directly with NGOs.   Other UN agencies
with strong ties to women's NGOs, are UNICEF, UNESCO, UNFPA,
and UNIFEM.

The role of external funding does raise questions about the self-
reliance and viability of organizations and the extent to which they are
grassroots and indigenous bodies, and about the extent to which
women's organizations could become self-financing or obtain financing
at the community, national, or regional levels. Moreover, much of the
external funding was associated with preparations for the Beijing
Conference, and decreased following the immediate follow-up
activities in 1996.   However, questions about NGO self-reliance are not
necessarily resolved in the case of women's organizations which
receive governmental funding.   In these cases, a separate set of
questions is raised regarding independence and the extent to which
these are truly *non*-governmental organizations.   For example,
CAWTAR is funded largely by Arab sources, but for that it has paid a
price in terms of its autonomy.   The organization has had a troubled
past; its first director angrily resigned because of her lack of
maneuverability, and its second director was fired for being too radical.
Heavy-handedness on the part of the Tunisian host government has
alienated many of the past staff members.[28]

In many countries, women's NGOs face legal constraints and restrictions on their activities. In Egypt, Law 32 of 1964 provides a comprehensive regulatory scheme for NGOs (called PVOs) in which the Ministry of Social Affairs (MOSA) is empowered to do the following: prescribe the charter and the bylaws; review and approve board membership, and appoint up to 50% of the board members; dissolve an association without court order, or decree that two or more NGOs should be amalgamated; restrict association activities to one category of a prescribed list of eight activities (expanded to 12 in 1986). MOSA may also strike down any decision of an NGO board of directors that it considers in violation of Law 32.

Another example comes from Iran. In preparation for the Fourth World Conference on Women, a Women's NGO Coordinating Office was formed. It produced a booklet, *The National Report on the Women's NGOs in Iran,* which lists a total of 50 women's NGOs. The booklet report that women's NGOs are organized around the following issues or constituencies: (1) religious minorities; (2) migrants; (3) international NGOs; (4) charity-cultural issues; (5) socio-political NGOs; (6) cultural-training issues; (7) governmental NGOs; (8) trade and specialized NGOs; and (9) publications. Although many of these NGOs perform important tasks, there is no indication that any of the NGOs is truly independent of government control and interference, especially in light of what we know about the state's excessive interest in the activities of individuals and organizations.

By contrast, women's organizations appear to be the most independent, institutionalized and "indigenized" in Turkey. There they have become an important part of the political landscape and they are credited with having made significant contributions to the process of democratization during the 1980s. According to Yesim Arat, "In the 1991 General Election, women's issues became a visible item on the campaigns and party programs of all the major parties. This development was unprecedented in Turkish politics."[29] Arat also believes that the NGOs dealing with women's rights and human rights questions can be especially effective in promoting equality.[30] In recent years secular feminists have had to mobilize against creeping Islamization. In February 1997 thousands of women protested in the streets of Ankara against Prime Minister Necmettin Erbakan's effort to give Islam a greater role in public life. According to press accounts, more than 8,000 protesters chanted, "We are women, we are strong, we are against Islamic law", and carried banners proclaiming "Join hands for democracy."[31]

The most serious constraints faced by women's organizations are found in Algeria, where Islamist violence has forced the women's groups underground or in exile. (See below.)

It should be noted that the women's organizations in the Middle East and North Africa are not mass movements and do not include the participation of urban poor, working class, and rural women as they do in, for example, India and some Latin American countries. Their constituency is limited and it is possible that in the case of some women's NGOs, their *raison d'etre* is rather self-interested. Organizational and managerial problems also exist, and these include insufficient coordination and cooperation between NGOs, poor volunteer recruitment, and inadequate technical abilities, especially in the fields of documentation, information retrieval, and computerization.

Case Study: The Algerian Women's Movement

The growth of independent women's organizations in Algeria illustrates the framework for analysis presented in this paper. The demographic, economic, political, and international factors stressed above are all present in the Algerian case; the Algerian women's movement falls within the human rights/women's rights type of women's non-governmental organization; the Algerian case exemplifies the constraints that women's organizations face in their mobilization and political activities.

Following the death of Boumedienne in later 1978, the new government of Chedli Benjedid initiated the process of profound economic and political change. This was a conservative move at women's expense. The introduction of a draft Family Code in 1981 alarmed many Algerian women, who saw it as an attempt to placate a growing Islamist tendency by institutionalizing second-class citizenship for women. The Algerian feminist movement has its origins in this period of protest against the draft Family Code, organized largely by educated women employed at the University of Algiers. Feminists point out that the Family Code, which was hurriedly adopted in 1984 before the women's organizations could remount their mobilization, contravenes the equality clauses of the Constitution, the Labor Code, and international conventions to which Algeria is a signatory. Among other things, the Family Code requires a husband's permission as a condition for a wife's employment.

The Benjedid government went on to slowly institute changes to the system of agricultural production and to the status of state-owned industrial enterprises, ostensibly as a way of tackling rising unemployment and debt servicing in the context of the falling price of oil. But these measures only exacerbated the economic crisis by raising prices, and resulted in the riots of October 1988. Benjedid's response was to usher in a brief period of political liberalization, but this was disrupted by the rise of the Islamist movement *Front Islamique du Salut* in 1990 and their victory in the 1991 elections. The proscription of the FIS ushered in a period of violent civil conflict. At the height of the political turmoil in the early 1990s pitting the government and military against Islamist extremists, Algeria's economic and political transition appeared uncertain, and the state seemed vulnerable to collapse. Algeria's feminists were caught between the devil of statism and the deep blue sea of Islamism, but they focused their political energies against patriarchal and violent *integrism*. During 1994 protests and demonstrations were organized by such groups as the Rassemblement Algerien des Femmes Democrates, Triomphe, l'Association Solidaire avec les Victimes du Terrorisme, la Commission femmes MPR (Mouvement pour la Republique), and SOS Femmes en Détresse. After one public protest in the spring of 1994, the independent *Al Watan* wrote: "Tens of thousands of women were out to give an authoritative lesson on bravery and spirit to men paralyzed by fear, reduced to silence. ... The so-called weaker sex ... refused to be intimidated by the threats advanced by 'the sect of assassins'".[32]

The Algerian feminist movement has received widespread support, from international NGOs and from transnational feminist networks. But the constraints women face – in the form of GIA terrorism and FIS intimidation – are considerable. Khalida Messaoudi is a former math teacher, a feminist leader and a democrat who helped to form Triomphe and who backed the Algerian Government's decision to stop the FIS from winning the 1991 parliamentary elections. For that, as well as for her criticisms of FIS policies toward women, the FIS officially condemned her to death. For some time she lived in hiding. Nabila Diahnine, an architect and president of a feminist group, was 35 years old when she was assassinated in February 1996 while on her way to work in the northern city of Tizi Ouzou. In June 1994 a bomb exploded during a march, after which public demonstrations of women's groups were rare for a while, and meetings were held in secret.[33]

The outcome of the November 1995 elections showed that the government retained considerable popular support, and this came as a relief to many who feared that Islamists had a wide social base. For its turn, the government of President Zeroual now had to acknowledge and accommodate Islamist and secular opposition forces. During 1997 the Islamist underground continued to carry out terrorist actions, but in a show of resilience and determination, democratic women ran for parliament and won seats. Remarkably, Khalida Messaoudi, a candidate of the Rally for Culture and Democracy, was among those women elected to parliament.

As disruptive and violent as the political crisis has been, that and the economic crisis have paradoxically given new life to Algeria's civil society. Layachi describes how interaction between the state and elements of the nascent civil society intensified after 1993:

> The High State Council met with the leaders of the moderate Islamic party, Hamas, the Islamic Supreme Council, the National Association of Imams, the National Association of Zaouias, the National Union of Public Enterprises, the Federation of the Management Associations of Local Public Enterprises, the Association of the Friends of Algiers, Protection of the Casbah, the Culture and Progress Circle, the National Syndicate of Algerian Jurists, the Lawyers National Order, and the Rally for Culture and Democracy.[34]

Missing from this list is the array of women's organizations that emerged in Algeria during the early 1980s and grew during the 1990s, as we saw above. Ever since the struggle around the Family Code, the growth of feminist activism has become a defining feature of Algeria in transition. Women's organizations are now an integral part of the democratic movement that gained momentum in the 1990s, and they constitute a significant part of civil society.

Summary and Conclusions

The changing political dynamics in the Middle East and North Africa include internal processes such as liberalization, Islamization, shifts in state-society relations, and the proliferation of non-governmental organizations. These processes have a gender dimension which is often overlooked but which should be integrated in research and analysis if they are to be understood and explained. In this article we have drawn attention to the growth of women's organizations in the region, and have situated it in socio-demographic change, economic and political liberalization, the fundamentalist threat, and global feminism. We have identified several types of women's organizations and highlighted the radical nature of those with a feminist and human rights agenda. Women's organizations are the new political voice in the region.

Though the constraints and limitations on the women's organizations in the Middle East and North Africa are considerable, they should not be perceived as sources of debilitation or delegitimation. That many women's NGOs are elite, professional, and middle-class bodies does not mean that they do not have a wider impact. In Middle Eastern societies, where the public sphere has historically been the province of men, where male-female gaps are still huge, where economic decision-making is entirely male, and where women's participation in formal political structures and in elections – whether as candidates or as voters – is still low and in some cases declining, the very existence of women's NGOs challenges the patriarchal order in rather profound ways. To the extent that women's organizations contribute to the democratization process, the creation of a democratic civil society and a civic culture, and seek to participate in the development process and in politics, they are important in and of themselves. The opening up of political space and the diffusion of once centralized economic power and resources will allow for the articulation of more feminist demands, including women's perspectives on economic policy and planning. In addition, the changing political economy in the Middle East and North Africa will challenge the women's NGOs to forge alliances and articulate the interests and needs of women workers in the evolving new economic order. That Middle Eastern women are now engaged in an array of activities is itself highly significant. And that the women's organizations are so diverse – ranging from the professional associations to those specializing in development issues to those that fight for human rights and women's rights – is historically unprecedented. Women's organizations represent a recognized role for women in the development process *and* they represent changing state-society relations and definitions of citizenship.

Notes

1. See Mustapha K. El-Sayyid, "The Third Wave of Democratization in the Arab World", pp. 179-190 in Dan Tschirgi, ed., The Arab World Today, (Lynne Rienner, 1994).

2. The Palestinian NGO position paper was reprinted in Civil Society, Vol. III, Issue 33 (Sept. 1994), pp. 10-11. Civil Society, is a magazine published by the Ibn Khaldoun Center, Cairo.

3. The description which follows is from the unedited English translation of the Arabic original, which was made available to participants of the expert-group meeting and high-level (inter-governmental) meeting that took place following the NGO Forum. I attended the meetings at the invitation of ESCWA, the main organizer, in my capacity as an expert and as a UN staff member.

4. See Al-Raida, (Beirut), Vol. XII, No. 69, Spring 1995, pp. 4-5.

5. See Al-Raida, Vol. XII, No. 69 (Spring 1995), p. 7, and Vol. XIII, Nos. 74/75 (Summer/Fall 1996), p. 2.

6. The three publications were given to me by an Algerian member of the Collectif. The publications were produced with the cooperation of the Friedrich Ebert Foundation and the European Union.

7. "Declaration of the Arab NGOs participating in the Fourth World Conference on Women", mimeo, distributed on 14 September 1995, Beijing.

8. Rami Khouri, "A Kick in the Pants: Women Call for Democracy", *Jordan Times,* reprinted in Women's International Net Magazine, December 1997 (via Internet).

9. Janet S. Chafetz and Gary Dworkin, Female Revolt: Women's Movements in World and Historical Perspective, (Totawa, NJ: Rowman and Allanheld, 1986), p. 191.

10. See Margot Badran, "Gender Activism: Feminists and Islamists in Egypt", in Valentine M. Moghadam, ed., Identity Politics and Women: Cultural Reassertions and Feminisms in International Perspective, (Boulder, CO: Westview Press, 1994).   On Iran see ch. 6 in Valentine M. Moghadam, Modernizing Women: Gender and Social Change in the Middle East, (Boulder, CO: Lynne Rienner Publishers, 1993).

11. Valentine M. Moghadam, "Feminist Networks North and South", Journal of International Communication, vol. 3, no. 1 (July 1996): 111-126. The quote appears on p. 114.

12. Cherifa Bouatta, "Evolution of the Women's Movement in Contemporary Algeria: Organization, Objectives, and Prospects", paper prepared under external contract for UNU/WIDER, Helsinki, 1995.

13. Sawsan El-Messiri, "Women and the Law in the Near East: Legal and Regulatory Constraints to Women's Participation in Development. Research on Women, Law and Development in Egypt", mimeo, 1994.

14. Information from Women's Environment & Development Organization News & Views, Vol. 8, No.1-2, (June 1995), 5. WEDO is an international women's NGO based in New York that has been active since the Earth Summit (Rio, 1993).

15. UNIDO, "Women in Industry: Tunisia" (Vienna: UNIDO, 1993).

16. See, for example, Civil Society, vol. III, issue 31 (July 1994), which focused on "Egyptian Women and Democracy".

17. Sawsan El-Messiri, "Women and the Law in the Near East " op. cit.

18. See, for example Ziba Mir-Hosseini, "Stretching the Limits: A Feminist Reading of the Shari'a in Post-Khomeini Iran." Forthcoming in Islamic Law and Feminism, ed. Mai Yamani (London: Ithaca Press, 1996).

19. Kandil, Civil Society in the Arab World, 63.

20. UNIDO, "Women in Industry: Tunisia".

21. El-Messiri, "Women and the Law in the Near East ".

22. Ibid.

23. Author's interview with Mr. Hussein Hassan, International Labour Relations Department, ETUF, Cairo, 9 February 1995.

24. See contributions in Valentine M. Moghadam, ed., Gender and National Identity: Women and Politics in Muslim Societies, (London: Zed Books, 1995).

25. For an elaboration, see Yesim Arat, "Purple Roof Women's Shelter Foundation", op. cit.

26. Ghena Ismail, "The Jordanian Women's Struggle", Al-Raida, Vol. XIII, Nos. 74/75, summer/fall 1996, pp. 32-34.

27. Bouatta, "Evolution of the Women's Movement in Contemporary Algeria: Organization, Objectives, and Prospects".

28. Interview with a former CAWTAR staff member, Amman, November 1996.

29. Yesim Arat, "Toward a Democratic Society: The Women's Movement in Turkey in the 1980s", in Women's Studies International Forum, Nos. 3-4 (1994), pp. 241-248.

30. Yesim Arat, "Changing the Political Climate and Creating Conditions to Promote Equality: The Role of Non-governmental Organizations", paper prepared for the International Workshop on National Machinery to Promote Equality between Women and Men in Central and East European Countries, Ljubljana, Slovenia (30 Nov. - 2 Dec. 1994).

31. See, for example, Boston Globe, Feb. 16, 1997, and WIN News, Vol. 23, No. 2 (Spring 1997), p. 74.

32. "Algeria: Women's Revolt", World Press Review, July 1994, p. 34.

33. "Women's Bodies in Algeria: The Deadly Political Game", Village Voice, Nov. 28, 1996 (reprinted in Shirgat Gah, WLUML Newssheet, Vol. VIII, No. 1&2, 1997, pp. 10-11.

34. Azzedine Layachi, "Algeria: Reinstating the State or Instating Civil Society?", in I. William Zartman, ed., Collapsed States: The Disintegration and Restoration of Legitimate Authority, (Boulder, CO: Lynne Rienner Publishers, 1995), p. 187.

Chapter 7

Refighting the Cold War: Containment as the Foundation of America's Post-Cold War Political-Military Posture in the Middle East

Laura Drake

Introduction

Regional containment, intended as a full-blown strategic doctrine for the Middle East area, is a product of the Clinton administration's national security team. It was originally conceived in 1993 under the name "dual containment," which has since devolved into multiple disconnected threads of containment. The strategy in its initial conception is the invention of Dr. Martin Indyk, President Clinton's first director of Middle East affairs at the National Security Council. He first introduced it as a comprehensive American strategy for the Middle East in a May 1993 address to the pro-Israel Washington Institute for Near East Policy, which he founded. It subsequently became the third pillar of then-National Security Advisor Anthony Lake's short-lived global policy of "enlargement": expanding the reign of democracy and free markets in most parts of the world, while preserving America's

* An earlier version of this chapter was published under the title "Still fighting the last war: A cold war policy for a postwar Middle East," Middle East Insight, Vol. 10, No. 6, September/October 1994, this updated and expanded chapter appears here with their permission.

traditional assets and interests in the Middle East and containing those states and non-state actors that present a threat to them.

At the broader level, containment policy as such is of Cold War origin. Dual containment, complete with its own East-West paradigm, transferred the defining global doctrine of the Cold War era to a post-Cold War regional setting. Iraq and Iran, both of which are led by governments that "pursue policies fundamentally hostile to US interests,"[1] were posited as the twin evil empires, while "extremism" – not Islamism – became the new "ism"[2] to be confronted as the parallel to communism in a post-Cold War era.[3] However, "extremism" was and still is an "ism" in which any form of Islamist political opposition bearing a military option is automatically also included, not because of its Islamic character, but because of its willingness to use force to oppose America's foreign policy objectives and political-military hegemony in the region. Israel, along with Washington's Arab allies Egypt, Jordan, and the GCC states, despite their authoritarian systems, are held out as representatives of the regional free world equivalent, because of their client status and their sympathy with Washington's positions in foreign affairs.

In other ways, however, regional containment differs radically from US efforts to encircle the Soviet Union during the Cold War. The US-USSR relationship was one of relative balance, between two states of roughly equivalent strength and stature in every way that mattered. The only possible strategy toward the rival superpower was one of 'defensive containment,' a passive strategy built on the twin foundations of deterrence at the center and proxy-wars on the periphery to simultaneously prevent a devastating nuclear conflict between the superpowers and the expansion of the Soviet sphere of influence around the world. Unlike superpower containment, the containment of Iraq, Iran, and other dissenting entities is an example of 'offensive containment' – possible only in a hegemonic global environment – where the main instruments are economic sanctions, arms embargoes, and political isolation, all of which are targeted directly at the core of the home country.

In its conception, however, the objectives of the current US Middle East strategy are much broader in scope than those usually associated with a posture of strategic containment. Middle Eastern containment in its initial form of "dual containment" represented a fully-integrated and structured framework intended to encompass the entire eastern part of the Middle East region (the Mashreq), or the area that spans

Refighting the Cold War: Containment as the Foundation   175
of America's Post-Cold War Political-Military Posture
in the Middle East

approximately from Iran to Israel (i.e., excluding North Africa and the Arabian peninsula), subdividing it into two geographical "halves" – east and west – and, implicitly, into two corresponding functional spheres – peace and containment.[4] Today the basic strategic mode of thinking in terms of the spheres of peace and containment survives, though the structured aspects originally envisioned in the strategy have long since dissipated.

Iraq and Iran, which constituted the eastern half of dual containment, were to be the objects of containment. Rather than balancing the two off against each other, building up one in order to counter the other, dual containment aimed to preserve the effects left behind by two Gulf wars and the Soviet collapse in which "a [new] regional balance of power between Iraq and Iran has been established at a much lower level of military capability," making it "easier to balance the power of both of them."[5]

The western half, encompassing Israel and the Arab cordon states, was to represent the arena of peace. The Clinton administration's premise was and is that the two spheres are interdependent and mutually reinforcing: "Containing the threats posed by Iraq and Iran in the east will impact on our ability to promote peace between Israel and its Arab neighbors in the west; similarly, promoting Arab-Israeli peace in the west will impact on our ability to contain the threats from Iraq and Iran in the east."[6] Thus was created a Middle Eastern variation of President Reagan's Cold War dictum of "peace through strength" – a policy of peace through containment.

It is possible to broaden the analysis and address the implicit geopolitical dynamics initiated during the dual containment phase. One has been the facilitation and solidification of Israel's status as the region's unchallenged hegemon. This can be said because the outlines and priorities of dual containment did not precisely follow those of America's traditional interests in the Middle East. Except peripherally and in passing, the strategy reserved no role other than that of chief protectee and passive recipient of security for the GCC countries, which are normally conceived as being of "vital interest" to the United States. The area lacked a category of its own in the dual containment structure; it was not explicitly included geographically in either the eastern or western half. In spite of this omission, it would be logical to assume that the southern Gulf monarchies, despite their geographical position on the eastern side of the line, actually belonged to the western half because of their alliance with the United States, their support for the peace process, and their objective fears regarding the regional powers Iraq and Iran. However, the marginalization of the GCC in the overall scheme of things to the role of passive protectorate rather than active participant is more representative of how the region looks from the Israeli vantage point than from that of the United States.

The western half

Dual containment initially bore important similarities to Israel's "eastern front" doctrine, a core military-strategic prescription dating back to the 1950s. In following that strategy, Israel sought by whatever means to prevent the emergence within the Arab Mashreq (eastern) subregion of any credible political-military alliance composed of the confrontation states situated to Israel's east. In particular, Israel feared a future potential alliance of Iraq and Syria, with Jordan (perhaps under a post-Hashemite regime) as a second-level partner and territorial launch point. The difference in the 1990s was that the 'front' had shifted a bit further eastward: the "line of confrontation" as the late Yitzhak Rabin used to call it had effectively moved from Jordan's western border to its eastern border, while the threat of massing armies has since been replaced with long-range surface-to-surface ballistic missiles armed with unconventional warheads. The mechanisms of embargo and isolation which are used to implement containment, as well as the explicit choice of Iraq and Iran as the foremost targets of the new policy, made Dr. Indyk's invention a most effective framework for neutralizing this new threat.

Israel also stood to benefit from the removal of both Iraq and Iran as strategic alternatives for their weaker Arab neighbors, one of the stated objectives of the original dual containment strategy.[7] Severed from their natural hinterland and deprived of what they have always considered to be their strategic depth and sources of leverage, it was thought that Iraq and Iran might someday be compelled to enter a regional peace constructed largely on Israeli requirements. Thus, dual containment promised, over the long term, to strengthen the Israeli position in the region by bringing about its normalization at minimal cost, while simultaneously keeping the states that might challenge it in an enfeebled position. In this aspect containment has been successful, though it has yet to bring about a full surrender in the basic foreign policy positions of these countries.

Refighting the Cold War: Containment as the Foundation   177
of America's Post-Cold War Political-Military Posture
in the Middle East

Israel also found in dual containment the rationale it needed to
continue as America's strategic ally in the post-Soviet era, by implicitly
becoming one of its regional enforcers. Israel immediately assumed and
was granted a new role for a new era: that of a Western or pro-Western
outpost standing on the front lines of what was then viewed as mostly
Iranian-sponsored Islamist extremism. dual containment allowed Israel
to defend its own interests while also serving an American policy
objective. For instance, in strafing Hezbollah bases in Lebanon, Israel
could claim to be containing Iranian ambitions and promoting the peace
process at the same time as it was defending its own security. Israel's *ex
post facto* justification of its 1981 bombardment of the Iraqi nuclear
reactor at Tuwaitha falls into the same category, as will any parallel
attack Israeli might decide to launch in future years against Iran's
nuclear facilities. Generally, however, Lebanon remains the region's
primary battleground just as it has been since the late 1970s. This is
probably not a coincidence. Still lacking a true geopolitical identity of
its own, the vacuum of Lebanon attracts political conflicts from one
end of the region to the other, serving as the ground where all its
contradictory tendencies converge.[8]

Syria stands at the strategic crossroads between dual containment's
regional "east" and "west." It is the only point on the map where the
eastern and western halves intersect in an independent alliance between
two powers of substance, in what its opponents sometimes call the
"Tehran-Damascus axis." Despite such characterizations, Damascus
remains perched atop the proverbial fence. Although it was the implicit
objective of dual containment to minimize independent contact
between the two halves, and now between any two hostile or neutral
major regional states, Syria has managed to preserve its strategic link
with Iran, and with it, a valuable source of leverage. President Assad is
still in possession of cards of real value to Israel and is therefore able,
unlike his weaker neighbors which have already surrendered all their
cards, to resist peace at any price. He has the luxury to take his time, be
patient, and wait for an equitable trade-off, but only if he can ensure the
ascension of a successor who will definitively continue his policies and
basic strategy after he is gone.

The Syrian leader has repeated many times that Damascus considers
peace to be a strategic option rather than a tactical one, and Israeli
leaders indicated early on in the peace talks that they believed him.[9]
Yet the Syrian president continues to maintain his close ties with
Tehran for leverage and insurance against the failure of the peace

option. Iran obviously benefits as well. Through Syria, Tehran is able to project its influence from the east to the far west in Lebanon, all the way south to that country's border with Israel, and to maintain that situation with minimal effort on its part. The Israeli government however continues to remind President Assad that holding onto 'hot cards' is not without risk. Every now and again the Israelis strike out at the Syrian-Iranian alliance by attacking the Iranian-backed Hezbollah in Lebanon, attacks which are usually followed by threatening statements directed at Syria, over which Israel holds a tremendous military advantage. Deprived of both strategic depth and a reliable supplier of advanced military technology, Syria fears nothing more than the next war with Israel.

The eastern half

That dual containment attempted to draw a line through the region at a place where a line did not belong constituted one of its major weaknesses. This is not to say the division was arbitrary, just that it was based upon a questionable ordering of American priorities rather than on local long-term geopolitical conditions.

Iraq shares linguistic, ethnic, and historical bonds going back centuries with the Arab peoples to its west, as well as a mutual antipathy toward the Persian state to its east, also going back centuries. Families, customs, and even political sentiments straddle Iraq's border with Syria, regardless of the personal animosity between their respective heads of state. Iraq not only belongs to the Mashreq (the Fertile Crescent) but is probably the most important state in that area due to its massive oil reserves (second only to Saudi Arabia), its abundance of water, its agricultural and industrial capabilities, and its substantive population base (currently 22 million). Under normal conditions, the balance of people to resources in Iraq is in exactly the right proportions: the population is large enough to provide a natural source of strength to the country but not so large as to constitute a burden on its resources, a situation which makes Iraq unique among Arab states. Iraq has also achieved a higher degree of technological progress and industrial potential than any other Arab country. For this reason, regardless of who is in power, Arab states to the west of Iraq, particularly Syria and Jordan, have traditionally depended on Baghdad as a 'strategic reserve,' – a natural counterbalance to Israeli power.

Refighting the Cold War: Containment as the Foundation   179
of America's Post-Cold War Political-Military Posture
in the Middle East

Yanking Iraq out of the Arab Mashreq would be like isolating the Russian Federation from its "near abroad": American efforts in that direction have served only to create a latent atmosphere of nervous tension which hangs heavy over regional decisionmakers who realized that the situation was hardly sustainable or desirable over the long-term. Surrounding governments know even today that Iraq must eventually either disappear into the world of failed states or return someday as a major regional factor, and they have found it difficult to make accurate calculations while such a key variable remains undefined. Generally, most regional bets seem to be on the eventual return of a strong Iraq rather than on its permanent demise.

Indeed, the Syrians have struck back quite effectively against this unreality by gradually and quite deliberately re-building their ties with Iraq, thereby defying the very premise of dual containment. As a result, Iraqi-Syrian relations, which constitute the center of gravity between regional east and west and the front line of dual containment's attempted severance, have been better during the period of dual containment and since than they have been at any time since the brief rapprochement during the Camp David-inspired Arab crisis in 1979. Diplomatic contacts, initiated at the lower levels, have since reached up to the levels of foreign ministers, while the land crossing on the Baghdad-Damascus highway has been re-opened to officials and to some commercial exchanges. There is even serious discussion around the re-opening of the Iraqi-Syrian oil pipeline, severed by Syria during the Iraq-Iran war in 1982. Both Iraq and Syria realized that they needed each other for strategic leverage, and that the alternative was permanent strategic and economic isolation (in Iraq's case) and vulnerability to political isolation followed by military destruction (in Syria's case).

The effort to perpetually enforce the isolation of Baghdad from a region in which it has played such a pivotal role has required constant attention and frequent adjustments in the instruments of American force. Whenever Iraq came close to meeting formal conditions for lifting sanctions, Washington moved the goalposts by adding new conditions.[10] Other permanent members of the Security Council, motivated primarily by economic considerations but also worried about the long-term consequences of Iraq's slow but progressive internal decay, have tried to recognize what they viewed as Baghdad's partial compliance with the cease-fire resolution, United Nations Security Council Resolution 687, by drafting statements and advocating the establishment a timetable for ending sanctions. Each time, the Clinton administration quashed their efforts. Over time, after it finally became obvious to everyone that the American conditions were fluid – and hence unattainable in principle – the administration began to find it increasingly difficult to justify its actions both to the Europeans and to Iraq's neighboring states, including those in the southern Gulf, with the exception of course of Kuwait and to a lesser degree, Saudi Arabia. The rest of the world, including the Iraqis themselves, had always assumed, probably erroneously, that Washington's conditions were meant to be fulfilled.

The international community, especially the Europeans and the Arab states, apparently understood from this experience (it is made explicit in Martin Indyk's comments, in the discussion surrounding fn. 14 below) that any parallel effort against Iran would most probably be based on the same principle, and this time, notably, they refused to go along.

Herein lay one of the basic reasons for the downfall of dual containment and the separation of the artificial Iraq-Iran duality into its components. This effect was further accelerated by the election of the obviously moderate President Mohammad Khatami in Iran, rendering the containment of a hostile and violently anti-Western Iran an anachronism in the calculation of most world leaders.

The neighboring countries are already losing enough in the way of trade and re-payment of debts because of the apparent permanence of the embargo against Iraq. Turkey and Jordan are the two regional states that have faced the brunt of it, though France, Russia, and other extra-regional actors that are owed money by Iraq are able neither to collect their much-needed balances (especially Russia) nor to resume the normal ties of what was a lucrative trade. Within the region, Iraq was Jordan's largest trading partner, while Turkey depended on Iraqi pipeline fees and trade in agricultural products. Economics aside, the Turks note that Kurdish nationalism has re-asserted itself on an unprecedented scale because of the power vacuum the sanctions have created in northern Iraq, resulting in several waves of instability accompanied by thousands of deaths in the southeastern Turkey. Most of America's allies in the region, including Jordan, Egypt, Turkey, and now Saudi Arabia, fear the further spread of Islamist opposition in the absence of an Iraqi buffer. President Assad, regardless of his personal feud with President Saddam Hussein, feared that the permanent loss of Iraq would deprive Syria forever of its strategic depth – non-Arab Iran being an adequate but not optimal substitute – and thus President Assad

Refighting the Cold War: Containment as the Foundation   181
of America's Post-Cold War Political-Military Posture
in the Middle East

took calculated steps to prevent it. For all these reasons, pressures from within the region to allow Iraq to return to a condition of normality are ever-present. The sanctions are considered by many in Europe and the Middle East to be more or less obsolete. This is especially true among the region's populations, who also consider the sanctions to be inhumane because they punish the people of Iraq rather than the Iraqi regime. The sanctions are also widely perceived as a strategic failure precisely because they have not succeeded in causing the removal of President Saddam Hussein from office. At the same time, no one has any illusions about the sanctions ever being lifted in any context other than that of large-scale political change in Iraq.[11]

Unlike Iraq, Iran is not an integral part of the Mashreq, first and foremost because it is not an Arab state. Bordered by the eastern Arab countries on one side, Iran forms the junction of several different regions in the Muslim world. Iran is divided from the Arab countries not only by geography but also by the historic Persian-Arab rivalry and the fundamental, age-old religious schism between the Sunni and Shi'i branches of Islam. Iran's recent connection to the Mashreq states and its emergence in dual containment as a virtual "eastern front" power despite its non-Arab status – today it is arguably the leading "eastern front" power – is a direct result of its pan-Islamist ideology but is not necessarily a permanent phenomenon. Tehran leaped beyond its natural geopolitical environment in taking advantage of local turmoil in Mashreq and Maghreb alike so as to create a new sphere of influence in the heart of what it viewed as a broader Muslim world. But its level of active participation in the Arab East has been on the decline for some time now. While severing Iran from the Mashreq might be viewed with alarm by a group like the Lebanese Hezbollah, which is totally dependent upon its financial and military largesse, Iran's departure or gradual disengagement – whether it results from an intensification of the means of containment, a Syrian-Israeli peace, or a dramatic change of policy in Tehran under Khatami – will not affect the region's overall integrity as has Iraq's long period of isolation. Much more dangerous is Iraq's downward slide toward state-failure. Iraq as a nation-state, as a political concept, an identity, has already been destabilized to the point where its existence into the next century has been called into question.[12]

The international trade embargo against Iraq has destroyed both the country's economy and its social and political coherence, while no-fly and safe-haven zones continue to segment its territory. Ethnic, sectarian and tribal identities have been heightened as a result of both factors; economic, social, and political structures are losing their meaning. In its current predicament, Iraq's structure is akin to a triangle: its sides are the regime, the sanctions, and the state. Given the strength of both the sanctions and the regime, it is the ultimate viability of the Iraqi state itself which constitutes the weakest link.

The state of decay is most advanced in the north of the country. The Iraqi Kurdish political tapestry responded to the loss of central authority by breaking down into rival armed militia factions engaged in battles for primacy and survival, for no particularly good political reason. Ominously indeed, there are no discernable differences in either ideology or grand-strategic objectives among the two most important militias, the Kurdish Democratic Party (KDP), led by Massoud Barzani, and the Patriotic Union of Kurdistan (PUK), led by Jalal Talabani. The significance of this second-level segmentation should have been driven home to anyone watching the Department of Defense briefings during this time, in which northern Iraq was represented on the Pentagon maps in the form of rival territories shaded in two different colors, green and yellow, and labelled with the acronyms KDP and PUK, respectively – thus bringing up the specter of Lebanon, and what it would mean if the phenomenon were to ultimately replicate itself throughout the whole of territorial Iraq.

The leaders of these two main Kurdish factions, in their battle for local and/or personal power, if it can be called that, began to seek out 'foreign' patrons to back them, as participants in civil wars are prone to do. And this is in an area whose political existence is already darkened by the shadows of three regional giants cast simultaneously onto it (three and a half if one includes Syria). The Kurdish area, forming the main point of intersection for these regional powers, also has the potential to serve as a convenient and low-cost political battleground for any two of them, or perhaps even for all of them together. Iraq and Iran, for various reasons, were the most natural choices for 'foreign' patronage from an objective, strictly geopolitical standpoint. One of the Kurdish factions, that of Talabani, succumbed to the temptation and momentarily disrupted the balance by stepping too deeply into the Iranian shadow, only to find the entire Kurdish framework had been swallowed whole and re-absorbed back into Iraq. This occurred, paradoxically, with the consent of the other Kurdish faction, the KDP, which ultimately came to view Jalal Talabani and the PUK as posing more of a threat than Saddam Hussein. And thus, in a stunning turn of

Refighting the Cold War: Containment as the Foundation   183
of America's Post-Cold War Political-Military Posture
in the Middle East

history, Massoud Barzani, the Kurdish leader, volunteered to serve as
the instrument of the Iraqi armed forces. The KDP was duly employed
to balance the Iranians by turning back the advance of their local
proxies, and at the same time, to deliver all the Iraqi Kurds back into
the hands of Saddam Hussein. Hence, the Kurds, who had a chance at
real autonomy for the first time since the 1970s, and who had attained
the partial symbols of independence – a parliament and an armed force
– ended up losing the territorial safe-haven zone itself, for all intents
and purposes, as the penalty for their apparent near-sightedness. And
that alone had been their historical break which had made everything
else possible.

Iraq as a whole contains the seeds of the same scenario that nearly
befell its northern territory, if central authority is suddenly or gradually
lost without the benefit of an immediate emergence of an obvious and
effective replacement. If the country eventually breaks up into well-
defined fragments or, alternatively, if it falls into a state of civil
dissolution and anarchy, a chain of events could ensue with broad-
ranging and unpredictable consequences. As in Lebanon from 1975-
1990 and northern Iraq from 1994 onward, Iraq could find itself broken
down into a plethora of local, former opposition forces trying to attain
internal primacy in a new, post-Saddam Iraq. Necessarily they would
seek the help of neighboring states to tilt the balance in their favor. And
needless to say, most of the states in question – at this point one could
add Jordan, Saudi Arabia, Syria and even Israel and the United States
to the mix – would be eager to add to their spheres of influence by
scavenging whatever portions of Iraq's remains were made available to
them, directly or indirectly, by local forces. The Lebanon-implosion
scenario may not be the most likely future for Iraq, yet as a worst case
scenario it must not be ignored: if the Iraqi state falters, Washington
could find itself in the unenviable position, along with most or all of the
area's primary actors, of trying to contain a regional black hole – a task
eminently more difficult than that of containing Iraq.[13]

Even in a scenario whereby Iraq remains intact, however, instability
is still likely to persist because the traditional balance between Iran and
Iraq has been disrupted, perhaps permanently, or at least for a very long
time. The Clinton administration claims that "a regional balance of
power between Iraq and Iran has been established at a much lower level
of military capability," but the earlier admission that "a structural
imbalance... exists between the measures available to contain Iraq and
Iran" carries the practical consequence that the balance has been

destroyed and Iran has in fact emerged stronger than Iraq.[14] Since the international community has refused the duality of containment in both theory and practice, Iran has been able to extend its projection of regional power, not just in spite of Iraq but also at its expense.

Iranian support for Islamists in other countries, an affinity based on religious (if not sectarian) commonality, and more importantly, on shared foreign policy goals, is aimed at altering the political systems and/or regional strategic postures of numerous states across the region, creating permanent new allies for itself, a friendly external environment as it were, and thereby securing a comfortable political future for itself as an Islamic republic in the Middle East region. It is notable that this extension of Iranian influence within the region and its constitution by American and Israeli strategic affairs analysts as a clear and manifest threat became apparent and achieved potency only after the destruction and subsequent political-military-economic quarantine of Iraq. Not only has the military balance been thrown askew, but the ideological balance has been tipped as well. For whatever embers of Arab nationalism still remained alight, however precariously, following the disappearance of Egypt into the wilderness of Camp David, were totally consumed by the fires of 1991: the legacy whose torch was carried from one end of the region to the other by Egypt's President Nasser was finally snuffed out and buried, once and for all, under the ashes of Ba'thist Iraq. Revolutionary, revisionist, and 'reformist' Islamism have flourished in the Arab world in the absence of the secular-nationalist counterweight represented most recently by Iraq, filling the ideological and geopolitical void left by the disappearance of Arab nationalism from the Middle Eastern map, the political philosophy through which the Ba'thists in Baghdad had projected their country's regional power for almost a quarter of a century.

Here, in the domain of political Islam, in which modern Islamist ideology presents itself as a comparatively youthful and singularly dynamic contender for national and regional power, as well as for moral authority, America's Middle Eastern containment posture finds itself inadvertently lending a programmatic framework to Samuel Huntington's "clash of civilizations."[15] US officials, in an effort to avoid the full-blown regionalization of the Great Satan phenomenon, went out of their way to denounce the Huntington theory and to explain that the enemy is not Islam, or even political Islam, but political "extremism" in the name of Islam.[16] In practice, however, the subtleties are too slight to survive the translation process: they enter regional

Refighting the Cold War: Containment as the Foundation   185
of America's Post-Cold War Political-Military Posture
in the Middle East

perceptions as an exercise in petty semantics at best and an exercise in deception at worst. Subsumed within the posture of containment, whether intentional or not, is a Middle Eastern version of the Cold War domino theory, starting with the presumption that the primarily Islamist form of extremism (or the extremist form of Islamism) is a radical menace exported in the first instance from Iran in the east to Arab states in the western part of the Mashreq (and beyond into North Africa) in order to expand Iran's regional power base and cause harm to American interests. The same principle held true for Iraq, in the view of US officials, except that its point of mass mobilization was secular-nationalist rather than Islamist radicalism. This led Washington to conclude that the phenomenon of "extremism," whether dressed in religious or secular nationalist clothing, must be contained at its point(s) of origin.

However, there is a difference between a state or states constituting a major strategic threat versus their having some differences of opinion over foreign policy issues. For although Iran may now be artificially stronger than Iraq, its strategic capabilities – with or without the radical politics – are in no way up to presenting a clear and present danger to America's vital interests in the area (the Gulf oil and its protectorate regimes). Armed with an antiquated patchwork arsenal of American, Soviet, and Chinese weapons bereft of an adequate supply of spare parts, saddled with an enormous short-term debt burden which is crippling its economy, and beset with increasing demands for liberalization from the leading elements of its citizenry, Iran is not now in a position to present a major strategic threat to anyone except perhaps to Iraq. Baghdad maintains that Iran has been actively destabilizing both the north and the south by supporting Islamist insurgents in both areas.[17] While Iran may be theoretically capable of overrunning the entire Persian Gulf, the direct presence of an uncontested global superpower within the arena, one which has proven its determination to crush any country which comes near it, has rendered any such possibility unrealistic to say the least.

More importantly, indications are that Tehran is losing interest, as compared with past years, in the affairs of what used to be called the Arab world (again with the exception of Iraq). Islamists active in the area point out some causes of tension between themselves and Iran, which they say is increasingly motivated by geopolitics, that is, they say it sometimes tries to pull local cadres into the service of its own agenda instead of primarily helping them to realize theirs. The

Hezbollah, which has become a virtual appendage of Iran in addition to pursuing its own main objective specific to Lebanon, is the only group in which Tehran seems to take serious and lasting interest.[18] None of this should be interpreted to mean that Islamist ideology is on the decline in Arab countries, that Iran is no longer supporting or aligning itself with local Islamist movements, or that Tehran does not realize the value of the Arab Mashreq as a secondary strategic environment. It only means that for Iran, as is true of all states in the international system, national interests as determined by geopolitical realities have taken precedence over national interests defined by ideological imperatives on the overall scale of priorities.

What Iran provided was an initial inspiration and leading-edge vehicle for Arab people to challenge their governments. The real problem is not Iranian expansion; it is the chronic legitimacy crisis of regional governments. Iran's experience provided disaffected and demoralized Arabs with a jump-start to re-group under a new umbrella and renew their activities. It played the role of initial facilitator and gave them a model to emulate. Tehran provided Arabs with a way of expressing their opposition to their governments and a credible political ideology around which to organize a mass following, something which had been lacking ever since the decline of secular pan-Arabism (and socialism to a much lesser degree) left a gaping ideological vacuum in the anti-system camp. But to try to contain this phenomenon now by containing Iran is obsolete in its conception. The Iranian storm has long since passed through the area, leaving its permanent mark and giving birth to its own dynamic processes. Indeed, the phenomenon has already generated an entire spectrum of second-level effects which have absolutely nothing to do with Iran. The Clinton administration, in focusing its containment efforts on the point of inception, the phenomenon's point of origin, is still trying to combat yesterday's problem, still fighting the last war.

Furthermore, Iran's declining influence in the Arab Mashreq is not a reflection of the success of the Iranian component of dual containment in isolating Iran or controlling its ambitions; rather, it has resulted from a gradual shift in Tehran's strategic priorities in light of the grand new world of possibilities that has opened up to it since the end of the Cold War. The vast Muslim region of Central Asia on Iran's northern borders is much more enticing as a playing field than the distant regions to the far west. Still in their infancy, these six former Soviet republics – Kazakhstan, Kyrgyzstan, Tajikistan, Uzbekistan, Azerbaijan, and

Refighting the Cold War: Containment as the Foundation   187
of America's Post-Cold War Political-Military Posture
in the Middle East

Turkmenistan – are open-minded, impressionable, and Islamic. Iran has been expending enormous amounts of energy in building the economic and cultural foundations for close, long-term relations, mutual co-operation, and ultimately, strategic influence within this very important global crossroads.

Central Asia is much more logical as a primary strategic environment for Iran than are the states of the Arab Middle East for both geographic and ethnic reasons: Tehran is closer to the former in both regards. The revolutionary Islamic Republic stands on the far-eastern periphery of the Arab-Muslim battleground: some of the countries currently up for grabs are over 1,000 miles away. The closer ones, Jordan, Lebanon, and Palestine, are geopolitical lightweights which cannot provide Iran with any lasting benefits unless they are collectively realized. Certainly Egypt would be a prize, but it is too far away, it is Sunni, it is historically unique, and it is a leader rather than a follower nation, similar to Iran itself. Furthermore, Egypt's Islamic movement is a rebellion of the young, arising out of that country's own unique historical and political circumstances and sharing little in common in pragmatic terms with the old-generation clerics who rule in Tehran. Rebellious guerrilla activity in Egypt is directed more against the corruption, indifference, and bureaucratic authoritarianism that have beset President Mubarak's government than in favor of any particular political ideology, although the rebels happen to be Islamist in their socio-religious orientation and have found the existing Islamic structures to be the most potentially effective vehicle through which to make their voices of protest heard.

And as for the idea of Iraq falling into the same category as Iran, there is a certain conceptual flaw in Washington's characterization of Iraq as an "extremist" state in "secular garb." Arab nationalism, the founding ideology of the Iraqi Ba'th, suffered a crushing setback in the aftermath of Camp David. At approximately the same time, Iraq ceased being a revolutionary ideological state. Its pan-Arabism began to acquire a moderate and settled character as a result of prevailing realities in the region. As the political unification of the Arab world fell further and further out of the realm of the possible, and even out of the realm of the conceivable, Iraq gradually transformed itself into a 'national interest' state, motivated primarily by the default considerations in international politics, namely, pragmatism and objective balance of power considerations. Ideology became secondary as an impetus to policymaking, taking a backseat to these more urgent pressures.

The change is reflected in Iraq's actions since that time and in government statements adjusting the meaning of pan-Arabism to fit the hard reality of Arab disunity. Take, for instance, this astonishing quotation by Iraqi President Saddam Hussein some 16 years ago:

> The question of linking unity to the removal of boundaries is no longer acceptable to the present Arab mentality. It could have been acceptable 10 or 20 years ago. We have to take into consideration the change which the Arab mind and psyche have undergone. We must see the world as it is. Any Arab would have wished to see the Arab nation as one state... But these are sheer dreams. The Arab reality is that the Arabs are now 22 states, and we have to behave accordingly.[19]

Since then, Iraq has acted according to what it considers to be its vital national interests and its perceived status as a regional power, though in its basic *raison d'etre*, it retained its Arab nationalist coloring, signified by its Ba'thist label and Iraq's pan-Arab regional orientation. Indeed, national interests, not ideology, were most likely the primary factors behind Baghdad's invasion of Kuwait in 1990. Israel acted likewise according to similar criteria in 1982 when it invaded Lebanon. The United States did it in Grenada and Panama and was prepared to repeat it in Haiti. In Iraq's case as in these others, the method – invasion – was extreme by its very definition, but the ideology itself was not.

Moreover, there is no evidence, contrary to the conventional wisdom of the time, that Baghdad perceived or derived any strategic benefit from creating instability for its own sake, nor did it generally sacrifice geopolitical interests for ideological considerations, although if the two were complementary, so much the better. In short, Iraq had factored ideological considerations out of those strategic equations in which ideology and geopolitics came into conflict: witness Baghdad's involvement and support for the 'wrong side' in Lebanon to weaken the influence of President Saddam Hussein's archrival President Assad of Syria, and his role in returning Egypt to the Arab fold ten years after Camp David, both of which occurred precisely because they were in Baghdad's short-term interests at the time. Containment of Iraq as containment of "extremism in... secular clothing" exposes Washington's failure to understand that Iraqi policy is reactive as is the policy of most states in the international system; thus it addresses the wrong problem.

Refighting the Cold War: Containment as the Foundation   189
of America's Post-Cold War Political-Military Posture
in the Middle East

The real problem is not that of containing a secular extremist state but of finding a way to reconcile what Iraq considers to be its vital interests with those of the United States, interests which clashed when Iraq invaded Kuwait and could conceivably do so again at some point in the future, even if a different Iraqi government were to eventually assume power.[20]

America's Middle East containment posture today: an assessment

Bilateral relations between the US and Iran on the one hand and the US and Iraq on the other are like two parallel continua, both of which are lacking a zero point: these two pairs of countries can be conceived either as friends or enemies of the United States, but there is so far no conceptual room in US thinking for mutual neutrality, not even with Iran under a Khatami presidency. Such is reflective of the basic structure of containment as a strategy, even when it includes a provision for dialogue as it does in the case of Iran, as it did similarly in the case of the Soviet Union at the height of the Cold War.

This brings up a very important complication that infuses all bilateral relationships among international political actors, but which is particularly apparent in the case of a relationship guided by containment and the defense against it. What one party sees as the conduct of normal affairs, the other party may be inclined to interpret as hostility. An instructive example is that of Washington's perception of 'rogue' Iraq, the latter's move into the Kurdish north in September 1996, and the events which then transpired between the United States, Iraq, Iran, and the two Kurdish factions, the KDP and the PUK. Every time President Saddam Hussein so much as flinches, even within his own country, a steady stream of analysts appears on the American television asserting that "Saddam is poking us in the eye again" or some other type of argument implying that Saddam Hussein's every move is conducted for the sole purpose of annoying the United States. What one or the other analyst thinks of the Iraqi president is entirely beside the point. Most sober analyses understood Iraq's move in backing up the Barzani faction with military force as having been motivated by local geopolitics, specifically, in that case, to balance Iran and its re-armament of the other Kurdish militia, that of Jalal Talabani, which had taken place just a few weeks earlier. These apparently faulty interpretations   occurred   because   the   Iraqi   move,   however indeliberately, affected Washington's regional policy objectives in a negative way. Washington perceived its interests as having been deliberately targeted rather than merely affected, thereby necessitating a response of some sort. Very often, hostility as seen from its point of origin is not directed specifically against all those whose interests might conceivably be affected by it, either directly or indirectly, but toward some wider (or narrower) goal.

This is as true in the case of the United States pursuing its own regional interests at the expense of local actors as it is in the case of Iraq directing hostility at a small and rather insignificant local adversary – namely, the Patriotic Union of Kurdistan – only to find itself under attack by a global superpower. The very same principle of course applies equally to Iraq's initial invasion of Kuwait in 1990; it is indeed in the nature of human beings to be self-centered. Hostility is in the eye of the beholder.

This concept of geopolitical self-centeredness – the Ptolemaic view of the political universe, of which all international political actors are equally guilty – makes it all the more likely that suspicions of hostility where they exist among a given pair of international political actors will be mutually reinforced by subsequent actions, even if unintentionally so. For although any specific act of hostility emanates from only one point of origin, and although it may be directed at only a single endpoint, the proliferation of its physical and political effects and their diffusion into a spectrum of divergent directions after the fact, as light passing through a prism, opens the possibility that the effective recipients of a hostile act directed at a single party may in fact be several. Nor are the results of unintentional hostilities any less potent than hostilities administered deliberately, as Iraq discovered to its utter dismay when it invaded Kuwait, with no particular intention of angering the United States.

By acting in the 1996 crisis in a way that was perceived internationally as an overreaction to Iraq's (mis)perceived hostility, however, Washington exposed the contradictions in its policy in front of its own allies and risked subverting the future of its own program. One example of the incapacity of what was then "dual containment" to respond to real changes on the ground is that the strategy left America unable to support either of the Kurdish factions during that flare-up of hostilities because both of their patrons had been tagged as enemies. The net effect was that the United States unwittingly removed itself (at least temporarily) from the regional interplay surrounding the political

Refighting the Cold War: Containment as the Foundation   191
of America's Post-Cold War Political-Military Posture
in the Middle East

future of the Kurds in northern Iraq. Given this context, it is not surprising that those observers who were then pronouncing the impending demise of dual containment almost unanimously marked the events of September 1996 as the beginning of the end.

Whatever the ultimate US objective regarding the future of the Islamic Republic system in Iran, the policy toward that system is essentially built around the arbitrary and case-specific qualities of what has become known as the 'rogue state.' The actions and policies specific to Iran, according to United States policy, have matured into approximately the following: 1/ Iran is a primary sponsor of terrorism and provides military, economic, and logistical support and safe-haven to terrorist organizations; 2/ Iran opposes the Arab-Israeli peace process and supports the continuing use of force against Israel and its occupation by Palestinian and Lebanese opposition groups; 3/ Iran is posing a threat to Middle East regimes friendly to the United States by means of subtle internal subversion; 4/ Iran is actively seeking a nuclear option and may be developing other unconventional weapons capabilities, as well as the means for their delivery; and 5/ Iran does not respect the human rights of its own people and works actively against their freedoms, through both repression at home and assassination and intimidation of dissidents abroad.[21]

Tehran has made clear that it opposes the Arab-Israeli peace process in the political sense but that it is not Iran's policy to generate active, physical opposition with the aim of disrupting or destroying it. According to former Iranian president Hashemi Rafsanjani: "Practically speaking, we do not take any action against the peace plan. When we see this whole process is unjust, we state our opposition as a matter of principle."[22] Perhaps the Iranian-sponsored conference held in October 1991 as a counter to the Madrid conference[23] held at the same time would qualify as generating opposition, but not in the sense of anything other than intellectual warfare. It is enough that Iran opposes the process as a matter of public policy, that is, in the political sense, to qualify it as a 'rogue state,' and hence, a state that needs to be contained (opposed). After all, the principle of mutual reinforcibility between the peace process and the containment of 'rogue' international political actors forms the largest theoretical foundation stone and one of the major arguments in favor of containment from an American political-military point of view (the political objective is the peace process, while the military objective is to perpetuate US control of Gulf oil). Therefore, it was enough that Iran had friendly links to groups actively opposing the peace process to qualify it as an enemy, even if Tehran was not itself initiating this activity.

On the issue of Iran's threat to the southern Gulf, the previous accusations of Iran presenting an overt military danger to that area have been dropped for the most part, after having been mostly discredited by military and political-military analysts. People began to wonder how an Iran whose arsenal was still built around shah-era weapons systems devoid of spare parts, and which had been defeated by the same Iraq that was so easily destroyed by the United States, could possibly pose a serious threat to anyone, especially with the US forces in the Gulf taken as a given. Political-military circles in Washington began to assert that at least the conventional aspect of the Iranian threat had been exaggerated. This, according to the military analyst Anthony Cordesman, "has led to a great deal of commentary on Iran which is simply not supportable by the facts;" the overall Iranian threat assessments, he said, were "grossly out of proportion."[24] Graham Fuller, likewise, said that "the Iranian threat has been considerably exaggerated in our policy statements."[25] This would suggest that the policy was either overly pessimistic or politically inspired; in any case, it seems this problem has for the most part been corrected. Thereafter, the main focus on the military side switched to Iran's development of unconventional weapons capabilities, particularly in the nuclear realm, while Washington's understanding of the primary threat posed by Iran changed from that of conventional military invasion in the southern Gulf *a la* Iraq to the issue of deliberate internal subversion by Iran, either directly or indirectly, through proxy or at least parallel Islamist movements that enjoy support from Iran.

On the last point, however, Iran's relations with the southern Gulf states – the same states whose security the US claims to be so worried about – are not as bad as it may appear at first glance. Although there is a basic adversarialism, and although many of the political elites in these states harbor a substantial and genuine fear of Iran, most of them are even more fearful of the consequences of the American containment posture and its potentially negative effects on them. In particular, it threatens to disrupt their relations with Tehran, which they regard as an important neighbor and regional power. The idea of provoking a country like Iran needlessly is viewed from ground zero as a reckless, ultimately counterproductive, and unwise exercise. The American policy is seen as making the Gulf states complicit in precisely that, in addition to intensifying the overall level of regional tension,

Refighting the Cold War: Containment as the Foundation   193
of America's Post-Cold War Political-Military Posture
in the Middle East

endangering Iran's internal stability – hence rendering it less predictable – and even increasing the likelihood of the improbable but dreaded Iranian-Iraqi rapprochement.[26] For it is precisely these states in the southern Gulf that would be the first victims of any self-fulfilling prophecy; therefore, they, like the Europeans, tend to prefer dialogue and 'constructive engagement' over the short term, while hoping for a general improvement in US-Iranian relations over the long term as the best guarantor of regional stability.[27]

There may also be a growing resentment within certain segments of the Gulf states elite that the United States is exploiting their oil wealth, not by taking their oil directly but by compelling them to undertake excessive arms purchases, thereby keeping the US arms industry going during a time of generalized decline. Dr. Abdullah K. Alshayeji, professor at Kuwait University and advisor to the Kuwaiti parliament, quotes a Saudi official wondering aloud as to whether the US might be trying to make the southern Gulf states go bankrupt. His remarks suggest the problem may be becoming more pronounced and generalized:

> There is growing restlessness among the intelligentsia and the Islamist elements that the West is using its military influence and protection power to twist the arms of the GCC elites to secure economic and political favors, and military contracts and concessions.... The citizens of the Gulf are revolted by being looked at for per capita income....

Under these circumstances, he writes, it is "extremely important" that Washington and its allies be careful not to "overplay their hands in pushing the GCC states too far or abuse their role as guarantors and protectors."[28]

Another important issue featured in the American containment paradigm, that of Iran's ongoing pursuit of unconventional military capabilities, is inextricably linked in time and space with the Egyptian-Israeli conflict over Cairo's efforts to force Israel to sign the Nuclear Non-Proliferation Treaty in 1995, at a time when the treaty was coming up for permanent renewal. The affair was complicated by the fact that Washington was the initiator and major backer of permanent NPT renewal, and by the additional fact that Cairo's opposition was not a result of any problem with the treaty itself but of Israel's own non-adherence to it. Israel, in order to justify its continuing rejection of the treaty in the context of a comprehensive regional peace process, was compelled to resort to arguing that it could not afford to shed the nuclear option because of the 'long-distance' threats it was still facing from Iraq, Iran, and Libya. As Iraq was disabled and under a permanent and extremely intrusive U.N. inspection regime, and since Libya was and is a geopolitical lightweight, Iran alone remained plausible as a serious threat.[29]

During the latter part of the Shimon Peres term in Israel one could notice an almost apocalyptic language emanating from Tel Aviv in regard to Iran's emerging nuclear capabilities.[30] However, a disagreement emerged between Israeli and US officials regarding the intelligence assessment of this threat. During a visit by former Defense Secretary William Perry to Israel, a credibility gap opened between Israel's assertion that Iran would have the bomb by the year 2000 or slightly thereafter[31] and the American assessment that Iran was, in actuality, "many, many years" away. The compromise that emerged was a confounding joint estimate that Iran, under normal circumstances, that is, without sanctions, would be 7-15 years from acquiring a nuclear capability.[32]

Once Shimon Peres dropped out of the picture and Benjamin Netanyahu took his place, the temperature in Tel Aviv *vis-a-vis* Iran immediately came down a notch,[33] thereby enabling, for the first time since its inception, the possibility of re-assessment in Washington of the strategy of dual containment, at least insofar as it applied to Iran. Unless and until a full and complete re-evaluation of bilateral relations is undertaken on both sides, however, the atmosphere in the US-Iranian relationship in the coming years will continue to be poisoned by the lasting effects of the inverse relationship phenomenon. As Iran's hostility toward Washington began to gradually and steadily decrease during the final phase of the Rafsanjani era, the hostility of the United States gradually and steadily increased, only to spiral out of control with the advent of President Clinton and his administration. This was a peculiar kind of spiral in that it differed from the ordinary phenomenon of the escalatory spiral in international politics in that only one side was doing the escalating, while the other was apparently engaging itself in a counter-effort to defuse tensions. Two factors have led American hostility to finally level off: 1/ the active opposition of the Europeans and other US allies (except Israel) to most aspects of the Iranian containment; and 2/ the surprise democratic election of Mohammad Khatami, Iran's Gorbachev, to Iran's second highest office, the presidency.

Refighting the Cold War: Containment as the Foundation   195
of America's Post-Cold War Political-Military Posture
in the Middle East

The policy of the United States in containing what it still views as a dictatorial and expansionist Iran, however, is increasingly disconnected from the realities on the ground in Tehran. The trend of disconnection, which began to emerge just before Khatami's election, accelerated suddenly in the aftermath of that event. It accelerated further in the wake of President Khatami's publicly televised initiatives and his show of moderation toward the American people and government. Iran has not only gone out of its way normalize its relations with the general world community – including its relations with the governments *and especially the peoples* of 'the West,' as well as with the 'threatened' Gulf states to its south – but it has also been undergoing an unprecedented period of internal and international political and economic opening, if not yet liberalization. Iran's *perestroika* has involved the opening of Iran to Western markets and investment, and its readiness to serve as a bridge connecting those new markets to the developing resources in Central Asia. Iran's *glasnost*[34] has involved not merely a symbolic opening as has happened in some regional countries, but rather, the door has been thrown open to public and intellectual consideration of most of the controversial issues of the day. Toward the United States and 'the West,' Iran's *glasnost* showed itself in Tehran's successful efforts to achieve the release of all the American hostages in Lebanon, as well as economic breakthroughs with major political significance such as the Conoco deal, in which an American company accepted an unprecedented invitation to go in and help develop Iran's oil fields, only to have it revoked by presidential decree (one of Clinton's executive orders). The changes in Iran are not progressing entirely without obstacles, and the obstacles are still formidable, but the direction of change is apparent and visible to any reasonably informed observer.

Freedom House disagrees that anything important is happening in Iran: it still rates the country as "unfree," the lowest possible category, while on the ground, Iran is considerably freer than most regional countries. Freedom House, however, remains an American institution, and as such, it may not be entirely aware of the process of change that has taken place in Iran during the past several years. Indeed, it is indicative of the lack of widely-disseminated information about Iran that the Freedom House rating for Iran has remained static during this period of Iran's unprecedented political and economic change.

Although Iran had fully completed its revolutionary transformation by 1989, the fact of that transformation began to generate its own dynamic as experienced by the second political generation. Iran began passing through a gradual transition from what Hooshang Amirahmadi calls "Islam-Islam" – the height of the Khomeini era – through a stage of "Islam-Iran" and on to the current situation: "Iran-Islam." He predicts that when the young generation comes of age the transformation will go full circle to "Iran-Iran" – which means back to the future – and that, stranger yet, the impetus could even be coming from the clergy itself.[35] The process of evolution has been so great and so rapid that one analyst went so far as to refer to post-Khomeini Iran as the "Second Republic."[36] This could, in fact, be modified to 'Second Islamic Republic,' for Iran is still the same state that Khomeini built, but, as always, the death of the founder allows for the next generation to step in and continue the evolutionary process.

While there is no freedom of religion and hence, association in Iran, and while Iran still has significant human rights difficulties, the situation in both of these domains is certainly no worse (and is, in reality, much better) than in Saudi Arabia, a US ally. Hence Iran's response to the American human rights critique, to the effect that Washington "accuses every country that is not under its hegemony of being a violator of human rights."[37] Nor are political parties yet legal in Iran, which might contribute to the flat rating of the Freedom House; this however fails to record the fact that their legalization has recently become one of the many hot topics now being subjected to active and open discussion and debate.[38] Iran, with its active and changing parliament and semi-free elections (candidates are still screened, though a plurality of opinion does emerge) – in addition to its relatively lively newspapers, journals, and unrehearsed lectures on the vital social, economic, and political issues of the day – is arguably one of the most democratically-minded states, relatively speaking of course, in the Middle East today. That is:

> Meaningful political opposition is confined to factions within the system who have an interest in not overturning the boat. Organized opposition aimed at overthrowing the system is mainly within the exile community in the US and Europe.[39]

However, the public debates in Iran have recently reached a point where they have broken out of the bounds of the strict theocratic paradigm that once contained them. Topics under debate in today's Iran are of a nature that touch the very core of the Islamic Republic's identity. According to the author of a pamphlet published by the Council on Foreign Relations:

Refighting the Cold War: Containment as the Foundation   197
of America's Post-Cold War Political-Military Posture
in the Middle East

This debate centers around previously untouchable subjects at the heart of the revolutionary ideology itself. Today, students, professors, journalists, and political activists are discussing and challenging the current role of Islam in politics, including the legitimacy of the participation of clergy in government. They are also discussing the merits of pluralism, political participation, and interaction with the outside world, including the West.[40]

Other subjects currently under debate include the compatibility of Islam with democracy, sensitive gender issues, the government's handling or mishandling of the economy, and major foreign policy matters, especially what Iran's political posture should be toward the United States and 'the West.' Substantive and relevant political analysis, and even critical statements about government policies, can be found within the pages of Iran's foreign policy journals – something unheard of in most Middle Eastern countries – many of which do not even have such publications except as colorless propaganda vehicles for the government.

It is a cause for optimism for the future of US-Iran relations that the coming generation of Iranian intellectuals is not encumbered with the bitter memories of the covert intervention carried out by the CIA back in 1953 to restore a detested and democratically ousted shah back to power, and the intense hostility this action generated toward America at the mass level in Iran. This hostility became so deep that it acquired historical proportions: it was allowed to spill into the next generation by virtue of another decade of short-sighted American policies, pursued mainly during the 1970s, designed to bolster and strengthen the regime of the reinstated shah – the same man was still in power some 20 years later. The Americans were remembered for having built up and trained his ruthless intelligence apparatus, the SAVAK, and for expending enormous efforts to hold the Iranian dictator in power against the obvious wishes of his own people. The third generation of young Iranians, those coming of age today, do not have any personal memories of these events and hence, the views of its members toward the United States are less intense. There is a degree of open-mindedness on their part, born of both curiosity and a desire to gauge American intentions in the present tense rather than the past. However, they too can be made to hate the United States, that is, if Washington is intent on giving them a new reason to do so. A posture of strategic containment, which strikes most profoundly at Iran's macro-economy, and hence, directly into the pocketbooks of these young Iranians, provides a running start in that direction.

Contrasting the developments toward more openness inside Iran with the official American discourse on the country has inevitably led to the emergence of a credibility gap on the subject between the academy and the policy community, as Gary Sick has already pointed out, while according to Anthony Cordesman, a parallel gap has emerged between the top policymakers and the intelligence community.[41] Even before Khatami, people began to question the sense of urgency that permeated the policy atmosphere. They began to wonder where is the crisis that has placed Washington on a veritable war footing with regard to Iran. Reasonable people began to ask themselves: does Iran *really* constitute "an unusual and extraordinary threat to the national security, foreign policy and economy of the United States?"[42]

The discourse in the Congress even surpasses this mild but growing sense of cognitive dissonance that characterizes the rest of the official discourse. Consider the following assessment of the current situation in the Middle East that provides the opening statement of a report released in December 1996 by the Washington Task Force on Terrorism and Unconventional Warfare, an office of the United States Congress:[43]

> Approaching the end of 1996 the Middle East may well be on the verge of a major regional war. Numerous sources in the region report that the supreme leaders – both civilians and military – in most Arab states, as well as in Iran and Pakistan are convinced that the present vulnerability of Israel is so great that there is a unique opportunity to, at the very least, begin the process leading to the destruction of Israel. These circumstances are considered to be a historic window of opportunity the Muslim World should not miss. Therefore, these Muslim leaders have finalized numerous strategies and tactical alliances heretofore non-existent in the region.

The inquiry goes on to formulate something which, had it been written in the Middle East, were inexplicably called a conspiracy theory. Compiled for the benefit and information of Members of Congress, the document asserts the existence of what amounts to a grand alliance currently making preparations for an all-out combined military effort against Israel. This alliance includes Iran, Syria, and Iraq – working together – having also recruited the Palestinian Authority, Pakistan, Egypt, and Crown Prince Abdallah of Saudi Arabia, the latter

Refighting the Cold War: Containment as the Foundation   199
of America's Post-Cold War Political-Military Posture
in the Middle East

of whom – jointly with the Syrians, we are told – "initiated the bombing in Dhahran." The report reveals the existence of a "joint command" (presumably secret) involving the "coordination of the activities of Iran, Iraq, and Syria" which held meetings throughout 1996, we are informed. In addition, the Iranian contingent conducted a war preparation exercise that same year, code-named "Velayat" (presumably named either after the Iranian foreign minister or for the generic term meaning 'states'). Of course, "The entire Iranian top leadership and high command were present at the exercise." And, if all this were not enough, the US Congress was also informed that

> Iran has nuclear weapons.... Irrespective of skeptic 'expert opinion' in the West, they – the decision-makers in Tehran – operate on the basis of their own conviction that Iran has operational nuclear weapons.[44]

Despite the general constitutional provisions granting the executive branch the primary responsibility for foreign policy, congressional entities and individual representatives concerned with Middle East affairs have been allowed to seize the initiative on much of Middle East policy formulation. And they used this opportunity to tighten the grip of Iran's containment yet another notch. They were consistently walking a full step ahead of the White House on the escalatory ladder – and approximately the same distance behind it on the reality scale – with the administration in a constant struggle to keep up. Indeed, if an escalatory spiral began during this time, a spiral which continued to gain momentum right up until the day of Khatami's election, its dynamic was generated not in the relationship between the United States and Iran, but in the relationship between the US Administration and the US Congress, and from there was projected out into the relationship between the United States and an increasingly bewildered Iran.

Conclusion

Perhaps the largest problem with America's post-Cold War containment strategy is its dependence on the ambiguously-defined concept of Middle Eastern "extremism" and the casting of it as a primary strategic nemesis for the United States in the post-Cold War era. Extremism, if one wanted to attempt to define it, is a label for categorizing state and non-state international political actors that share the following broad characteristics: 1/ opposition to the prevailing internal or regional geopolitical status quo; 2/ willingness to use force to change it, especially where the other available means have been exhausted; 3/ expansive revolutionary ideologies to focus the energies and rally the enthusiasm of adherents, and to increase their numbers; and 4/ inherent distrust of US intentions, generated by heavy accumulation of past experience, and the resultant opposition in principle to American involvement in the region. If we accept the use of the term "extremism" to describe this combination of phenomena, it can be said that as long as substantive grievances remain toward the regional status quo and America's role in perpetuating it – just as with the shah toward the end of his reign – there will always be a market for extremism.[45]

The suppression of extremism through the combination of military and diplomatic force, the justifying principle of post-Cold War containment, will only change the way in which protest sentiments toward the regional order express themselves. But they will express themselves. Trying to contain them without addressing their fundamental causes is akin to plugging up a leaking pipe: at some future point in time an even larger leak develops in a different location. The successful suppression and destruction of secular pan-Arabism led many Arabs to look for a replacement in Islamic fundamentalism; suppression of Islamism and its revisionist objectives will lead to the emergence of something else. But the same pressures always remain: the presence of extreme ideologies is symptomatic of the feeling of general malaise which pervades the Arab world and the peoples of the Middle East at large.

Today, two contradictory trends are competing with each other in the Middle Eastern state system: 1/ a pervasive regionwide regime legitimacy crisis calling for systemic change; and 2/ the resolution or pacification of the region's historic confrontations, especially the Arab-Israeli conflict. These two trends are lines on a plane that have been moving along separately, each in its own track, yet they are not parallel. They are heading for intersection in the not-too-far future. The question to be determined is whether the revolutionary line will fuse with the peace-integration line and move together in a single direction, or whether the revolutionary line will cross over the peace-integration line, unaffected by it, and continue on into the future without it.

This geometric metaphor implies that the first trend, that of revolution or reformist evolution within individual regional states, will

Refighting the Cold War: Containment as the Foundation   201
of America's Post-Cold War Political-Military Posture
in the Middle East

be the defining factor. It should be safe to say that the region's political systems are heading for a major internal transformation of some kind: they have not yet responded to post-Cold War stimuli but pressures are growing. The political dynamic in most of the region's nation-states had been frozen by at least the late 1960s or early 1970s and held there ever since, while the substance of leadership has dissipated with the passage of time. Most regional governments have long ago abandoned their founding ideologies in practice and are now surviving almost solely on their physical attributes of power. The legitimacy of most rulers was based on these ideologies, now either reduced to hollow shells or swept out of existence by successor regimes. Even more regressive are some of the kingdoms and sheikhdoms in the southern Gulf, which appear to be frozen several centuries further back in time. The only real exceptions to the overall regional pattern are Lebanon, which tried democracy but succumbed to a combination of internal and regional pressures; Jordan, which is attempted evolution from above only to descend back into back into its old pattern of forcible repression of peaceful expressions of dissent, especially dissent in foreign policy matters; and Yemen, which turned to democracy following its re-unification until it too succumbed to civil war. However, it is virtually inevitable that the leadership structures in most Arab countries will eventually be brought up to date – 30 years all in one stroke.

The second trend – that of peace with Israel and regional political and/or economic co-operation – may or may not be the wave of the future. Instead of addressing the concerns of the people or nation-states as a whole, peace is being constructed in such a way as to be totally dependent upon the currently prevailing but nevertheless obsolescent leadership structures. Many in the region see the likely endgame of US-led conflict resolution processes as the coercive integration of the Middle Eastern peoples, especially Arabs and Iranians, into a structure of local and regional hierarchies chosen by Washington and Tel Aviv instead of by themselves. Taking short-cuts to peace by dealing with local client leaders while ignoring the wishes of the peoples involved, especially that of self-determination, results in reconciliation between leaders, accompanied by continuing hostility between peoples and the intensification of popular hostility toward the leaders, who are blamed for allowing the region to change in such a way that leaves their grievances unaddressed and in some cases, even aggravating them.

One thing is certain: the parties making the peace of today will not be in power tomorrow. The citizens of the Middle East have their own priorities: they want their systems to move forward, they want their leaders to be both relevant and independent, to take an interest in solving their economic problems, and to reverse their international political predicament in which their national pride and aspirations have suffered so greatly. They want their governments to be less subservient to foreign powers, especially Washington, and to re-gain their political independence. They want more domestic political participation and a greater flow of ideas, more accountability in government, more transparency, more freedom. And equally, they want real economic development, more efficient bureaucracy, more jobs, and less corruption. These are the primary considerations, which is why most of these governments, unless they begin addressing the issues their people care about, must eventually fall. They will not necessarily fall to extremist elements, but they will fall.

The real question is whether or not the successor governments will be supportive of the peace-integration track or will stand against it. America's forthcoming policies will have a large degree of impact on whether the region's inevitable revolutions or gradual revisions will take place within the peace-integration paradigm or the Islamic confrontationalist paradigm. The latter is currently the only vital and credible system-opposition force in the region today. The reasons: 1/ the modern Islamist solution has never been tried before in the Arab world and has therefore not yet had the chance to fail and be discredited; and 2/ it is perceived as genuinely independent of any foreign powers. If Washington is seen as ignoring these realities, or of standing in the way of change, progress, and natural evolution, or if it is seen as containing change in the name of containing extremism, or defending unrepresentative government in the name of defending peace and moderation, then the name of peacemaking as well as that of the United States will be identified with the region's obsolete rulers and will fall right along with them.

However, the initial inclusion of dual containment in the Clinton administration's short-lived global "enlargement" doctrine proscribed US support for the development of secular-nationalist or democratically-minded Islamist forces of the kind that appear in the region from time to time, because that would mean abandoning the regimes it has been counting on to uphold its "vital strategic interests,"[46] as the shah of Iran once did. In his 1993 address introducing enlargement, then-National Security Advisor Anthony Lake mentioned every relevant region in the world except the Middle

Refighting the Cold War: Containment as the Foundation   203
of America's Post-Cold War Political-Military Posture
in the Middle East

East in the context of democratization.[47] Instead of advocating democratization and free markets as in the rest of the world, it appears that America's overriding objective in the Middle East is still "to protect our friends and promote our interests and their interests in peace and stability in the Gulf and the Middle East."[48]

The framers of America's strategy of containment toward the Middle East would presume that the Arab Middle East can march forward without Iraq, its key player to the east, it imagines that the Persian Gulf will be able to enter the 21st century without a strong Persia, and it assumes that a newly independent Central Asia will at once reach out to embrace the grand new world that has opened up to it, while at the same time sealing off its own natural gateway to that world – also Iran. Probably the most fatal assumption of containment strategy is the idea that an Arab-Israeli peace can be achieved by smoothing out differences between leaders, by suppressing the voices of dissent and then professing surprise when they reach new heights of violence, and most importantly, continuing to ignore the real grievances held by the larger populations that will be most affected by this peace, which constitutes the initial condition of dissention. And at the same time, successive US administrations have spent the greater part of the last decade creating a new set of grievances among what is about to become an entire new generation in Iraq. This is the 'sanctions generation,' the Iraqis of tomorrow who have already spent the formative early childhood years suffering under US sanctions, and who are holding the United States – as the primary author of the sanctions regime – responsible for the progressive decay of their country under the still-comprehensive trade embargo. A parallel process very nearly threatened to play itself out in Iran (again), a process that briefly threatened to degenerate into all out war and which was driven most forcefully by the passions of an American Congress that had lost its way.

The US containment strategy in the Middle East, beginning with "dual containment" and continuing until today as a more simple, disaggregated and generic 'containment,' is nothing less than a refighting of the Cold War, only on a smaller, regional basis. The difference is that the purpose is not merely deterrence but also compellence: containment is applied in an overt effort to force changes in the governments or policies in the region that do not agree with the United States in the area of large-scale foreign policy objectives. Rather than pointing the Middle East to a brighter and more peaceful future, post-Cold War containment may instead facilitate an illusory peace based on nothing more profound than 'might makes right,' not only in the Arab-Israeli arena but also in the Gulf, and in the upcoming internal political contests that are expected to take place between some regional governments and their peoples. The region will therefore have to look forward, given this kind of political environment, to a growing sense of political uncertainty, agitation, and anxiety, both within the individual countries and in the region at large, accompanied by frequent earthquakes and upheavals of differing magnitudes, that is, new rounds of active hostility and violent rebellion emerging from within the peoples most affected by these policies. Although the Soviet Union is dead and buried, and although Washington sees fit to interact with the rest of the post-Cold War world on an increasingly normalized basis, the Cold War paradigm framing US foreign policy continues to remain alive and well in the Middle East.

Refighting the Cold War: Containment as the Foundation   205
of America's Post-Cold War Political-Military Posture
in the Middle East

Notes

1. Martin Indyk, Address at a symposium of the Middle East Policy Council entitled: "Dual Containment: US Policy Toward Iraq and Iran," Washington, 24 February 1994.

2. The US renunciation of Islamism as the new enemy ideology, the new "ism," is in Edward P. Djerejian, "The US and the Middle East in a Changing World," Address to the Meridian House International, Washington, 2 June 1992.

3. See National Security Advisor Anthony Lake, "Confronting backlash states," Foreign Affairs, Vol. 73, No. 2, March/April 1994, pp. 45-55, for a direct analogy between Soviet containment and dual containment: "Forty-seven years ago, George Kennan... made the case for containment of an outlaw empire. He argued that the United States had within its power the means to 'increase enormously the strains under which Soviet policy must operate' and thereby generate the 'break-up or gradual mellowing of Soviet power.' Today, the United States faces a less formidable challenge in containing the band of outlaws we refer to as 'the backlash states.' It is still very much within our power to prevail."

4. The structure of dual containment resembles in some of its important aspects the outline presented by Dr. Kadhim Niama, an Iraqi strategic thinker who heads the international relations department at the University of Baghdad. Dr. Niama told the author during a May 1994 visit to Iraq that "the United States is trying to permanently divide the Middle East into four separate areas - the Maghreb, the Mashreq, the Persian Gulf, and Iraq/Iran - in order to control each one through its own separate dynamic."

5. Martin Indyk, address to the Middle East Policy Council's symposium on dual containment, 24 February 1994, op. cit.

6. Martin Indyk, Address to the Soref Symposium, Washington Institute for Near East Policy, Washington, 18 May 1993.

7. "[I]f the balance of power in the region should shift again in favor of radical forces led by Iraq or Iran, this [peacemaking] effort is likely to fail as the military option appears more viable to some of the participants in the negotiations." Ibid.

8. During a visit by the author to Lebanon in June 1994, the most common theme expressed by Lebanese was that of conflicting foreign identities pervading their country. Their conception of Lebanon as suffering from a

problem of "multiple personalities" was reinforced by this author's drive south, along the coastal road: approximately five miles outside Beirut stood a billboard with a large picture of the Ayatollah Khomeini waving to supporters, followed about 100 yards down the road by another billboard advertising suntan lotion for sunbathers on the beach, followed by a third advertising running shoes. Then Khomeini again, then the suntan lotion, then the running shoes, a veritable feedback loop of contradiction.

9. See for example, comments by Israel's then US Ambassador, Itamar Rabinovich, who also headed the Israeli delegation on the Syrian negotiating track: "[I]t is clear to us today that we have a serious partner - not only for negotiations, but also for an agreement." Interview on Qol Yisrael Radio, translation cited in Foreign Broadcast Information Service: Near East and South Asia, 6 August 1993.

10. This was acknowledged in a Washington Post, editorial of 16 February 1994: "The adding of new conditions when a party gets within range of meeting old ones is known as raising (sic) the goalposts. Usually it is unfair.... But Iraq is different." And the Administration confirms that even a change in government would not be enough: "We will not be satisfied with Saddam's overthrow before we agree to lift sanctions." Quoted in Martin Indyk, Address to the Washington Institute, 18 May 1993, op. cit.

11. See, for example, the comment by spokesman Nicholas Burns of the State Department that it will be "a long, long time" before the sanctions are lifted, quoted in "New Iraq row said to ensure sanctions stay," Reuters, 11 June 1996. On the growing dissention among some of Washington's Middle Eastern allies, see Michael Georgy, "UAE to push for lifting of Iraq sanctions," Reuters, 22 May 1996; for the changes in Egypt and the GCC states see John Lancaster, "Arabs reconsider exclusion of Iraq," Washington Post, 1 December 1996: A36; in reference to Tansu Ciller of Turkey see Lally Weymouth, "Saddam's new friend," Washington Post, 30 July 1996: A13; on Tunisia's opposition see "Christopher firm on keeping sanctions intact," Reuter, 25 September 1995; and for the doubts of Saudi Arabia's Prince Khaled bin Sultan, joint commander of coalition with Norman Shwartzkopf in the 1991 Gulf war, see Michael Hedges, "US ally calls sanctions outdated," Washington Times, 23 May 1995.

12. See, for example, Graham Fuller, "Iraq into the Next Decade: Will Iraq Survive Until 2002?" published by the RAND Corporation, Santa Monica, California, 1993.

Refighting the Cold War: Containment as the Foundation   207
of America's Post-Cold War Political-Military Posture
in the Middle East

13. For a full elaboration and conceptualization of the implosion scenario on the Lebanese model, see Laura Drake, "Implosion of Iraq?" Middle East Insight, March/April 1996.

14. The "structural imbalance" results from the fact that "Iran does not *yet* face the kind of international regime that has been imposed on Iraq" [emphasis added]. Martin Indyk, Address to the Washington Institute, 18 May 1993, op. cit.

15. See Samuel P. Huntington's pathbreaking article, "The Clash of Civilizations," Foreign Affairs, Vol. 72, No. 3, Summer 1993.

16. "[O]ur common foe is oppression and extremism, whether in religious or secular guise." Anthony Lake, "Middle East Moment: At the Heart of Our Policy, Extremism is the Enemy," The Washington Post, 24 July 1994.

17. Personal interview with Isam Mahboub, head of the First Political Directorate, Iraqi Foreign Ministry, during visit to Baghdad, May 1994.

18. These revelations came during personal discussions with Islamists both here and overseas who must obviously remain anonymous.

19. Baghdad Radio, 10 September 1982. Cited in Christine Helms, Iraq: Eastern Flank of the Arab World (Washington: The Brookings Institution, 1984), p. 114.

20. It should be remembered in this context that Iraq came extremely close to invading Kuwait in 1961, seven years before the current Iraqi regime took power. Baghdad was dissuaded from doing so at the last moment by the diplomatic intervention of other Arab states.

21. Clearly the matter of Salman Rushdie falls into this last category; it has been a primary irritant in Iranian-European relations, as have the assassinations of Iranian oppositionists taking refuge in their countries. Israel has used unconventional tactics against its opponents as well; however, the Europeans appear to be consistent in opposing the execution of such tactics on their soil regardless of who the perpetrators are. For Iran's efforts to distance itself from the Rushdie fatwa without rejecting it outright, see Yousef Azmeh, "Iran woos friends to blunt US hostility," Reuters, 24 May 1995.

22. George A. Nader, Interview with President Hashemi Rafsanjani, Middle East Insight, Special Issue on Iran, v. 11, no. 5, July/August 1995, pp. 7-14.

23. Elie Rekhes, "Terrorist connection: Iran, the Islamic Jihad and Hamas," Justice, v. 5, May 1995, Abstract of a lecture delivered in a colloquium on Iran: Foreign Policies and Domestic Constraints, Moshe Dayan Center for Middle Eastern and African Studies, Tel Aviv University, 3 April 1995. Cited on Israel Information Service Gopher, Israeli Foreign Ministry: israel-info.gov.il.

24. Anthony Cordesman, Middle East Policy Council Symposium on dual containment, Capitol Hill, Washington, 24 February 1994; Anthony Cordesman, presentation at the Woodrow Wilson Center seminar entitled "Should the United States deal with Iran?" 15 June 1995, respectively.

25. Graham Fuller, Middle East Policy Council Symposium on dual containment, Capitol Hill, Washington, 24 February 1994, respectively.

26. Emma C. Murphy, "The impact of the Arab-Israeli peace process on the international security and economic relations of the Persian Gulf," Iranian Journal of International Affairs, 8(2), Summer 1996: 420-48; Haleh Vaziri, "The Islamic Republic's policy in the Persian Gulf: who's containing whom, how, and why?" Middle East Insight, Special Issue on Iran, Vol. 11, No. 5, July/August 1995, pp. 76-9.

27. Richard W. Murphy, "It's time to rethink the US-Iran relationship, Christian Science Monitor, 18 July 1996: 18; "Oman calls for talks not isolation of Iran, Iraq," Reuters, 28 May 1996.

28. Abdullah K. Alshayeji, "Stability in the Gulf region: clash of visions," Iranian Journal of International Affairs, 8(2), Summer 1996: 320-52. Also see Shibley Telhami's critique, "How to lose friends in the Persian Gulf," Los Angeles Times, 5 June 1995.

29. Some analysts have pointed out that any Iranian unconventional arms effort is directed primarily against a future threat from Iraq, which used chemical weapons against it during the Iraq-Iran war. Although this does not rule out their also being deployed against Israel, Iran sees any potential deployments of this nature as being primarily for defensive purposes due to Israel's (until recently) bellicose posture toward Iran.

30. Especially outstanding in this regard was the appearance by then Israeli Prime Minister Shimon Peres on Ted Koppel's "Nightline," 29 April 1996.

Refighting the Cold War: Containment as the Foundation 209
of America's Post-Cold War Political-Military Posture
in the Middle East

31. For the five year estimate, see Ibid; also see Chris Hedges, "Iran may be able to build an atomic bomb in 5 years, US and Israeli officials estimate," New York Times, 5 January 1995, p. A10.

32. Clyde Haberman, "US and Israel see Iranians 'many years' from A-bomb," New York Times, 10 January 1995: 3; Steve Rodan, "What the US is whispering to Israel about Iran," Jerusalem Post, 13 January 1995, p. 9.

33. Aluf Ben, "A change in Israeli-Iranian relations," Ha'aretz, 10 November 1996: A1, A10; "'Senior source' says Israel to re-examine its relations with Iran," Israel Defense Forces Radio, BBC Summary of World Broadcasts, 11 November 1996. According to the latter report, the change was brought about as a result of Netanyahu's election and his decision to "stop attacking Iran during talks with international elements."

34. Eric Hooglund, "The pulse of Iran today," Middle East Insight, Special Issue on Iran, v. 11, no. 5, July/August 1995: 40-7.

35. Hooshang Amirahmadi, "Iran: from political Islam to secular nationalism," Muslim Politics Report, Council on Foreign Relations, No. 4, November/December 1995, pp. 1-2.

36. Eric Rouleau, "The Islamic Republic of Iran: paradoxes and contradictions in a changing society," Middle East Insight, Special Issue on Iran, v. 11, no. 5, July/August 1995, pp. 54-8.

37. "Iran top judge rejects US human rights criticism," Reuters, 10 February 1997.

38. Bahman Baktiari and W. Scott Harrop, "Tables turn on Iran's Islamic extremists," Christian Science Monitor, 16 April 1996, p. 18; Hooglund, "The pulse of Iran today," op. cit.

39. "Iran quarterly report no. 17," MEED Quarterly Report, September 1994.

40. Valla Vakili, "Debating Religion and Politics in Iran: The Political Thought of Abdolkarim Soroush," Council on Foreign Relations, Studies Department, Occasional Paper Series, no. 2, 1996, p. 3.

41. Gary Sick, "The United States and Iran: truth and consequences," Contention, 5(2), Winter 1996, pp. 59-78; Cordesman, presentation at the Woodrow Wilson Center, op. cit.

42. The quotation is that of President Clinton upon banning all US trade with Iran in 1995, quoted in Ian Black, "Giant of the Gulf calls the shots," The Guardian, 9 March 1996.

43. The author of this rather sensational document is Yosef Bodansky, an official of the US Congress based in the office of Rep. Jim Saxton (R-NJ-3), Chairman of the aforementioned Task Force and Member of Congress since 1984. The work is sponsored as a joint effort by several subcommittees, including the International Relations Committee of the House Foreign Affairs Committee.

44. Ibid.

45. Anthony Lake seems to recognize this in some sense: "Extremism takes many forms but has a common source - political, economic, and social alienation and exclusion." Yet instead of addressing its causes, he suggests that "[w]e must respond by working with willing nations to build regional bulwarks against extremism." See The Washington Post, 24 July 1994, op. cit.

46. "Our strategy must be pragmatic. Our interests in democracy and markets do not stand alone. Other American interests at times will require us to befriend and even defend non-democratic states for mutually beneficial reasons." Anthony Lake, "From Containment to Enlargement," Address to the Johns Hopkins University, School of Advanced International Studies, Washington, 21 September 1993.

47. Namely, the former Soviet republics, Central and Eastern Europe, Latin America, the Carribean, the Asian Pacific, and sub-Saharan Africa. Ibid.

48. Dr. Martin Indyk, Address to the Middle East Policy Council, 24 February 1994, op. cit.

Chapter 8

Post-Soviet Russian Foreign Policy toward the Middle East

Mark N. Katz

Introduction

Since the breakup of the USSR in 1991, there has been significant change in Moscow's Middle East policy. During much of the Cold War, Moscow sought to project Soviet influence throughout even the far-off Arab region of the Middle East. In the post-Cold War era, though, Russian foreign policy has focused on that part of the Middle East closest to the former USSR – the Northern Tier. This article will examine the major aspects of post-Cold War Russian foreign policy toward the Middle East in order to identify Moscow's multiple goals in the region and discuss Moscow's capacity for achieving them. First, though, a brief review of the different stages of Imperial and Soviet foreign policy toward the region is necessary in order to show the extent to which post-Cold War Russian foreign policy toward the Middle East has and has not changed.

Imperial and Soviet Foreign Policy toward the Middle East

For purposes of this discussion, it is important to note that the "Middle East" for the Russian Empire, the Soviet Union, and the Russian Federation has included the Muslim regions of the Caucasus and Central Asia.

Imperial Policy

There were many differences in Tsarist policy toward the Middle East from the late eighteenth century (when Russia emerged as a great power) until the fall of the monarchy in 1917. Still, there was a degree of consistency in the aims pursued by the Tsars toward the Middle East during these years as well as the means by which they pursued them. This was the period when Russia, like many West European states, established its colonial empire. During this period when the Tsars were expanding Russian power in the Caucasus and Central Asia, their foreign policy toward the Northern Tier focused, to a greater or lesser degree, on seizing territory from and attempting to limit British influence in Turkey, Iran, and Afghanistan. Tsarist foreign policy also attempted to extend Russian influence into the Arab world on occasion — notably at the time of the French revolution and then in the 1890s and early 1900s, but these efforts achieved little in the face of more determined competition in the region from other European states as well as the emergence of serious threats from Europe demanding Russia's full attention.[1]

Except for the fact that the West European colonial empires were established overseas while the Russian one was established overland, the processes of colonization employed by Imperial Russia were not dissimilar to those employed by Western Europe: seizure of territory from weaker states, co-optation of local rulers, playing off local rivals against each other, and the settlement of large numbers of colonists from the "mother country" in the colonies. Tsarist policy toward the Caucasus and Central Asia, then, was not particularly different from the policy of other European colonial powers in the areas where they predominated. Nor did Russia, being an autocracy, suffer from the contradiction of a nation enjoying democracy itself ruling other nations by force which would increasingly afflict, and contribute to the downfall of, the colonial empires of Britain, France, and other democratic West European states.   The success of Tsarist policy, though, did depend on the ability of Russia to maintain its influence by force, and when this came to an abrupt end with the dissolution of the Tsarist regime in 1917, Russia lost control of the Caucasus as well as its ability to influence even the northern tier Middle Eastern states.

Lenin's Policy

Lenin radically transformed Russia's foreign policy, seeking not simply to gain an important place for Russia within the existing system of international relations, but to overthrow that system altogether and replace it with a revolutionary socialist one.   The Leninist foreign policy toward the Middle East, however, bore a remarkable resemblance to previous Tsarist policy. After winning the Russian civil war, the Bolshevik regime moved quickly to restore Russian control in the Caucasus and put down rebellion against Soviet rule in Central Asia.[2]   Lenin also sought to ally with anti-Western but non-Marxist regimes in Turkey, Iran, and Afghanistan.   Moscow even ended its support to a nascent Marxist regime in northwestern Iran – the Gilan Soviet – in an apparent effort to improve its relations with the Iranian monarchy and prevent it from increasing its reliance on Britain for fear of the Soviet threat.[3]   Although Moscow expressed support for revolution against West European rule in the Arab world, it took few practical steps to foment it under Lenin.

The Soviet Union under Lenin, then, used force to reassert Russian rule where it could, sought alliances against the West with the Northern Tier states, and virtually ignored the rest of the Middle East where it lacked the ability to seriously involve itself.   Despite its professed revolutionary aims, this was a relatively prudent foreign policy.

Stalin's Policy

Stalin's foreign policy underwent several dramatic reversals, depending on whether he thought he was in a position to damage the West or whether he needed its cooperation.   His foreign policy thinking was often characterized by overoptimism about Moscow's ability to manage events in other countries in a way that would benefit the USSR.   Preoccupied by his ambitious domestic projects as well as with events in Europe and the Far East, Stalin paid considerably less attention to the Middle East. To the extent that Stalin had a foreign policy toward this region, it too was mainly concerned with the Northern Tier countries.[4] Stalin made only minimal effort to project Soviet influence into the Arab world. In the late 1920s, he established diplomatic relations with the conservative Saudi and North Yemeni monarchies and hoped to cooperate with them on the basis of common opposition to British colonialism, but nothing came of this scheme.[5]

Shortly after the German attack against the USSR in 1941, the Soviet Union and Great Britain cooperatively occupied Iran. When the British were withdrawing their forces from southern Iran as per the Anglo-Soviet agreement on terminating their occupation after the war ended, Stalin appeared unwilling to withdraw Soviet forces from the northern part of the country. He also supported the emergence of Marxist regimes in Iranian Azerbaijan and Kurdistan. Yet despite the fact that the West could do little to force him to, Stalin did in fact withdraw his troops from northern Iran and allowed the two "Soviet" republics there to collapse in exchange for what he apparently hoped would be close relations with the Shah's regime – an expectation that was dashed soon after the completion of the Soviet withdrawal.[6]

Far from being an example of aggressiveness, Stalin's foreign policy toward Iran in the aftermath of World War II was remarkably restrained considering that he did not face serious constraints from the West here. Similarly, although Stalin demanded a Soviet base in the Turkish Straits and the award of a UN Trusteeship over Libya, he did not press for these aggressively (he was not in a strong position to do so).[7]

In light of strong Soviet support later for the Arab side in the Arab-Israeli dispute, Stalin's support for the creation of Israel in 1948 appears curious.[8] Far from foreseeing that Israel would eventually receive strong support from the United States and so create an opportunity for Moscow to ally with the Arabs (as some conspiracy theorists argue), Stalin's support for Israel appears to have been based on assumptions that 1) Britain and France would remain predominant in the Arab world; and 2) Jewish hostility toward Britain before Israeli independence would endure afterward, thus creating the opportunity for the USSR to ally with Israel. Both these assumptions, of course, proved inaccurate.

Khrushchev's Policy

It was under Nikita Khrushchev that the Soviet Union was first able to sustain an active foreign policy in the Middle East as a whole. Several factors made this possible. Unlike during the nineteenth century and much of the 1920s, Soviet control over the Caucasus and Central Asia was quite firm from the 1930s until the Gorbachev era. Similarly, unlike the 1910s, 1930s, and much of the 1940s, Russia was not under direct attack or the threat of it from Germany. In addition, the rapid progress of the Soviet nuclear weapons program gave Moscow increased confidence that the USSR would not be directly attacked by any other nation either.

It was this growing strength of the Soviet Union that made those Middle Eastern states closest to it increasingly fearful and hence willing to join Western-sponsored security alliances. Hence during the 1950s, Turkey, Iran, Iraq, and Pakistan all joined Western-sponsored security pacts.[9]

Increased Soviet strength, then, was counter-productive to Khrushchev's efforts to increase its influence in the Northern Tier since this greater strength led these states to fear Moscow. What gave Khrushchev the opportunity to play a larger role in the region was the rise of Arab nationalism. Arab nationalism was highly anti-Western due to Western colonization of the Arab world as well as support for Israel and pro-Western Arab monarchies. In its confrontation with the West, Arab nationalist leaders – especially the foremost one, Gamal Abdul Nasser of Egypt – sought support from the Soviet Union, and Khrushchev readily gave it.[10]

In addition to Egypt, Arab nationalist regimes came to power in Syria, Iraq, Algeria, and North Yemen before Khrushchev's ouster in 1964. Although there were differences over various issues between Moscow and all of them, in general these states were pro-Soviet. This was also the period when Moscow acquired military facilities in the region, especially in Egypt. Khrushchev also tried to improve Moscow's relations with conservative pro-Western Arab regimes at this time, but these efforts were generally (though not completely) unsuccessful due to these states' fear of their Arab nationalist neighbors.[11] In a sense, though, this did not worry Moscow since these conservative Arab governments all appeared highly vulnerable to being overthrown and replaced by pro-Soviet Arab nationalist regimes also. Although mainly the result of American pressure, Arab public opinion credited Nasser and Khrushchev for having forced the British and French to withdraw from the Suez Canal and the Israelis to withdraw from the Sinai Peninsula after their tripartite intervention in 1956.[12]

Khrushchev's Middle Eastern policy appeared to be highly successful. It depended, however, on several factors. The first of these was that Arab nationalist regimes would remain pro-Soviet. This, in turn, depended on their continuing satisfaction with the extent of economic and military assistance they received from the USSR. But Khrushchev made the point repeatedly that while the USSR was willing to assist Third World revolutionaries, it was not willing to do so to the point where this risked a Soviet-American confrontation.[13] Although this self-limitation on Soviet behavior would be made manifest in other regions before Khrushchev's ouster (most notably during the 1962 Cuban missile crisis), it would only be later that Moscow's Arab nationalist allies would come to understand that there were definite limits to Soviet military assistance for them.

Brezhnev's Policy

The contradictions in Soviet foreign policy toward the Middle East (especially the Arab world) inherited from the Khrushchev era would become apparent in the Brezhnev era – though not right away. In fact, Soviet influence in the Arab world would at first expand under Brezhnev in the aftermath of the 1967 Arab-Israeli war. Their defeat that year served to greatly increase Arab hostility toward the United States for, unlike in 1956, having so strongly supported Israel in this conflict and afterward. Many Arab governments broke diplomatic relations with the US at the time. Already anti-American Arab nationalist regimes moved closer to the USSR, accepting a greater Soviet military presence in their countries in exchange for increased shipments of Soviet arms with which they hoped to defeat Israel in a future encounter. Even many conservative Arab states distanced themselves from the US and moved closer to the USSR. These conservative Arab states did this partly to placate anti-American public opinion in their own country which could have jeopardized their survival if they were too closely identified with the US But they also improved relations with the USSR in order to give Moscow an incentive to moderate the hostile policies of Moscow's radical Arab allies toward their conservative neighbors. And those conservative Arab states which remained hostile toward the USSR (Saudi Arabia and the smaller emirates of the Persian Gulf which Britain withdrew its protection from in 1971) appeared to be vulnerable to guerrillas supported by South Yemen – the one Arab state where a Marxist-Leninist regime had come to power.[14]

By the beginning of the 1970s, the USSR appeared well on its way toward becoming the predominant external power in the Arab world. Over the course of the 1970s, however, Brezhnev's foreign policy would experience numerous setbacks stemming from the contradictory nature of its foreign policy in this region. To begin with, Moscow never considered Arab nationalism to be anything but a way station on a road that would ultimately lead to the establishment of Marxist-Leninist regimes in these states. When Arab nationalist forces were strong and Marxist-Leninist ones weak, Moscow acquiesced to the suppression of the latter by the former. And when Marxist-Leninist (or more pro-Soviet) Arab leaders succeeded in ousting Arab nationalist (or less pro-Soviet) ones, Moscow benefited, as in 1978 in South Yemen when the pro-Soviet faction in the South Yemeni ruling party ousted and executed the pro-Chinese one.[15] But when such attempts failed (as when the more pro-Soviet Ali Sabri attempted to overthrow Anwar al-Sadat in Egypt after the death of Nasser, and when the Sudanese Communist Party launched an abortive coup against the Arab nationalist regime of Jafaar al-Nimeiry in Sudan), this contributed to the reorientation of once pro-Soviet regimes away from Moscow and toward Washington.[16]

In addition, the Arab defeat in the 1973 Arab-Israeli conflict made clear the limit to which Moscow would risk a broader conflict with the US in order to support the Arabs against Israel. This limit had been evident in 1967, but on this earlier occasion the Arabs blamed their defeat on American support for Israel. By contrast, the Arabs generally blamed their 1973 defeat on the inadequacy of the weaponry Moscow had supplied them with. There was also a general sense that since the USSR could not be relied upon to provide the Arabs with the strength necessary to push Israel out of occupied Arab territory, the Arabs needed to enlist the help of the US in order to persuade it to do so.[17] While their defeat in 1967 led to a Soviet diplomatic victory in the region, the Arab defeat in 1973 led to an American diplomatic victory there. Despite the unhappiness of many Arab states over the Egyptian-Israeli accords signed at Camp David in 1978, Washington succeeded at excluding Moscow from all but a pro forma role in the politics of Arab-Israeli peace-making from the aftermath of the 1973 war onward.

Toward the end of the 1970s, events in two Northern Tier countries at first appeared to provide important gains for the Soviet Union, but would soon prove to be serious losses for it. The first of these apparent gains occurred in 1978 when a Marxist-Leninist regime came to power in Afghanistan. But not only did this new regime elicit strong domestic opposition, its leadership was also seriously divided. In order to prevent the regime from falling from power or out of the Soviet orbit, Brezhnev ordered the Soviet invasion of Afghanistan in December 1979. This decision turned out to be disastrous for three reasons: 1) unlike the Hungarians in 1956 or the Czechoslovaks in 1968, the Afghans put up a fierce resistance which Soviet forces were never able to defeat; 2) detente with the West – and the benefits which Moscow derived from it – came to an end; and 3) the Muslim world in general (including the Middle East) came to see the USSR as the enemy of Islam. Not only were several conservative Arab states able to capitalize on rising anti-Soviet sentiment in the Arab world to move closer to the US despite its support for Israel, but the anti-American regimes in Iraq and (after 1979) Iran also condemned the Soviet intervention in Afghanistan, thus complicating Moscow's relations with them.[18]

The second event – the Iranian revolution of 1979 – was welcomed by Moscow since it brought about the downfall of one of America's staunchest allies in the region. The Brezhnev regime hoped to ally with the Ayatollah Khomeini on the basis of a common anti-American foreign policy, and that the Islamic fundamentalist regime which replaced the Shah's would itself soon be replaced by a Marxist-Leninist one. However, not only did the Islamic fundamentalist regime remain firmly in power and defeat its communist and other leftist opponents, but Khomeini's foreign policy was as anti-Soviet as it was anti-American.[19] Given Soviet involvement in and then invasion of Afghanistan on Iran's eastern border as well as Moscow's massive supply of Soviet arms to Iraq, whose forces poured across Iran's western border in 1980, it is hardly surprising that Khomeini saw the USSR as an enemy. From Moscow's perspective, the new regime in Iran was a serious problem since it represented a competitive revolutionary ideology which threatened pro-Soviet as well as pro-Western regimes in the Middle East, and even had the potential to spread to the Muslim regions of the USSR itself.

By the first half of the 1980s (encompassing the last years of the Brezhnev era and the short reigns of his two immediate successors,

Andropov and Chernenko), the Soviet position in the Arab world had become considerably weakened. Its only allies were isolated or beleaguered radical regimes in Syria, Iraq, Libya, and South Yemen. In addition, Moscow's ambition to extend its influence in the Northern Tier states was frustrated both by the tenacious resistance to the Soviet-backed Marxist-Leninist regime in Afghanistan and to the emergence of a formidable revolutionary challenger in Iran.

Gorbachev's Policy

Between 1985 and 1987, Gorbachev's new foreign policy logic had not fully evolved, and Moscow still competed with the US for influence in the Middle East (and elsewhere). By 1988, however, it was evident that Gorbachev had decided to subordinate Soviet policy toward the Middle East to both his policy of seeking detente with the West as well as his ambitious domestic goals when the USSR agreed to withdraw its forces from Afghanistan by February 1989. In 1990, Gorbachev also acquiesced to the dissolution of the Marxist-Leninist regime in South Yemen through its merger with non-Marxist North Yemen; considering that the Soviet Union under Gorbachev had decisively intervened in South Yemen's 1986 civil war to prop up the Marxist-Leninist regime there, this was a remarkable policy turnabout in the space of four years. It was also during this period when the USSR came to support American-sponsored Arab-Israeli peace efforts instead of trying to promote its own Middle East peace plan in competition with the US But the most spectacular example of the extent to which Gorbachev subordinated Moscow's policy toward the Middle East to its relations with America and the West came during the 1990-91 crisis over Kuwait. Although the USSR did not send troops itself, Moscow supported American-sponsored UN Security Council resolutions condemning Iraq, imposing sanctions on it, and finally, authorizing the use of force to end the Iraqi occupation of Kuwait.[20]

There was an inherent logic to Gorbachev's refashioning of Soviet policy toward the Middle East (and the Third World as a whole) so as not to contradict Soviet foreign policy toward America and the West, which he had also refashioned to support his ambitious domestic agenda. Unfortunately for Gorbachev, his domestic agenda was riddled with inconsistencies and ultimately led to his downfall as well as the breakup of the USSR. Why this happened cannot be recounted here; the story is well known anyway. Vis-a-vis the Middle East, however, it is important to note that Gorbachev's domestic policies inspired the rise of non-Russian nationalisms, including in Russia's own Middle East: the Caucasus and Central Asia. Although much stronger in the former than in the latter, the breakup of the Soviet Union at the end of 1991 meant that the uncontested Russian control over these two regions which had been maintained since the Stalin era had come to an end.

Post-Soviet Russian Foreign Policy toward the Middle East

It is only with this history in mind that continuity and change in Russia's post-Soviet foreign policy toward the Middle East can be adequately assessed. Yeltsin's foreign policy toward the Middle East immediately after the breakup of the Soviet Union was a continuation of Gorbachev's: cooperation with America and the West in this region based on the Russian desire to obtain Western resources needed for Russian economic reform and growth. But two important changes have occurred since the breakup of the USSR that have strongly affected Russian foreign policy in general as well as toward the Middle East in particular: 1) the impact of Russian economic as well as military decline; and 2) the rise of Russian nationalism.

The first of these changes, the decline of Russian economic and military strength, has led to Russia no longer being willing or able to involve itself in costly military conflicts abroad or to give away large quantities of military and economic assistance to impecunious allies the way the USSR did from Khrushchev to Gorbachev. Russia is still willing to transfer arms abroad, but only to those states which can pay for them in hard currency.

The second change that has affected Russian foreign policy – the rise of Russian nationalism – has occurred for several complex reasons, not least of these being the decline in Russian economic and military strength. Popular expectations raised by Yeltsin's government just after the breakup of the USSR that market reform would quickly lead to a higher standard of living for the Russian population were not fulfilled. Indeed, for the majority of Russians, the standard of living has declined. There is also massive popular disappointment over the loss of Russia's superpower status and its empire. Non-democratic forces have risen up which blame the West – and both Gorbachev's and Yeltsin's efforts to have good relations with it – for this double loss.

As a result of the serious deterioration in his health occurring around the time of his re-election as president in mid-1996, Boris Yeltsin has only sporadically been able to direct Russian government policy since then.   The person who has actively managed Russian foreign policy toward the Middle East since then has been Yevgeniy Primakov – whom Yeltsin appointed as his foreign minister in early 1996 and later as prime minister in mid-1998.

Primakov in particular appears determined to reassert Russian influence over the South Caucasus and Central Asia in the aftermath of the collapse of the Soviet Union.   Yet while he has devoted considerable attention to this goal, he has faced many constraints in pursuing it.   First and foremost, the significant degree of democratization that has occurred in post-Soviet Russian politics has meant that public opinion now matters.   And public opinion in Russia, just like in other countries, can be contradictory.   While many Russians, for example, favor the restoration of the USSR, they came to increasingly oppose Yeltsin's failed military effort to defeat Chechen secessionists, ultimately forcing Yeltsin to withdraw Russian troops from this region in 1996.   Ironically, it was one of the leading Russian nationalists, Alexander Lebed, who negotiated an end to the fighting and the Russian withdrawal during his brief stint as Yeltsin's national security adviser.[21]

What happened in Chechnya has had a profound impact on Russian policy toward the South Caucasus and Central Asia.   For if the Russian public will not tolerate protracted military intervention to keep Chechnya within the Russian Federation itself, it appears highly unlikely that it would tolerate protracted intervention to keep areas outside Russia, such as the South Caucasus and Central Asia, under Russia's influence.

Similarly, Russia has intervened militarily in Tajikistan to defend "ex-communists" against an "Islamist" forces from 1992 to the present. Unlike the intervention in Chechnya which was done with mainly Russian conscript troops, the Russian intervention in Tajikistan has been more akin to the "Foreign Legion:" while the officers and NCOs of this 18,500 man force are predominantly Russian, the enlisted men are predominantly Tajik.   Even then, Russian public opinion has taken a negative view of this intervention, and in 1997 Russia negotiated a cease-fire and power-sharing agreement in Tajikistan.[22]

Post-Soviet Russia, then, cannot resort as easily to the use of force as Imperial Russia or the Soviet Union did to gain and retain control over the South Caucasus and Central Asia. Russia, however, is still able to exercise powerful means aimed at preventing the new states of South Caucasus and Central Asia from becoming too independent from Moscow. These include limited military intervention (as when Russian troops drove government forces out of Abkhazia, a breakaway region of Georgia), the ability to destabilize these weak regimes, and considerable leverage over the choice of export routes for the petroleum wealth that some of them possess.[23] Yet because post-Soviet Russia has neither the will nor the capacity to undertake prolonged, large-scale military operations in these regions like Imperial or Soviet Russia, and because the countries of the South Caucasus and Central Asia are all independent and some are rich in petroleum, Moscow's continued influence over them is now dependent on how it manages its relations with the countries just to their south: Turkey, Iran, and Afghanistan.

The Northern Tier

Because of their geographical proximity to the South Caucasus and Central Asia as well as their varying combinations of linguistic, ethnic, and religious links with some of them, Turkey, Iran, and Afghanistan could potentially undermine Russian influence in these areas of the former USSR. Indeed, when the USSR broke up at the end of 1991, it was widely predicted that Turkey and Iran would actively compete for influence in the Caucasus and Central Asia and that Russia would no longer play a strong role in them.[24] These forecasts have clearly proven to be inaccurate: Russia remains the predominant power in the South Caucasus and Central Asia while Turkey and Iran have achieved only a relatively modest degree of influence there so far. Still, there is now in the post-Soviet era a potential that did not exist during the Soviet period for the Northern Tier countries to play an important role in the South Caucasus and Central Asia.   This potential may increase if changes in these parts of the former USSR create opportunities for the Northern Tier states.

Russian foreign policy, then, has sought to ensure that such opportunities do not arise through managing Russia's relations with the Northern Tier states in such a way that these states do not have the incentive, or barring this, the opportunity to challenge Russia's position in the South Caucasus and Central Asia. So far, Moscow has pursued this set of objectives vis-a-vis the Northern Tier countries relatively successfully. Considering the very recent history of the Soviet invasion and occupation of Afghanistan, it would not have been surprising if the Islamic regime that ousted the Marxist one in Kabul was extremely hostile toward Russia. In fact, the Afghan regime that came to power in 1992 was quite hostile toward Russia at first. It allowed Tajik Islamic forces to operate from Afghan territory in their struggle against the ex-communist Tajik regime which Russian forces had helped restore to power.[25] But as this regime became increasingly beleaguered by the increasing powerful Taliban forces, Moscow and the Rabbani government in Kabul found that they shared common interests. Before its downfall, Russia reportedly provided military assistance to the Rabbani government, which in return ended its support for the Tajik Islamic opposition and began cooperation with the Russian-backed Tajik regime.[26]

Russian relations with the Taliban after they came to power in Kabul in 1996 have been extremely poor. Russian officials have expressed the fear that, after subduing northern Afghanistan, the Taliban intend to spread their brand of Islamic revolution into former Soviet Central Asia. Moscow has continued to provide assistance to the remaining Afghan forces that continue to hold onto northeastern Afghanistan.[27] If in fact the Taliban do represent a threat to the stability of Central Asia, the Russians have so far succeeded in containing it within Afghanistan.

Russian-Turkish relations have had a complicated evolution in the post-Soviet era. On the one hand, there has emerged an unprecedented degree of cooperative interaction between the two countries. Turkish businesses, for example, are actively involved in the growing private sector of the Russian economy. On the other hand, many in Russia fear the possibility that Ankara may be able to displace Moscow as the pre-eminent power in the ex-Soviet republics with linguistic links to Turkey (Azerbaijan in the Caucasus and Kazakhstan, Kyrgyzstan, Uzbekistan, and Turkmenistan in Central Asia). The Russian nationalist strain in Moscow's foreign policy has identified Turkey not only as a threat to Russian interests in these states, but also in the Muslim regions of the Russian Federation.[28] Russian nationalists frequently claimed that Turkey supported the Chechen independence movement.[29] The ultra-Russian nationalist leader, Vladimir Zhirinovsky, appears to regard Turkey as Russia's primordial enemy.[30]

Turkey has, in fact, attempted to extend its influence into the South Caucasus and Central Asia. There have been several obstacles, however, to the spread of Turkish influence to these regions. To begin with, Turkey does not directly border on any of the predominantly Turkic former Soviet republics (except for its very short common border with Azerbaijan's Nakichevian exclave which itself is geographically discontiguous from Azerbaijan). In addition, Turkey's economy is not particularly strong and there are severe constraints on the aid and investment that Turkey can provide to these former Soviet republics. Further, Ankara's cultural campaign to link these republics more closely with Turkey was largely unsuccessful, resulting instead in resentment over Turkey's perceived cultural arrogance.[31] So far, Turkish efforts to spread its influence to these republics have been limited both by Turkey's distance from them (especially the ones in Central Asia), the lack of sufficient resources that might enable Ankara to spread its influence, and perhaps most importantly, Turkey's unwillingness to damage its relations with Russia by aggressively seeking to displace its influence in the South Caucasus and Central Asia.[32]

In sharp contrast to Moscow's wary relationship with Turkey, Russian-Iranian cooperation has developed to such an extent that some observers see an alliance emerging from it. Underlying this increased Russo-Iranian cooperation are several convergent interests which make such an alliance a real possibility.

One of these convergent interests is economic. Russia wants to increase its hard currency export earnings, but has few opportunities for doing so. Iran wants to buy arms and nuclear reactors, but is unable to get these from the West due to American pressure on its allies not to sell these items to Tehran. It is not surprising, then, that Russia has been eager to sell Iran – a country which can pay in hard currency – goods which Iran cannot obtain from the West.[33]

In addition, Russian and Iranian interests converge in a number of broader political areas. Moscow and Tehran share one important common interest vis-a-vis the US: neither wishes to see American influence grow in the Caucasus or Central Asia. Nor do Russia and Iran wish to see the influence of Turkey grow in these regions either. Further, Russia and Iran are both multi-ethnic states which seek to forestall all secessionist movements within their borders from gaining ground.

Russia's policy of keeping Azerbaijan weak and impoverished serves Iranian interests perfectly. What is now independent Azerbaijan is the northern part of a larger area where Azeris predominate; the southern part is in Iran, and more Azeris live there than in the north. The independence of what was Soviet Azerbaijan has already led to an upsurge of nationalist feeling among Azeris to the south who seek secession from Iran and unification with Azerbaijan.[34] Although difficult to gauge just how powerful this movement is among Iranian Azeris, it does not seem to be particularly strong at present. Obviously, though, it is something that the Iranian government wants to discourage.

The authorities in Tehran fully understand that Iranian Azeris would be far more attracted to a peaceful, prosperous, democratic Azerbaijan than a war-torn, poverty-stricken, dictatorial one. Thus, Tehran has a strong incentive to acquiesce in Moscow's efforts to keep Azerbaijan poor and weak.[35]

Similarly, the Iranian government had relatively little to say concerning the brutal Russian use of force in Chechnya. This may seem somewhat surprising, considering that this was a case of non-Muslims suppressing Muslims.[36] But whatever concerns Tehran may have had about this appeared overshadowed by the common Russian-Iranian interest in preventing secession. Tehran may reasonably fear that an internationally recognized independent Chechnya could encourage secessionist movements in Iran.

Tehran did nothing to help the democratic/Islamic government that briefly came to power in Tajikistan in 1992. Nor did Iran do much to assist the increasingly radicalized Islamic opposition to the Soviet-style apparatchik regime that was restored to power and kept in place with the help of Russian armed forces.[37] While not uncritical of Moscow's use of force here, Tehran has worked with Russia to arrange a political settlement among the warring factions in Tajikistan.[38]

It may seem especially surprising that Iran would not avail itself of the opportunity to support Islamic revolutionaries, especially in Tajikistan – the one former Soviet republic in which, like Iran, Farsi is the predominant language. Tajikistan, though, provides yet another instance of Russian and Iranian interests converging.

Moscow fears that if Islamic revolution is successful in Tajikistan, it could sweep not only through Central Asia, but also through the Muslim regions of the Russian Federation. While Iran in theory favors Islamic revolution in other countries, it has become unenthusiastic about Islamic revolutionaries who do not recognize Iranian leadership. The Iranian leaders appear to have concluded that it makes little sense for Tehran to support the Islamic opposition in Tajikistan at present when Iran would not necessarily gain an ally even if a Tajik Islamic regime did somehow come to power.

But while Iran is at best indifferent toward the Tajik Islamists, its relations with the Taliban have become openly hostile. The Taliban have condemned the Islamic Republic for being insufficiently Islamic. Tehran, for its part, has accused the Taliban of being agents of the CIA. Iran fears that the Taliban, if allowed the opportunity, would compete with Iran for the leadership of the international Islamic revolutionary movement. Just like Russia, Iran has supported the remaining anti-Taliban forces in northern Afghanistan.[39] After the killing of several Iranian diplomats by the Taliban, Iran reportedly massed over 200,000 troops along its border with Afghanistan in September 1998.[40]

The Yeltsin-Primakov policy toward the Northern Tier – especially Iran – appears to be highly successful so far. Not only has Russia succeeded in preventing Turkey or Afghanistan from displacing Russian influence in the South Caucasus and Central Asia, but it has gained something akin to a willing ally in Iran – something that previous Soviet leaders never succeeded in transforming Iran into. Russia's diminished post-Soviet circumstances have obviously not prevented it from conducting an active foreign policy vis-a-vis the Northern Tier countries.

The Farther Middle East

This has not been the case, however, with regard to Moscow's foreign policy toward what for Russia is the "farther" Middle East – the Arab states and Israel. Under Yeltsin's first foreign minister, Andrei Kozyrev, Russia came to play only a minimal role in this region. Kozyrev essentially continued Gorbachev's policy of cooperation with the West. Although Russia continued to officially co-sponsor the Arab-Israeli peace negotiations with the US, Moscow no longer played any significant role in this process. It clings to this role mainly so that Moscow can point to it as a sign that Russia is still a great power.[41]

Russian policy changed, though, when Kozyrev was replaced by Primakov as foreign minister in early 1996. When fighting erupted between Israeli and radical Arab forces based in Lebanon during the spring of 1996, Primakov attempted to act as a mediator to the conflict.

His efforts, however, failed when all parties to the dispute accepted American mediation instead.[42]

Primakov was attempting to reassert an independent role for Russia in the Arab-Israeli arena. It must be noted, though, that he was not trying to re-establish Russia's military presence in the region, but its diplomatic one. What is noteworthy about his failure was that even Moscow's long-time ally, Syria, did not see dealing with Russia as an alternative to dealing with the US Although Primakov sought to reassert a Russian role in the Arab-Israeli arena, he was unable to sustain this effort.

To the extent that Moscow still has a sustained policy toward the farther Middle East, it is primarily an economic one. It has sought improved relations with Israel[43] and the conservative Arab states not in an effort to displace the US as the predominant political power in the region, but for the sake of increased trade with them.

Moscow would like to increase its exports (especially of arms) to Iraq and Libya, the two remaining radical Arab states possessing significant oil wealth.   Although the Russian government has frequently urged they be lifted, Moscow has observed the UN Security Council-imposed restrictions on trade with Iraq and Libya (which are far stricter with regard to the former).[44] Despite the obvious economic benefit that would accrue to Moscow from increased trade with these two states, Moscow has not broken the sanctions regime against them primarily because of the negative effect this would have on Russian relations with the West as well as conservative states in the Middle East.   Under Yeltsin, Russia has virtually ended arms transfers to former allies in this region which cannot afford to pay for them.[45]

Primakov stepped up his efforts to involve Russia in diplomatic efforts concerning Iraq with the crisis that emerged following Baghdad's heightened non-compliance with the UN-mandated weapons inspection program and its efforts to end American participation in it. When the crisis emerged, Primakov launched an active campaign to forestall the American use of force against Iraq and to cajole Baghdad back into compliance with the inspection program. As an incentive to Iraq, Primakov proposed – and won grudging American acceptance for – easing the UN-imposed restrictions on Iraqi oil exports.[46]

Primakov's efforts, however, proved to be futile as the crisis re-emerged several times. Despite the increased oil export quota that Russian diplomacy won for him, Saddam Hussein decided once again not to comply with the weapons inspection program but to create a crisis situation instead. Even high level Russian Foreign Ministry officials admitted that the Russian diplomatic effort had failed.[47]

Conclusion

The success of Yeltsin and Primakov in maintaining predominant Russian influence in the South Caucasus and Central Asia as well as managing relations with the Northern Tier states is an impressive accomplishment, especially given Russia's economic and military decline. Yet despite Primakov's concerted efforts to revive an important diplomatic role for Russia in the farther Middle East, Russia has been unable to achieve it. This represents a return to the pattern of Russia seeking to play an important role in this region but being unable to sustain it which existed from tsarist times through the Stalin era. In retrospect, then, Moscow's success in playing an important role in the farther Middle East under Khrushchev and Brezhnev may have been an aberration for Russian foreign policy.

Whether this proves to be the case, or whether Moscow will return to playing a more aggressive role in the farther Middle East in the future cannot, of course, be foretold. It was observed earlier that it has only been when Russia has been firmly in control of the Caucasus and Central Asia that it could sustain an active Russian presence in the farther off Arab world. Since the time the USSR broke up in 1991, however, this condition has again been absent.

Notes

1.On Tsarist foreign policy toward Turkey and Iran, especially in relation to Russian expansion in the Caucasus and Central Asia, see Hugh Seton-Watson, The Russian Empire, 1801-1917, (Oxford: Oxford University Press, 1967), pp. 41-51, 57-62, 289-311, 430-45.

2.Evan Mawdsley, The Russian Civil War, (Boston: Unwin Hyman, 1987), chs. 15-16.

3.S. Neil MacFarlane, "Successes and Failures in Soviet Policy toward Marxist Revolutions in the Third World, 1917-1985," in Mark N. Katz, ed., The USSR and Marxist Revolutions in the Third World, (Cambridge: Cambridge University Press, 1990), p. 12.

4."From 1919 to 1945, Moscow lacked the strength or opportunity to do otherwise than maintain the status quo with its southern neighbors." Alvin Z. Rubinstein, Soviet Foreign Policy since World War II: Imperial and Global, 4th. (New York: HarperCollins, 1992), p. 204.

5.John Baldry, "Soviet Relations with Saudi Arabia and the Yemen, 1917-1938," Middle Eastern Studies, Vol. 20, No. 1, (January 1984), pp. 53-80.

6.Rubinstein, Soviet Foreign Policy, pp. 66-7.

7.Ibid., p. 204.

8.Ibid.

9.Iraq, though, ceased its military cooperation with the West after the 1958 revolution which ousted the monarchy.

10.Rubinstein, Soviet Foreign Policy, pp. 212-14.

11.Although Kuwait established diplomatic relations with the USSR in 1963, none of the other conservative states of the Arabian Peninsula did so until the Gorbachev era.   On Soviet relations with the Arabian Peninsula states generally, see Mark N. Katz, Russia and Arabia, (Baltimore: Johns Hopkins University Press, 1986).

12.George Lenczowski, The Middle East in World Affairs, 4th ed. (Ithaca: Cornell University Press, 1980), pp. 534-6.

13.Mark N. Katz, The Third World in Soviet Military Thought, (Baltimore: Johns Hopkins University Press, 1982), pp. 18-21.

14.Lenczowski, The Middle East in World Affairs, pp. 784-7.

15.Katz, Russia and Arabia, pp.92-3.

16.Lenczowski, The Middle East in World Affairs, p. 787.

17.Galia Golan, Soviet Policies in the Middle East from World War II to Gorbachev, (Cambridge: Cambridge University Press, 1990), ch. 7. Sadat's disenchantment with Moscow was evident the year before the 1973 Arab-Israeli war when he ordered the removal of most Soviet military advisers from Egypt in response to, among other things, Soviet unwillingness to supply him with the advanced weaponry he wanted. Rubinstein, Soviet Foreign Policy, p. 215.

18.Other radical regimes friendly to Moscow (Algeria, Libya, Syria, and North Yemen) did not condemn the Soviet invasion of Afghanistan, but did not, like Marxist South Yemen and Ethiopia, support it either. Robert O. Freedman, Moscow and the Middle East: Soviet Policy since the Invasion of Afghanistan, (Cambridge: Cambridge University Press, 1991), pp. 71-80.

19.Golan, Soviet Policies in the Middle East, pp. 185-96.

20.Freedman, Moscow and the Middle East, ch. 4; Golan, Soviet Policies in the Middle East, ch. 17; and Rubinstein, Soviet Foreign Policy, pp. 218-28.

21.Vera Tolz, "The War in Chechnya", Current History, 95 (October 1996), pp. 316-21. On Russian public opinion on the war in Chechnya shortly before the 1996 Russian presidential elections, see US Information Agency, "Half the Russian Public Willing to Grant Independence to Chechnya," Russia/NIS Opinion Alert, L-14-96, March 6, 1996.

22.Muriel Atkin, "Tajikistan's Civil War," Current History, 96 (October 1997), pp. 336-40. On Russian public opinion concerning the war in Tajikistan, see US Information Agency, "Environment and Nuclear Proliferation Are Among

Russians' Top Concerns," Russia/NIS Opinion Alert, L-68-95, November 13, 1995.

23.Rosemarie Forsythe, The Politics of Oil in the Caucasus and Central Asia, Adelphi Paper no. 300 (London: International Institute for Strategic Studies, 1996); and Darrell Slider, "Democratization in Georgia," in Karen Dawisha and Bruce Parrott, eds., Conflict, Cleavage, and Change in Central Asia and the Caucasus, (Cambridge: Cambridge University Press, 1997), p. 172.

24.See, for example, William Drozdiak, "Iran and Turkey Vie for Political, Economic Influence in Soviet Muslim States," Washington Post, November 24, 1991, p. A27.

25.Rubin, "Tajikistan," pp. 216-19.

26."Russia is once again a significant arms supplier...to the government in Kabul controlled by Ahmad Shah Massoud, a former guerrilla commander who was the bane of Soviet forces in the Panjsher Valley north of Kabul." John F. Burns, "The West in Afghanistan, Before and After," The New York Times, February 18, 1996, p. E5.

27.Mark N. Katz, "Tajikistan and Russia: Sources of Instability in Central Asia," Caspian Crossroads, Vol. 2, No. 4, (Spring 1997), p. 13.

28.For example, according to "specialists" from the Russian Defense Research Institute, "'Turkey is acting as an instrument of American policy in the region, whose main goal is the establishment of Western control over the Caspian's energy...'" Lunev, "Russian Military Policy in the Transcaucasus."

29.The Turkish Welfare Party (the Islamic political party which gained the most votes in the 1996 Turkish parliamentary elections) does in fact publicly support Chechen independence.   Stephen Kinzer, "Ferry Incident Raises Turkey-Russia Tension," The New York Times, January 21, 1996, pp. 1, 10.

30."Zhirinovsky vs. the Turks," Middle East Quarterly, Vol. 1, No. 2, (June 1994), pp. 87-91.

31.Mesbahi, "Regional and Global Powers and the International Relations of Central Asia," pp. 21-20; and Kelly Couturier, "Discord Between Russia, Turkey Growing," The Washington Post, December 4, 1994, p. A44.

32.Malik Mufti, "Daring and Caution in Turkish Foreign Policy," Middle East Journal, Vol. 52, No. 1, (Winter 1998), pp. 32-50.

33.Robert O. Freedman, "Yeltsin's Russia and Rafsanjani's Iran: A Tactical Alliance," Middle East Insight, Vol. 11, No. 5, July-August 1995, pp. 88-9; "Russia to Increase Cooperation with Iran," Jamestown Foundation Monitor, [jf-monitor@andrew.cais.com], 12 April 1996.

34.David Nissman, "The Two Azerbaijans: A Common Past and a Common Future," Caspian Crossroads, No. 2 Spring 1995, pp. 20-3.

35.Thus, despite the fact that Armenians are predominantly Orthodox Christian and Azeris are predominantly Shia Muslim, Iran has not supported Azerbaijan in the ongoing Azeri-Armenian dispute over Nagorno-Karabakh. Leila Alieva, "The Institutions, Orientations, and Conduct of Foreign Policy in Post-Soviet Azerbaijan," in Adeed and Karen Dawisha, eds., The Making of Foreign Policy in Russia and the New States of Eurasia, (Armonk, NY: M.E. Sharpe, 1995), pp. 298-9.

36.Kenneth Katzman, "Iran, Russia, and the New Muslim States," Caspian Crossroads, No. 2 Spring 1995, p. 15.

37.Freedman, "Yeltsin's Russia and Rafsanjani's Iran," pp. 90-91.

38.Atkinson, "Tajikistan's Civil War," p. 340.

39.Ralph H. Magnus, "Afghanistan in 1996: Year of the Taliban," Asian Survey, Vol. 37, No. 2, February 1997, pp. 111-17; Terrence White, "Iranian Weapons Part of Arms Build-up on North-West Afghan Battlefield," Agence-France Presse, April 21, 1997; Reuter, May 10, 1997; and Xinhua, July 28, 1997.

40.Howard Schneider, "Cautious Iran Eyes Neighbor," The Washington Post, September 16, 1998, pp. A15, A19.

41.Robert O. Freedman, "Russian Foreign Policy in the Middle East: The Kozyrev Legacy," Caspian Crossroads, No. 4, Winter 1995/96, pp. 18-20.

42."Primakov Wants More Activist Policy in the Middle East," Jamestown Foundation Monitor, [jf-monitor@andrew.cais.com], 22 February 1996;

"Primakov Rebuffed in Israel," Jamestown Foundation Monitor, [jf-monitor@andrew.cais.com], 23 April 1996; and "Kremlin Slams United States for Mideast Peace Effort," Jamestown Foundation Monitor, [jf-monitor@andrew.cais.com], 24 April 1996.

43.In the spring of 1996, it appeared that Russian relations with Israel were about to deteriorate when some branches of the Russian government moved to halt the activities of the Jewish Agency--the organization assisting Jews who wish to immigrate to Israel. This was avoided, however, after these actions became publicized and the Yeltsin government acted quickly to allow the Jewish Agency to resume operations in Russia.   "Jewish Emigration Organization Alleged to Be Interfering in Russian Affairs," Jamestown Foundation Monitor, [jf-monitor@andrew.cais.com], 17 May 1996; and "Positive Signs for Jewish Agency," Jamestown Foundation Monitor, [jf-monitor@andrew.cais.com], 28 May 1996.

44.Freedman, "Russian Foreign Policy in the Middle East;" "Primakov Wants More Activist Policy in Middle East;" "Moscow Wants Libya Sanctions Reviewed," Jamestown Foundation Monitor, [jf-monitor@andrew.cais.com], 27 March 1996; and "Blockbuster Russian-Libyan Trade Deal?" Jamestown Foundation Monitor, [jf-monitor@andrew.cais.com], 29 March 1996.

45.For a general discussion of trends in post-Soviet Russian arms exports, see Andrew J. Pierre and Dmitri V. Trenin, eds., Russia in the World Arms Trade, (Washington, D.C.: Carnegie Endowment for International Peace, 1997).

46.Daniel Williams, "Putting Russia Back on the Global Map," Washington Post, January 25, 1998, p. A24.

47.Daniel Williams, "Russian Vows to Seek Iraqi Solution," Washington Post, January 31, 1998, p. A17. See also Daniel Williams, "Russia, France, Turkey Press Initiatives on Iraq," Washington Post, February 3, 1998, p. A13.

Chapter 9

Political Economy of European Union-Middle East Relations

Anoushiravan Ehteshami

Introduction

Fred Halliday has argued that since the end of the Cold War, "both fusion and fission have come again on to the order of the day".[1] In this chapter, I have tried to apply modified versions of these themes to my analysis of European Union (EU)-Middle East relations. The idea of fusion is particularly apposite to my analysis, where I regard western European democracies' attempts at integration as symbolizing the trend towards fusing their economies and some of their decision-making processes. The term fission, on the other hand, summarizes best the collapse of the Soviet Union, but it has also been used to explain the potentially explosive nature of European-Middle East relations in the post-Cold War era, where Europe's own regionalist momentum could arguably disrupt the political, economic and social rhythm of its southern Mediterranean neighbors. Fission could also be painting the turbulence of the crisis-ridden Middle East and North Africa (MENA) subsystem itself, where political elites are finding it increasingly difficult both to adjust to the post-Cold War international order and to respond to the economic and social challenges facing their societies.

This chapter argues that EU-Middle East relations are being forged in a climate where globalization on the one hand, and regionalization on the other are reshaping the international system. It argues, moreover, that while relations between the two regions have been entering a new phase, the EU's regionalist enterprise, and its increasing assertiveness, has been clashing with the neighboring MENA subsystem which, for a variety of reasons, has been suffering from a long period of malaise, compounded in recent years by deep fragmentation and sub-regionalist tendencies. It does, nonetheless, look forward to closer European-Mediterranean relations and to a more constructive European presence in the MENA region. Effects of a more determined European voice in international politics is assessed particularly in relation to the Arab-Israeli peace process, and in EU's Mediterranean policies.

The analysis begins with an assessment of the EU and its place in the international system, and continues with observations on the impact that systemic changes have had on Europe and on the Middle East. The EU's policies towards the MENA region receives attention from the two related fields of political and economic exchanges, and security issues. The key factors affecting the EU-MENA relations are discussed in relation to the changes that each region has undergone since the end of the Cold War.

Systemic Change and the European Union

Two, dynamic, rapidly evolving and inter-related forces can be identified as the main engines driving the European Union's development of its internal structures as well as the re-definition of its role and behavior in the international system. The first of these, which can be termed regionalization, is rapidly becoming a response to the second, commonly known as globalization.[2] The latter is a product of transnational capitalism, the most overwhelmingly powerful inter-national socio-economic force. It has been reshaping the international system in its entirety, imposing boundaries on the states' zone of influence on the one hand, and opening up tremendous economic opportunities in every corner of the world on the other.

Regionalism, by contrast, usually characterizes the inward movement of a fairly well defined geographical space, designed either to bolster the regional club against external pressures, or merely to strengthen the process of co-operation amongst neighboring countries which may have arisen from the convergence of one or more of the following: geopolitical factors, cultural likeness, political affinity, or territorial proximity.[3]

Taken together, regionalization and globalization have been forcing profound changes on state behavior world-wide. In a nutshell, whether it is in the realm of a country's foreign policy or that of its domestic social and economic environment, globalization is imposing limits on the autonomy of the state and forcing it to make compromises and sacrifices, even with its "soul", in the interest of prosperity in the post-Cold War economic order. Such a compromise is finding itself manifested in regionalism, that is to say the world-wide trend of regional co-operation and integration by geographically and/or culturally proximate states in their collective interests.

In addition to these global factors, other systemic changes have been helping to shape Europe's destiny. Two in particular are of great significance in the European context: the collapse of the Soviet Union (and its political and military departure from Eastern Europe), and the unification of Germany. Together, these developments, one centrifugal and the other "convergenal", have helped in what one commentator has called the dismantling of the "very structure of European stability".[4] They have further been responsible for stretching the very fabric of post-Second World War European political and economic order.

One western European response to these highly destabilizing developments has been to deepen the capitalist economic structures of Europe (namely the EU) and also to try and cocoon the Union from the global winds of change by surrounding it with a series of economic, political and security partnerships and alliances, of which the North Atlantic Treaty Organisation is only the most visible. Other initiatives, like the EU partnerships with its eastern and southern neighbors, the strengthening of the Western European Union and support for such multilateral gatherings as the Euro-Mediterranean Dialogue, can be seen as forming key elements of the same strategy. Much of this activity, it is fair to say, has been informed by the European realization of its need in the post-bi-polar world to find a collective, if not united, voice in responding to regional crises, such as the 1990-91 Persian Gulf crisis, and to major disruptions in the international system.[5]

The success of multilateral and bilateral agreements with its periphery, however, has always been conditional upon further successful integration of the western European economic club itself. The most significant aspect of such moves in recent years has been the creation of a single economic space in the capitalist heartland of Europe.[6]

Though the creation of a single market may not have been a new strategy - the decision to create a fully unified internal market was taken back in 1985 - the unification of Germany and the disintegration of the USSR caused a marked shift in focus within the EU and accelerated the rate of flow towards further European integration. The vision of a single European entity was being pushed at the time by key continental powers (Germany and France in particular) and was vehemently opposed by Prime Minister Thatcher of Britain, who found herself helpless in reversing the tide of creeping federation.[7]

Within a few years, albeit tentatively at first, the main western European powers and their EC partners started taking the first steps which were to mark the transitional process from the "Common Market" to the "Single Market" and finally towards the "Union".[8]

Combined with the logic of further European integration is the impact that regionalism will have on the EU's own institutions and policies, as well as on its international role. As to how the Union might change as it begins to respond to the forces of globalization, we need to consider, firstly where pressure is being felt and, secondly, how the EU is responding to such pressures. Beyond this of course, as will be shown below, EU responses to global challenges do have a direct bearing on the well-being and future development of the Union's neighbors (to the east as much as on those to the predominantly Muslim south, the countries of Middle East and North Africa), and it is here that some of the results of EU thinking on regional relations and strategies first appear. These are the territories, moreover, in which the EU may be fighting many of its global battles. For these states in turn, developments in Europe are of great significance, not only because the EU is a major global player[9] (see Table 1) and their main trading partner, but more particularly because most of the EU's decisions tend to have a direct impact on the prosperity of the more vulnerable societies around it.

Economic Player	Population (million)	Territory (1,000km)	Economy Share in world ($billion)	national product (%)
European Union	369	3,240	8,420	32.1
United States	260	9,372	6,952	26.7
Japan	125	378	5,110	19.5
Russian Federation	149	17,075	363	1.3
China	1,205	9,571	630	2.3

Table 1: Main Global Economic Players, mid-1990s
Sources: European Commission, and Dresdner Bank (Frankfurt).

Additionally, as these economies develop closer ties with the EU so they are increasingly being exposed to the same winds of change which have been blowing in the Union itself, including the contradictions - emerging from processes of integration, deregulation of markets and competition policy - which are embedded in the EU economic policy in terms of making the single market sufficiently efficient and competitive to take on the US and Japan as well as the other export-oriented economies of Asia. To realize this aim, Brussels has had to make the EU economic space "leaner and meaner", but, as O'Hearn argues, the increase in "the competitiveness of the largest and most technologically advanced firms, sectors, and regions [has threatened] to exacerbate uneven development among [EU] regions and, in particular, to marginalize the so-called European periphery".[10] In the same vain, it can be argued that a similar fate might be awaiting the EU's external periphery, where the contradictions of the EU's competition policy might spill over and lead not only to the "economic balkanization"[11] of the Arab system, but also to the "uneven denationalization"[12] of the MENA countries?

EU-MENA Relations in the Context of International Transformations

The international setting for EU-MENA relations in the post-Cold War order can be viewed as the end of American economic hegemony and the emergence of a truly multi-center economic order. In this order power has become a more fluid commodity, shifting from the post-1945 US-western Europe-dominated Atlantic international order to a still undefined, incoherent and evolving East Asian-dominated Asia-Pacific world in which Japan, China and the East Asian Newly Industrializing Countries (NICs) may be forming only the leading locomotive of a forward-moving Asian-Pacific economic train. In this brave new world, industrial western Europe is having not only to rise to and respond to the Asian challenge, but to contain the latter's on its home turf and in its own markets.

In this new world, the Middle East is once again finding itself at the cross-roads of the struggle between Europe and Asia. It is caught in the crossfire of a global economic battle between these two huge politico-economic spheres. For the United States, which has a strong military and economic presence in both regions, the "Euro-Asian struggle" can be of great strategic value, a moment of rich pickings as it were - as was the case in the decades following the Second World War. To take advantage of this "window of opportunity" it needs to maintain its presence in both while also keeping its own economy lean and responsive to global changes.

A prolonged Euro-Asian struggle, of course, could also very easily sour the US' carefully nurtured ties with either or both of these sets of economies, and thus compromise its strategic objectives in both the post-Communist European area, in which international liberalism that the US adheres to still holds sway, and the Asian economic grid in which the above American-championed paradigm of the last half century has been losing ground to the international mercantilist tradition of Japan and the Asian Tigers.[13]

In the new landscape, the Middle East forms part of a vital link between the two Eurasian geo-economic spheres, and as such is a significant global beachhead. Not surprisingly, therefore, it is where the US has been keen to play an active and holding role; to hold the balance of power and thus influence the calculations of its European and Asian partners and competitors. For the remaining military superpower dominating this strategically significant region is vital if it is to keep its European and Asian challengers at bay.[14] The US and its competitors fully realize that the Middle East and North Africa region is caught between two potential "heartlands" of uneven power, as Halford Mackinder would see it,[15] which are poised to control the "world island".

From another, complementary, perspective, the MENA region is caught between the marching force of the so-called Asian values-based economic organizational strategies (the Easternization of the workplace one might say) on the one hand, and the Westernization of the entire world (the adoption at the global level of the capitalist mode of production and its Western-based cultural heritage) on the other. Against the pressures exerted by these forces, the Middle East and North Africa region and its new periphery in the shape of Central Asia (MENACA), is, to paraphrase Frederick Starr, a pivotal region and key to the security of Eurasian landmass.[16] It is here that many global struggles are being played out, and important international battles lost and won.

Without stability in the broader MENACA region, long-term development in Eurasia cannot be sustained, nor can security for its many billions of people and many dozens of states be obtained. This point is clearly underlined by a list of so-called pivotal states drawn up by a group of American scholars.[17] It is noteworthy that of the ten Third World countries listed, four (Algeria, Egypt, Turkey and Pakistan) operate within the MENACA region and a total of six belong to Asia.

Yet, the MENA region itself is not only highly unstable, continuing to threaten in different ways the very stability of the post-Cold War order, but has been subject to many destabilizing external pressures as well.[18] The region's weak economic base adds to its fragility and vulnerability and seems to deter substantial foreign investment commitments,[19] in turn reinforcing the prevalent cycle of decline.

Region	Value ($million)	%
Far East	65,033	65.2
Latin America/Caribbean	26,560	26.6
MENA	4,230	4.3
Sub-Sahara Africa	2,895	2.9
Other	952	1
Total	99,670	100

Table 2: Foreign Direct Investment Flows to Developing Countries by Region, 1995
Source: UNCTAD, World Investment Report 1995 (New York: UNCTAD, 1995).

In concrete terms, five key developments can be identified as having defined the pace and nature of European Union involvement with the Middle East and North Africa region in the post-Cold War era. Two of the events earmarked for further analysis here accompanied the ending of the Cold War, and indeed may have accelerated its eventual end, helping in the process, to shape the order that followed. The first was the Iraqi invasion of Kuwait in 1990 and the Western/Soviet response to the Iraqi action. The second, and of more importance, was the implosion of the Soviet superpower itself. This event in itself has had a profound impact on the international system, particularly in the ways in which it has altered the very conduct of international relations and the way in which it has characterized the passing of bi-polarity. It is no wonder that the implosion of the Soviet Union has been dubbed as "the big bang" of the international system.[20]

The Soviet collapse also changed the geopolitical map of Asia (in particular in West and Central Asia), and with it the Cold War pattern of alliances; indeed the very balance of power in both Europe and West Asia.

The third development of note was the coming into force in Europe of the Maastricht Treaty on 1 January 1993. This treaty transformed the 12-member European Community into a "European Union" and prepared the way for the emergence of a single western European politico-economic space.

The fourth post-Cold War development of much importance to EU-Middle East relations is of course the Arab-Israeli peace process and the EU's role and expectations in that regard. Particularly important has been the EU's economic and security initiatives towards the Middle East (such as the call for a Conference on Security and Co-operation in the Middle East) and the ways in which it has attempted to address post-Cold War security concerns arising from its neighboring MENA region.

Finally, we need to ask what might be the implications for the Middle East of the numerical, and therefore spatial, expansion of the EU in 1995. This development will need attention particularly with reference to the changing balance of power within the Union between the Mediterranean and the continental states, first moving southwards in the mid-1980s and now moving northwards, and also in relation to the probable eastward expansion of the EU in the new millennium.

The Kuwait Crisis and its Aftermath

The Iraqi invasion of Kuwait in 1990 marked a major turning point in the history of the MENA region. Firstly, it sounded the death knell for Arab unity, and with it the region's ability to contain and resolve conflicts with its own resources. Secondly, it marked a new phase in the sub-regionalization of the entire MENA territory, a process of fragmentation which has been spreading itself in a restructuring Middle East subsystem.[21] This sub-regionalization has been accompanied by atomization of the region as well, whereby states no longer seek collective solutions to regional problems, and instead aim to maximize their own independence from regional powers in an effort to find "independent" solutions to their domestic and foreign policy dilemmas.[22]

The end result of these regional crises manifested itself in several ways. Firstly, came the isolation of certain key regional powers, most notably Iraq and Iran in the Persian Gulf sub-region. Secondly, it saw the pro-Western Arab regimes enter into comprehensive defense pacts with Western powers, most notably with the US, Britain and France. Thirdly, the western Europe powers were able to capitalize on the vulnerabilities of the MENA states to strengthen their own presence in the MENA region, and also, largely through the EC, to reach advantageous trade agreements with MENA states and MENA sub-regions. The process of regionalization which had accompanied globalization of the capitalist system, and had given birth to such sub-regional entities as the Gulf Co-operation Council, the Arab Maghreb Union and the Arab Co-operation Council, was merely reinforced by the EC's trade and investment agreements reached with MENA states after the Cold War.

Thus, into this polarized and fractured MENA arena settled the Western powers, headed by the United States. In the absence of the Soviet Union, they begun re-ordering the region, seeking, in the process, to make it more compatible with the New World Order. In short, the US-led Western alliance became the new power broker in the Middle East, with the US as regional hegemon.

The Western powers' demands for compatibility focused on certain economic and political issues: conformity in approaches to economic development (in the form of economic liberalization and structural adjustment), support for Western initiatives in the region (the Arab-Israeli peace process, Persian Gulf security, containment of anti-Western terrorism, suppression of Islamist movements and states, etc.), and development of pluralist and democratic institutions and processes. In return, the main Western powers agreed to underwrite the security of the most important Middle Eastern states, particularly where Western interests dictated a direct presence.[23] This policy brought overt American, British and French security guarantees for several Gulf Arab countries. Western security initiatives towards the GCC countries included the reactivation of the US' Fifth Fleet in the summer of 1995, combining access to naval bases in Bahrain and elsewhere with the prepositioning of much military hardware in the Persian Gulf.[24]

The Implosion of the Soviet Union

The implosion of the Soviet superpower a year after the Iraqi invasion of Kuwait was of considerable significance in the shaping of Euro-MENA relations. The end of the Soviet Union posed serious problems for many Middle Eastern countries, in particular for those who had developed a politico-military dependence on Moscow and the Warsaw Pact countries. In the first place, these countries (most notably Syria) had to readjust their foreign policies in such a way that it showed recognition of the US hegemony in this region. Their agreement to participate in the Madrid Arab-Israeli peace talks and in direct meetings with Israeli representatives stems in part from recognition of such realities.

But, while the implosion of the Soviet Union strengthened the hand of the Western powers in this region, it also provided the old "southern belt" countries and other MENA powers (like Israel, Saudi Arabia, Syria and Egypt) with the opportunity to extend their economic and political reach to new territories in the Caucasus and in Central Asia. The fact that many of the new states emerging from the former Soviet Union were largely comprised of Muslim peoples was an added bonus.

At another level, the implosion of the Soviet Union acted as a catalyst for further sub-regionalization of MENA. The political fallout of the Soviet implosion for the MENA region resulted in strategic vulnerability for the remnants of the so-called radical Arab regimes. In broader strategic terms, however, the end of the Soviet system resulted in several fundamental changes in Eurasia. As far as EU-Middle East relations are concerned, two developments are of particular importance. First, the Soviet collapse created a short-term power vacuum in the heart of Asia, which in turn encouraged further regionalist tendencies in this area as neighboring MENA countries scrambled to build new links to these new republics. This they did through extensive bilateral exchanges as well as through multilateral agencies such as Economic Co-operation Organization (ECO).

It allowed the non-Arab Muslim states of the Middle East (Iran, Turkey and Pakistan) to consolidate their relative position in the region's post-Cold War geoeconomic order by expanding the ECO to include all the Muslim republics of the former Soviet Union and Afghanistan. This thirteen member organization is unique, for not only is it the region's largest sub-regional organization, comprising solely of non-Arab Muslim states, but also it boasts huge territory and immense natural resources, with a potential market of over 300 million people. ECO, furthermore, is only one of several regional organizations with a Middle Eastern dimension which have emerged from the ashes of the Soviet Union; other notable sub-regional organizations includes the Black Sea Grouping and the Caspian Sea States Organization.

Secondly, Moscow's weakened geopolitical position allowed the Western countries to use European-based institutions, such as the Organisation for Security and Co-operation in Europe (OSCE) and Partnership for Peace, to extend their influence into the heart of Asia - even as far as the Pacific rim via Russia and to the western borders of China via Central Asia. Through such mechanisms as the OSCE and Council of Europe, the western European powers had acquired the institutional capability to take an active part in shaping the post-Soviet regional order. In the post-Cold War era, both directly (through such frameworks as the "5+5", Euro-Med., Euro-Arab, and EU-GCC Dialogues) and indirectly (largely through NATO and the OSCE), the EU has been able to enhance its capability to shape the emerging regional order in MENA proper as well as in MENA's new periphery, the landlocked territories of Central Asia. This it has done largely through economic (trade, investment and aid) measures based on negotiations between the EU and its MENA partners, and through its support for establishment of one or more over-arching regional bodies such as an (European-style) Organization for Security and Co-operation in the Middle East and the Organization for Security and Co-operation in the Mediterranean.[25] European support for the establishment of NATO-Mediterranean dialogue in early 1995, in which Egypt, Israel, Mauritania, Morocco and Tunisia are involved, is part of this same strategy of engagement.[26]

These economic partnership/association arrangements have taken the form of bilateral trade and investment agreements, or multilateral pacts which are designed to tie the MENA countries (in particular the Mediterranean states) to collective co-operative structures - dominated by the EU. The EU's role in this regard can hardly been exaggerated; the Union is the main economic partner of the MENA countries, a region in which inter-regional trade barely reaches 10 per cent of these countries' total trade.[27]

Country	Inter-Arab trade	Total trade	% of inter-Arab trade in relation to total trade
Algeria	202	9231	2
Bahrain	460	2656	17
Djibouti	54	89	61
Egypt	671	5562	11
Iraq	0	2	0
Jordan	226	1424	16
Kuwait	75	8445	1
Lebanon	435	737	59
Libya	404	7826	5
Morocco	376	4013	9
Mauritania	2	464	0
Oman	205	4831	4
Qatar	220	2913	8
Saudi Arabia	3674	45630	8
Somalia	105	130	81
Sudan	118	515	23
Syria	762	3151	24
Tunisia	379	4657	8
UAE	1709	20906	8
Yemen	45	1048	4
Total	**10122**	**124285**	**8**

Table 3: Inter-Arab Trade Relations, 1994 ($million)
Source: OAPEC Monthly Bulletin August/September 1996.

In the mid-1990s, the EU was taking over 40 per cent of all Arab exports and providing as much as 45 per cent of their imports. For the Maghreb states, as much as 50 per cent of each of the countries' trade is with the EU, rising to over 60 per cent in the case of Egypt.[28] In terms of their export markets, the Arab states are even more beholden to the EU. In Tunisian, Algerian and Moroccan cases, between 70 and 75 per cent of their exports are destined for EU markets, and in Egypt's case, the most populous Arab state, the figure is about 60 per cent. As far as Israel and Turkey are concerned, over 35 per cent and 50 per cent respectively of their exports are bound for the European Union, and no less than 50 per cent and 45 per cent respectively of their imports originate in the EU.[29]

The problems such trade dependence has generated have been compounded by the considerable trade surplus the EU enjoys with many MENA economies,[30] and the fact that the Mediterranean and the Persian Gulf account for no more than four per cent and 2 per cent respectively of total European trade.[31] Table 4 illustrates the extent of the existing imbalance in European-Mediterranean trade.

	EU exports to the Mediterranean	Mediterranean exports to the EU	EU balance
Agricultural goods	4.1	3.8	0.3
Manufactures	38.3	15	23.3
Energy	0.7	12.4	-11.7
Minerals	0.4	0.6	-0.2
Total	43.5	32.9	10.6

Table 4: Euro-Mediterranean Trade, 1992 ($billion)
Source: Bichara Khader, Le Partenariat Euro-Mediterraneen, Working Paper Series (Cairo: Economic Research Forum, No. 9523).

As is evident, despite its heavy energy dependence on the Mediterranean region, the EU enjoys considerable trade advantage in the vitally important manufacturing sector and a small advantage in the agricultural goods sector as well.

Maastricht and the MENA Region

The Maastricht Treaty was the long overdue response to the structural problems associated with the deepening and extension of European co-operation. As Hugh Corbet articulated the problem back in 1977: "Because of the economic differences between them, the countries of the European Community are affected differently by global problems, which means that their governments are bound to react in different ways. This provides a clue as to what must be done if the Community is to develop further".[32] The real momentum for the treaty, however, did not come from international economic pressures, but from within Europe itself, particularly from the federalist forces that German unification had unleashed in 1990.[33] These same forces, however, met their anti-thesis in another growing trend, that of "Euro-scepticism", which set about challenging the proposed strategy of integration through transfer of more decision-making power to EU institutions, the Commission and the Parliament in particular. Despite the problems associated with different European interpretations of the Maastricht Treaty, it was enforced on 1 January 1993.

The battle between the various tendencies has been absorbing much European energy in the 1990s, delaying to a degree the final steps of integration. Prior to and since Maastricht the arguments about further European integration have been internalized by national political forces as well, thus helping to split many national polities and European institutions. One result of these internal divisions in the post-Maastricht EU has been the Union's inability to advance the foreign policy and security aspects of the treaty. While, the treaty has established some of the structures for forging a common European foreign and security policy, it has not been able to create the conditions for the implementation of the same. Put another way, although the treaty has rationalized the mechanisms that enable the EU to attack problems as a united force, it has not successfully driven the system to complete the essential conditions for adopting common action. Different, and at times divergent, national objectives have proved far harder to overcome than previously anticipated, a problem which will arguably continue until the full implementation of monetary union. The problem of collective action though is not insoluble, nor absolute. The EU states are gradually responding to change and showing signs of collective action. On some important external policy matters, like at the WTO's multilateral trade liberalization negotiations, and fighting the US' 1996 D'Amato Bill, the Commission is already speaking for the Union.

Nonetheless, the treaty has had some direct, albeit subtle, effects on the MENA region.[34] Firstly, on the economic front, as George Joff notes, the single market has raised a series of non-tariff barriers against non-members' exports to Europe.[35] Economic pressures have ranged from requiring the MENA countries to raise the quality of their manufactured exports to the EU to European standards, to accepting the imposition of European regulations on their products and exports, to competing with each other to find a secure toehold in "fortress Europe". The EU's roundtable discussions with its MENA economic partners is a partial response to these problems and a way of addressing some of the economic consequences of the creation of the single market.

Secondly, on the political front, the treaty has introduced a series of new administrative structures and procedures of governance which provide the opportunity for western European powers to develop a collective and co-ordinated voice in international affairs. The EU's ability to develop and implement a "Mediterranean policy" is itself an example of this trend. But in other areas of policy too, the Arab-Israeli peace process, Persian Gulf security matters, political dialogue and so on, the treaty has enabled the EU to intervene with more confidence and assertiveness. This has been so because the Maastricht Treaty has given birth to a new "pillar" of decision-making in the EU; that of foreign policy, which allows for the evolution at the center of a "common foreign and security policy".[36]

Although the "Maastricht process" is unlikely to eliminate national competition amongst the EU countries - note for instance their rivalry for access to MENA markets (particularly in the highly profitable GCC arms markets), nor dilute their pursuit of their national interests, where their interests do converge (as in the Arab-Israeli conflict, for example), then we are likely to see more instances of collective action.

The last word on the treaty has to be that while it has created the conditions for collective European action in the foreign and security matters, it has not acted to distil the external interests of the EU countries in such a fashion as to formulate basic EU foreign policies. The EU remains largely reactive in this regard and has not emerged as the proactive superpower many of its Commissioners had wished for. Where the Maastricht Treaty's presence has been felt in the MENA region, however, is more in the economic sphere; in their trade and investment policies (particularly where the EU is their main partner), on their economic units (firms and industries), on their legislation (from competition law to intellectual property rights), market reform strategies, and regional co-operation and integration schemes.[37] These are important areas of national activity - of a neighboring region - whose workings the EU's own internal logic has been able to directly affect and shape.

The Arab-Israeli Peace Process

The renewed vigor and speed with which the US pursued the resolution of the Arab-Israeli conflict after the 1991 Gulf war owed much to the long over-due recognition by the Western allies that despite other tensions in the Middle East, this conflict had continued to destabilize the region. On this point there was complete agreement between Washington and Brussels, though, as we shall see below, consensus on the issues at stake was much harder to find.

The peace process itself of course was made possible because of the regional changes which had followed the multi-national alliance's war against Iraqi forces.[38] Direct European involvement in the Gulf war and its long-standing commitment to a just and peaceful settlement of the Arab-Israeli dispute (as enshrined in the Venice Declaration of June 1980) brought the Community into the game as a full player, despite the fact that the US and the USSR were identified as the sponsors of the historic Madrid peace talks. Following the first round of talks, however, the geographical momentum of the bilateral talks shifted towards the US landmass, with the EC countries being left in charge of some of the multilateral talks.

This situation, in which the EC found itself playing second fiddle to the US began to change in September 1993, with the signing of the Palestinian-Israeli Accords, which ushered in a new era in contacts between Israel and its Arab neighbors. The direction of the new era was emphatically underlined by the Jordanian-Israeli peace treaty of October 1994. In these new contacts between Israel and its Arab neighbors, the US had continued to reserve for itself the role of supreme political master while the EC was increasingly required to act as the paymaster for the parties engaged in the peace process. While the role of paymaster was generally welcomed by the Community,[39] allowing the Europeans not to have to address the thorny issue of a united policy on an important regional matter, it soon transpired that some of the key European powers were beginning to show signs of displeasure at not having a political voice to match their economic clout in matters which were so important to European security and to relations within the Mediterranean region in general. For the Europeans, it should be remembered, the process of reconciliation as a by-product of the post-Cold War world had allowed the rebirth of a multilateral era, the "UN era", in which they sought the opportunity to drive home their United Nations Security Council numerical advantage and, capitalizing on their two-member majority, to influence the resolution of regional conflicts around the world, including in the MENA region. The Middle East, therefore, had become for the Europeans not just the test case for assessing the limits of a common European foreign policy (so badly exposed during the Kuwait crisis), but the arena in which the EC should seek to apply its economic muscle to the resolution of thorny political problems.

The Palestinian and Jordanian peace accords with Israel provided the catalyst for a change of gear by the EC in formulating European relations with the MENA region, and also enabled it to emerge as the main economic sponsor of the evolving Palestinian entity.[40] First, the EC sought a more direct involvement in the peace process, both as mediator and enforcer. Secondly, the EC increased its interest in enhancing European-MENA trade, investment and political agreements based on bilateral and multilateral arrangements. Here, paradoxically, while the EC's posture was encouraging regionalization, its actual policies were reinforcing fragmentation, as these were based on finalization of bilaterally reached association agreements with MENA countries. The EU's action was also encouraging the creation of a new division in the MENA system between "ins" and "outs" - between those with access to EU markets and resources and those without such preferential access.

Thirdly, the EC introduced a series of Mediterranean initiatives which culminated in the introduction of the Euro-Mediterranean Partnership in 1994.[41] The idea of a partnership had emerged from the Lisbon European Council meeting of June 1992 which had proclaimed the Community's "strong interests in terms of security and social stability" in the Mediterranean region,[42] and the December 1994 summit of the European Council in Essen when the Mediterranean was declared "a priority area of strategic importance for the European Union". These new European initiatives towards the Mediterranean region stemmed from the concern, expressed in 1989, that the fall of the Berlin Wall had forced on the Commission a re-assessment of the EC's periphery, south and east.[43] On the southern front, the EC based its policy on economic co-operation,[44] which was increasingly contingent on Mediterranean non-member countries' efforts towards economic restructuring - the same principles as were applicable to its relations with the new democracies of Eastern Europe.

The EU's position on the Arab-Israeli peace process increasingly contradicted, and therefore complicated, its relations with the Clinton administration, whose policies were unashamedly pro-Israel. The Europeans were keen to increase direct pressure on Israel in order to encourage it to comply with the relevant UN resolutions on the conflict - or failing that, at the very least to live by the agreements reached with the Palestinian Authority - while the US appeared to be giving the Rabin-led Labor-dominated Israeli government a free hand in formulating its own policies towards its Arab neighbors - even at the expense of violating the spirit and letter of international norms and of the UN charter. It was not lost on European powers either that both the US and Israel were content to see the EC marginalized in the negotiations. Both parties, to different degrees, regarded the EC stance in the conflict as Arab-leaning and biased in favor of the Palestinians in the peace process.[45]

The tensions between the US and EU sides reached new heights in the second half of the 1990s. Few examples will suffice to illustrate the point. In 1996, the Israeli bombardment of southern Lebanon in April and the victory of the Likud-led coalition in Israel's May general election acted as a double wedge in US-EU approaches towards the Arab-Israeli conflict; while both developments were received with open dismay by the Europeans, the US was much more reserved in its assessment of the situation, post-Rabin. Their differences were further marked with the US's failure to invite the EU's American representative to the Arafat-Netanyahu Washington summit of October 1996, and the Palestinian leader's unscheduled stop over in Europe and his meeting with several senior Europeans on his way to the American capital.[46]

Relations between the new Israeli government and the EU, on the other hand, had also hit a new low by the middle of 1996.[47] These tensions flawed onto the streets as it were with President Chirac's high profile visit to Israel and the Occupied Territories in October 1996, where he not only snubbed the Israeli parliament and chose to become the first Western head of state to address the Palestinian legislative council, but also adopted the role of an EU peace maker ready to step in where Washington had failed. Relations between Israel and EU of course had already been damaged by the EU foreign ministers' strongly-worded statement on the Middle East in early October in which they had pointedly criticized many aspects of the Likud government's policies in the peace process.

Paris' position on the direction of the peace process was by this time being echoed by the EU over some of the most sensitive issues in the negotiations, the most central of which was East Jerusalem, where the European line - rejection of Israel's "unilateral annexation of East Jerusalem" - causing a further widening of the distance between the American and European positions on the one hand, and Israel and the EU on the other.

In 1997, relations took another turn for the worse, when in March an EU-drafted Security Council resolution expressing "deep concern" about Israel's proposed new housing project in East Jerusalem was vetoed by the United States.[48] This embarrassing episode, where the US rejected a position statement proposed by several of its NATO partners - and supported by the rest of the international community - highlighted more clearly than ever the growing rift between the Atlantic allies over conflict resolution in the Middle East, where their co-operation had been deemed essential at almost every G-7 Summit since the end of the Cold War. That the gap between th EU and the US over the peace was widening was again highlighted in the course of 1998. First came France's decision in May 1998 to set up a joint committee with Egypt, another of Washington's close Arab allies, to plan a new international conference to revive the peace process. France's initiative, co-ordinated almost entirely independently of Washington had come just as the US was preparing its own diplomatic assault on the stalemate on the Palestininan-Israeli track, and was easing its political pressures on Israel as a means towards encouraging Israel to make good the labour government's promises to withdraw from more of the west Bank. France's key role in the peace process was further underlined by president Asad's trip to Paris in July, his first to a Western capital in 22 years, during which President Chirac discussed the resurrection of the Israeli-Syrian track with the Likud-led Israeli government – something that Washington had been unable to do.

Then came Britain's decision (in July) to upgrade the status of the Palestinian diplomatic mission in London. With this highly political act, Britain joined the ranks of its European partners who had for years treated their own Palestinian missions as defacto embassies. London's decision to upgrade the PLO's status at the international body, put even more distance between the US's approach to the peace process and that of its European allies. With this act, Washington's closest European ally demonstrated how much closer to its European partners its attitude towards the Arab-Israeli conflict had drawn.

These European political moves, spearheaded by the two EU permanent members of the UN Security Council, were being made against the backdrop of mounting European pressure on Israel. In May, for example, when Israel was busy with its fiftieth anniversary celebration, EU representatives warned the country that if it continued with the practice of labeling goods originating in the Occupied Territories with "Made in Israel", thus gaining tax free access to the EU markets, then the EU would consider introducing a general boycott of such goods. In Israel this EU threat was seen as a direct attack on Israeli economy. More salt was added to Israeli injuries in June, when

EU foreign ministers demanded the full implementation of the EU trade co-operation with the Palestinian authority, which in effect was reinforcing Palestinian attempts to break the grip of Israel on their economy.[49]

The already imperfect US-EU relations over the peace process has been mirrored by the deepening tensions in EU-Israeli relations, where EU institutions and its high-level personnel increasingly express their dissatisfaction with Israeli policies, and act on it. The European Parliament's resolution in March condemning Israel's settlement policy was one such action, as were the comments made at about the same time by the European Commission's commissioner responsible for the Middle East, Manuel Marin, and the EU governments' Middle East envoy, Miguel Moratinos, on Israel's policies in relation to East Jerusalem.[50]

It is self-evident that the contrast between the European and American policies and approaches towards the peace process could not be sharper.

To make matters worse, EU-US relations were deteriorating further over the US' policies towards Iran, Libya and Cuba, with Washington has being keen to isolate the three named countries internationally through the levying of unilateral secondary sanctions against them. The main bone of contention has been whether "containment" of Iran is a superior strategy to the EU's declared policy of "critical dialogue". In the absence of an EU-US dialogue on this issue, not surprisingly neither side has been prepared to compromise on its chosen path. It is noteworthy that despite the negative impact of the Mykonos trial on EU-Iranian relations, the fact that the verdict of the trial was seen as a moral victory for Washington, the reality that the Iranian regime has been engaged in campaigns against its opponents overseas, and that "critical dialogue" was suspended by the Eurpoeans, neither the US nor the EU have been able to capitalize on this crisis to find a co-ordinated and common policy towards Iran.[51] Disputes over the treatment of Iran is yet another instance of the rift between the NATO allies over MENA-related matters.

In sum then, the EU has increasingly been seeking a political role in the MENA region to match its overwhelming economic position in Eurasia. Brussels has calculated that an enhanced political profile in Eurasia is likely to allow the EU to expand and enhance its global economic standing in relation to its main competitor regional organizations, North American Free Trade Area and Asia Pacific Economic Co-operation in particular.

The political role the EU has been contemplating is a reflection not only of its importance as a major regional organization in the post-Cold War international order, but also a recognition of the need for the Union to respond positively to the problems it identifies on its southern and eastern peripheries. Political empowerment of the Union, furthermore, is a manifestation of the desire of some its members to develop the institutions of the EU in order for it to be able to act unitedly in the interest of the collective.

Beyond the Arab-Israeli Peace Process

More than ever before, however, the European interest in the MENA region was being underwritten by security concerns,[52] many of which can be regarded as geopolitical[53] and therefore constant - territorial proximity of northern and southern Mediterranean countries, boundaries of three of the world's important strategic chokepoints, Black Sea maritime competition, etc. - and others as unwelcome features of the post-Cold War order - growing ethno-nationalism, particularism, sectarianism, human migration, and territorialism.

In concrete terms, European security concerns were being articulated in terms of the negative impact that inter-state conflict in the region could have on European interests, the destabilizing impact of the MENA region's continuing militarization and economic difficulties, a population explosion which could devastate southern Europe, and the possible fall-out from the march of political Islam in the southern Mediterranean countries and in Europe itself, with its own large (and largely of MENA-origin) Muslim communities.[54] On most of these issues and the potential threat to Western interests of Mediterranean instabilities the US not only concurred with its European allies, but was in full agreement with them.[55]

Ironically, just as the military threat has begun to recede on the European continent itself, reinforced by the prospects of NATO's expansion eastwards, the Mediterranean theatre has been emerging as a new "rectangle" of instability in the 1990s. In the eastern Mediterranean, the Balkans have been on fire for the best part of the decade, Albania has been in turmoil for some time, and Turkish and Greek horns have locked over Cyprus and other bilateral problems. Within the Middle East subsystem dimension of the Mediterranean, despite the Arab-Israeli peace process, the new military relations which have been emerging between Israel and Turkey have been threatening the post-Gulf war regional balance of power, worrying Syria sufficiently for it to try and strengthen its strategic alliance with Iran, tightening its grip on Lebanon, while also developing its post-1990 politico-security ties with Egypt and Saudi Arabia. Elsewhere, Libya's international isolation, the Algerian civil war and inter-state tensions in the Red Sea sub-region (between Egypt and Sudan, and between Yemen and Eritrea) all have contributed to making the Mediterranean area a less safer place in the post-Cold War period. All of this has been taking place against a backdrop of European concerns over the expanding armouries of MENA countries in general in terms of sophisticated and lethal weapons acquisition, and continuing high military expenditures by the key Mediterranean countries in particular.

Country	Defence expenditure ($billion)	Advanced aircraft	Advanced naval systems	Advanced SSMs	Non-conventional weapons
Algeria	1.3	some	yes	no	chemical
Egypt	2.4	yes	yes	yes	chemical
Israel	7.2	yes	yes	yes	nuclear/chemical
Libya	1.4	yes	yes	yes	chemical
Morocco	1.4	some	no	no	no
Syria	2.1	yes	yes	yes	chemical
Turkey	6	yes	yes	no	not applicable

Table 5: Military Profile of Main Non-EU Mediterranean Armed Forces, mid-1990s
Sources: IISS, The Military Balance 1996/97 (London: Oxford University Press for IISS, 1996); Anthony H. Cordesman, Perilous Prospects: The Peace Process and the Arab-Israeli Military Balance (Boulder, Colorado: Westview Press, 1996).

The need for an European Mediterranean initiative, therefore, had been well understood by the EU countries for some time,[56] but the crowning moment of these efforts did not come until the middle of the decade, with the Barcelona conference of November 1995 in which 27 countries participated, including eight Arab countries (Algeria, Egypt, Jordan, Lebanon, Morocco, Palestine, Tunisia, and Syria), Israel, Turkey, Cyprus, and Malta. The conference set about sketching the political and economic guidelines for future relations between the EU and its Mediterranean neighbors around three axis: (a) a common area of peace and security; (b) an area of shared prosperity; and, (c) cultural ties and exchanges between civil societies.[57] With much optimism, the EU also announced the launch of a region-wide free trade zone by 2010, covering 27 countries and up to 800 million people.[58] The conference's momentum was to be sustained through a series of "15+12" meetings to implement the agreed plan of action.[59]

It is in the mid-1990s also that the EU's political engagement begin to show signs of deepening, with countries like France seeking a more active role for the Union in Middle Eastern affairs.[60] Using words reminiscent of the American superpower, the French articulated EU's new assessment of the situation in the following way: "The Middle East is of essential, even vital, interest to us [the EU]".[61]

Much of the European debate about the EU's future role in the MENA region, however, coincided with fairly public disputes between the United States and some of its European NATO partners over other issues; the command structures and future role of NATO in Europe, the desirability of its expansion eastwards, and NATO's peace-keeping operations on the European continent. For France at least, strengthening of the European role in all the above was a given, a position which did not endear Paris to Washington, and which also threatened to open up a rift with France's own, less intervention minded and pro-American, European partners.

Implications of the 1995 EU Expansion for the Middle East Region. The EU's "Atlantic-Alpine"[62] (to include Finland, Sweden and Austria) enlargement of 1995 has again shifted the geographical balance of the EU, this time away from the Mediterranean in the south and towards the center/northern territories of the continent. The impact of this geographical shift, however, may prove to be smaller than at first feared by the MENA states. Firstly, the main threat to the security risk of Europe still comes from the south.

Secondly, within the EU, the southern European countries exercise much power. They have been able to place the Mediterranean firmly on the EU's priority agenda and have gone as far to form "an effective lobby, often using their veto power to gain additional resources for specific regional projects".[63] Thirdly, the new EU members do not benefit from the political advantages which could be derived from the weight of large population (a total of 24 million between them) or economy. As such, they are unlikely to be able to influence the EU's agenda in the short term. Fourthly, while the new Atlantic-Alpinal members may have had a greater interest in consolidating the EU's growing links with Eastern Europe, they have shown little interest in blocking the Union's Mediterranean initiatives. Indeed, the 1995 Barcelona conference, which took place in the first year of their accession, has been a powerful glue for keeping the Mediterranean arena attached to all EU agendas.

Over time, however, and as the Eastern European countries begin joining NATO and the EU, new alliances within the Union could emerge, which could encourage direction of EU funds in an eastward direction and could marginalize the Mediterranean as a priority EU area. Transfer of economic resources will be followed by some transfer of political power within the EU itself, which will inevitably have a knock-on effect on the EU's relations with the MENA countries.

Conclusions

As we have seen, the EU has been engaged in a protracted campaign of dialogue with its eastern and southern neighbors. While initially it was distracted by the collapse of the Warsaw Pact, the EU has, since the mid-1990s, been trying hard to follow a two-track (one based on economics and the other on security structures) policy towards its neighbors. Much of the EU's recent efforts have concentrated on finding a workable formula for absorbing the Eastern European countries, at the same time as formulating a new relationship with the non-member Mediterranean states and the GCC countries. The pre-requisite for this complex strategy is a cohesive Union. But divisions within the EU, which surface at virtually every summit meeting of its political leaders these days, have been hampering its efforts to found the broad Euro-Mediterranean environment which Brussels has been planning, and which is regarded as vital for the geoeconomic supremacy of the EU in the new Eurasian hemisphere.[64] The issues the European leaders are discussing on the eve of the new millennium, therefore, are not new ones. These questions are to do with fusion, economic integration and political compatibility, which have been openly discussed at least since the early 1970s (when the EEC expanded to nine), when it was being argued by some that the convergence of the economic and the political in Europe was a "functional inevitability".[65]

Apart from its internal difficulties, several regional problems also continue to hamper the fulfilment of the EU's MENA strategy. Chief amongst these is what used to be known as the "Eastern Question",[66] but is today seen in the dilemmas the EU faces in the southern Mediterranean countries' desire to join the European club. Here is where the EU's relations with its Mediterranean neighbours could turn sour. Indicative of some of the problems which may lie ahead of the EU's integrative Mediterranean strategy are its turbulent relations with Turkey, whose 1987 application to join the Community was rejected in December 1989. The Commission stated that Turkey's application had raised "very large questions".[67] In a detailed response, it basically argued that apart from its domestic political problems (human rights violations, absence of pluralism and democratic government, etc.), as a poor, territorially separate and culturally distinct country Turkey was an unsuitable candidate for membership: "Turkey covers an area exactly half that of the old "Nine" and the population [that]... by the end of century will be far larger than any Community state. There are obvious cultural differences which are far stronger than those between, say, Portugal and the Community; moreover, Turkey, apart from its small border with Greece, will never be contiguous with the rest of the EC. It is considerably poorer than any of the other Mediterranean EC members. The implications for the regional and social funds of the Community are literally unthinkable, unless membership is treated simply as part of a political bloc".[68]

These issues have continued to dog the EU's relations with Turkey, which the EU recognizes as an strategically important country, providing bridges to the east (in the Crimea as well as the Caucasus and Central Asia) and the south (the Middle East). Unlike the southern Mediterranean countries, Turkey claims to be a fully fledged European country which has had a close association with the European entity as far back as 1963. A generation later, the EU still shows reluctance to entertain the idea of Turkish membership. In March 1997 the German foreign minister stated the view of several EU members when he said; "Turkey will not become a member of the European Union in the foreseeable future".[69] To the dismay of Turkey, such views have surfaced at the time when the EU has agreed to admit to its ranks eight Eastern European countries in the near future.[70]

With virtually every other non-member Mediterranean country similar problems are likely to arise, particularly where high population growth, economic incompatibility and underdevelopment are in evidence, and the footsteps of political Islam can be heard (as in Turkey itself). Ironically, the debate over the opening of the EU to Turkey and other Mediterranean countries is causing tensions in the Atlantic alliance (between the US and the EU) and amongst the Union partners themselves,[71] holding up the taking of uncomfortable decisions by the Europeans about their own future as well as the future of their southern allies.

To avoid some of these inherent problems, the EU has tried to check the Mediterranean countries' aspiration for membership through its Euro-Med. initiatives, provision of easier access to EU markets, etc. Such initiatives have been designed to create zones of prosperity around the EU in such a way as to slow down to a crawl the pace of accession of these countries to the Union. They are being looked at along with other proposals, which include giving preferential treatment on trade matters, or creating a "two-tier" Union (which has already been proposed by some Euro-sceptic members of the EU about their own future role within the Union) in which some of the Mediterranean countries become full members of certain policies and institutions but remain outside of others; one foot in Europe and another out.

It should be clear from my discussion that we can no longer comfortably speak of an exclusively "European" space when, by virtue of the security questions arising from the collapse of the Soviet Union and the disappearance of the communist European bloc, such western European-dominated entities as the OSCE, NATO and the Western European Union can now reach the shores of the non-European Mediterranean states as well as the very heart of Asia, and by definition much of the region we call the Middle East. If geographical separation of territories is proving impossible in the post-Cold War order, it is even more problematic to separate economies and economic processes. In today's interdependent, dynamic, and global economic system, power can be gained as swiftly as it can be lost. Regional bodies such as the EU have recognized the salient features of such a globalized economic environment, and are working hard to try and protect their own corner, and competitive niches, in this highly competitive system.[72] At the same time though, the EU is unique amongst today's regional bodies in having to secure its interests and security through extended contacts with its (rather well integrated) peripheries. It has in a sense to accommodate some of the aspirations of its neighbors if it is to secure its own long-term interests and address many of the security concerns arising from its fragile and unstable southern periphery. The EU's own prosperity, therefore, depends on its ability to delay the fission on its doorstep.

With these factors in mind, it can be argued that at least part of the EU's policy has been based on what may be termed "enlightened self-interest". The EU assumes that if the economies on its periphery do well, not only will they become more stable polities, and therefore less of a threat to the EU, but the EU as their main trading partner could also benefit enormously from their economic prosperity. At heart, the EU's policy appears to be based on the notion that economic development offers the only real barrier to political instability and social decay in the MENA region. There is much truth in this view. Consider one fact: in order to be able to check just the negative economic impact of population growth, for instance, the Arab world would need to grow by as much as six per cent a year. To actually develop their economies, however, and prepare themselves for the next century, the highly populated Middle Eastern states would need to achieve sustainable growth rates well above this target. They would need, in short, to be able to emulate the achievements of the Tiger economies of Asia.

In the last analysis, the dynamic energy which the EU needs to harness if it is to guide developments in its MENA periphery, and to keep this region engaged, is that of the Mediterranean basin; its human and capital assets, as well as its vast natural resources. This much may be obvious. But, in the face of the immense weight that globalization places on EU economies, and the problems associated with NATO's restructuring and expansion, the hardest conundrum for the EU to solve will be how to manage its alliance with the US, consolidate its own vertical integration, and accommodate its planned horizontal expansion in the early twenty first century, while at the same time keeping what Jacob Kol refers to as its "pyramid of preferences"[73] - an architecture which is vital for EU's future relations with the MENA countries - from collapsing.

As we approach the twenty first century, the real test for the EU will be how to define the parameters which would allow it to assure its own solidarity without necessarily fragmenting the cohesion of its non-European neighbors.

Notes

1. Fred Halliday, "The End of the Cold War and International Relations: Some Analytical and Theoretical Conclusions", in Ken Booth and Steve Smith eds, International Relations Theory Today, (Cambridge: Polity Press, 1995), p. 44.

2. For some stimulating perspectives in the globalization debate see Malcolm Waters, Globalization, (London: Routledge, 1995), Paul Hirst and Grahame Thompson, Globalization in Question, (Cambrige: Polity Press, 1996), and Ian Clark, Globalization and Fragmentation: International Relations in the Twentieth Century, (Oxford: Oxford University Press, 1997).

3. For other definitions and detailed analyses of the phenomena of regionalism see Louise Fawcett and Andrew Hurrell eds, Regionalism in World Politics: Regional Organization and International Order, (Oxford: Oxford University Press, 1997).

4. Ronald Steel, "Europe after the Superpowers", in Nicholas X. Rizopoulos ed., Sea-Changes: American Foreign Policy in a World Transformed, (New York: Council on Foreign Relations, 1990), p. 7.

5. For detailed analyses of the impact of the Kuwait crisis on western European states and their security and strategic thinking see Nicole Gnesotto and John Roper (eds), Western Europe and the Gulf, (Paris: Institute for Security Studies of WEU, 1992).

6. Ernest Wistrich, The United States of Europe, (London: Routledge, 1994). See also Europe Without Frontiers - The Completing of the Internal Market, (Luxembourg: Office for Official Publications of the Communities, 1989).

7. Richard McAllister, From EC to EU: A Historical and Political Survey, (London: Routledge, 1997).

8. Martin J. Dedman, The Origins and Development of the European Union, 1945-95 (London: Routledge, 1996).

9. The EU accounted not only for just over 30 per cent of world output in 1995, but also for 20 per cent of world trade as well. See The Economist, 29 March 1997, p. 118.

10. Denis O'Hearn, "Global Restructuring, Transnational Corporations and the "European Periphery": What has Changed?", in David A. Smith and József

Böröcz eds, A New World Order? Global Transformations in the Late Twentieth Century, (Westport, Connecticut: Praeger, 1995), p. 71.

11. The rather apt term, economic balkanisation, has been borrowed from an Economist Intelligence Unit report entitled, "The Economic Balkanisation of Europe", European Trends, Vol. 2, 1983, pp. 31-5.

12. This term comes from Michael Zern, "The Challenges of Globalization and Individualization: A View from Europe", in Hans-Henrik Holm and Georg Sórensen eds, Whose World Order? Uneven Globalization and the End of the Cold War, (Boulder, Colorado: Westview Press, 1995), pp. 137-63.

13. Peter A. Gourevitch, "The Pacific Rim: Current Debates", The Pacific Region: Challenges to Policy and Theory, The Annals of the American Academy of Political and Social Science Vol. 505, September 1989, pp. 8-23.

14. A reality which may not be apparent by international trade statistics, in which the MENA region accounts for 3.6 per cent of world trade (below the Latin American and Eastern European totals). See Sinclair Road, "World Trade and the Middle East", Middle East International, No. 532, 16 August 1996, pp. 18-20.

15. Halford Mackinder ed., Democratic Ideals and Reality, (New York: W. W. Norton, 1962).

16. Frederick S. Starr, "Making Euroasia Stable", Foreign Affairs, Vol. 75, No. 1, January/February 1996, pp. 80-92.

17. Robert S. Chase, et. al., "Pivotal States and US Strategy", Foreign Affairs, Vol. 75, No. 1, January/February 1996, pp. 33-51.

18. Despite the Arab-Israeli peace process, in every year since 1990, the official end of the Cold War era, MENA related tensions have in one way or another threatened the stability of the international ssytem. It is not too surprising that of the six so-called "pariah" states in the world in the mid-1990s, four were Middle Eastern ones (Iran, Iraq, Libya and Sudan).

19. For a useful survey of foreign investment in the MENA region see Raed Safadi, Global Challenges and Opportunities facing MENA Countries at the Dawn of the 21st Century, Working Paper Series (Cairo: Economic Research Forum, No. 9624).

20. See IISS' Strategic Survey, 1991-1992 (London: Brassey's, 1992), p. 5.

21. For a discussion of the region's new restructuring phase see Yezid Sayigh, ""System Breakdown" in the Middle East?", in Martin Kramer ed., Middle East Lectures - Number Two, (Tel Aviv: Tel Aviv University, 1997), pp. 57-68.

22. Muhammad Faour, The Arab World after Desert Storm, (Washington, DC: United States Institute of Peace, 1993); Anoushiravan Ehteshami, "The Arab States and the Middle East Balance of Power", in James Gow ed., Iraq, the Gulf Conflict and the World Community, (London: Brassey's, 1993), pp. 55-73.

23. Apart from the obvious interest in the Persian Gulf region's hydrocarbon resources and markets, we can cite another attraction: it has been calculated by the Merrill Lynch that the GCC's 185,000 millionaires dispose of wealth of around $718 billion, with some two-thirds of it amassed by Saudi Arabia's 78,000 millionaires. Gulf States Newsletter, Vol. 22, No. 557, 24 March 1997, p. 10.

24. See Nader Entessar, "The Post-Cold War US Military Doctrine: Implications for Iran", The Iranian Journal of International Affairs, Vol. VIII, No. 2, Summer 1996, pp. 393-419.

25. For some of the ideas on this see Gerd Nonneman ed., The Middle East and Europe: The Search for Stability and Integration, (London: Federal Trust, 1993).

26. Lionel Barber and Bernard Gray, "Nato Turns its Attention to Turbulent Moslem South", Financial Times, 9 February 1995.

27. Michel Chatelus, "Economic Co-operation Among Southern Mediterranean Countries", in Roberto Aliboni, et. al. eds, Security Challenges in the Mediterranean Region, (London: Frank Cass, 1996), p. 85; Bichara Khader, "Les Échanges économiques Euro-Arabes", in Nazih N. Ayubi ed., Distant Neighbours: The Political Economy of Relations Between Europe and the Middle East/North Africa, (Reading: Ithaca Press, 1995), pp. 21-35. According to the Arab League, inter-Arab trade in 1992 stood at 8.6 per cent of the Arab countries' total trade. See "Euro-Arab Relations", Arabfile, Vol. 3, Issue 3, June 1993, pp. 5-7.

28. Tim Niblock, "North-South Socio-economic Relations in the Mediterranean", in Roberto Aliboni, et. al. eds, Security Challenges in the Mediterranean Region, (London: Frank Cass, 1996), pp. 115-136.

29. IMF, Direction of Trade Statistics, (Washington, DC: IMF, 1996).

30. Rodney Wilson, "The Economic Relations of the Middle East: Toward Europe or Within the Region?", The Middle East Journal, Vol. 48, No. 2, Spring 1994, pp. 268-87.

31. Roberto Aliboni, European Security Across the Mediterranean, Chaillot Papers 2, (Paris: Institute for Security Studies of WEU, March 1991).

32. "European Integration and the Integration of the World Economy", British Journal of International Studies, Vol. 3, No. 1, April 1977, p. 65.

33. Desmond Dinan, "The European Community, 1978-93", in Pierre-Henri Laurent ed., The European Community: To Maastricht and Beyond, The Annals of the American Academy of Political and Social Science, Vol. 531, January 1994, pp. 10-24.

34. For some early predictions on the impact of the treaty on the MENA region see Ellen Laipson, "Europe's Role in the Middle East: Enduring Ties, Emerging Opportunities", The Middle East Journal, Vol. 44, No. 1, Winter 1990, pp.7-17.

35. "The European Union and the Maghreb", in Richard Gillespie ed., Mediterranean Politics, Vol. I (London: Pinter Pubs, 1994), pp. 22-45.

36. "The Treaty of Maastricht: What it Says and What it Means", The Independent, Sunday 11 October 1992.

37. At the 34th session of the Federation of Arab Chambers of Commerce and Industry meeting in March 1997, for example, it was agreed that the Arab world would need to create a single trade and business environment, a common market of its own, if it was to emulate the successes of the European model. See Gulf States Newsletter, Vol. 22, No. 557, 24 March 1997, p. 10.

38. Emma C. Murphy, "The Arab-Israeli Conflict and the New World Order", in Haifa Jawad ed., The Middle East in the New World Order, (London: Macmillan, 1994), pp. 81-98.

39. See, for instance, EC Support for the Middle East Peace Process, (Brussels: Commission of the European Communities, 29 September 1993).

40. Francois D'Alancon, "The EC Looks to a New Middle East", Journal of Palestine Studies, Vol. XXIII, No. 2, Winter 1994, pp. 41-51.

41. The Commission Proposes the Establishment of a Euro-Mediterranean Partnership, (Brussels: European Commission, 19 October 1994).

42. Ibid., p. 1.

43. The re-assessment process resulted in a major report (with policy recommendations) produced in 1989 (updated in 1990) on the south, entitled Redirecting the Community's Mediterranean Policy, (Brussels: European Commission, 1989). The EC Council adopted the "New Mediterranean Policy" advocated by the Commission in December 1990.

44. Claire Spencer, The Maghreb in the 1990s, Adelphi Paper 274, (London: Brassey's for IISS, February 1993).

45. Rosemary Hollis, "The Politics of Israeli-European Economic Relations", Israel Affairs, Vol. 1, No. 1, Autumn 1994, pp. 118-134.

46. Shada Islam, "Europe Spurned", Middle East International, No. 535, 4 October 1996, pp. 6-7.

47. Ironically, in early 1996 the Israeli Labour government had welcomed the EU's more interventionist policy in the Middle East, hoping that through its trade negotiations with Syria it could encourage Damascus to return to the negotiating table.

48. The resolution was drafted by France, Portugal, Sweden and the United Kingdom. The US veto in the Security Council resulted in the tabling of an alternative resolution to the General Assembly, which was adopted on 13 March by a vote of 130 in favour and two against, with two abstentions. See News Summary, (NS/4/97) (London: UN Information Centre, 1-14/3/1997).

49. Journal of Palestine Studies, Vol. XXVIII, No. 1, Autumn 1998.

50. Shada Islam, "EU and Israel: Battered Relationship", Middle East International, No. 546, 21 March 1997, pp. 6-7.

51. The Mykonos trial refers to a four-year long legal and criminal investigation in Germany which ended on 10 April 1997. A Berlin court ruling on that day implicated Iran's senior leaders in the murder of four Iranian Kurds

in a Berlin restaurant in 1992, causing an immediate rapture in EU-Iranian relations. Ironically, the EU's steps to suspend critical dialogue and to reduce its diplomatic exchanges with Tehran coincided with the Clinton administration's review of its Iran policy and calls in the US for application of a more constructive policy towards the Islamic Republic.

52. See Richard Latter, Mediterranean Security, (London: HMSO, December 1991); Roberto Aliboni, European Security Across the Mediterranean, Chaillot Papers 2, (Paris: Institute for Security Studies of WEU, March 1991).

53. Bichara Khader, L'Europe et la Mediterrane: gopolitique de la proximit, (Paris: L'Harmattan, 1994).

54. Ghassan Salam, "Torn Between the Atlantic and the Mediterranean: Europe and the Middle East in the Post-Cold War Era", The Middle East Journal, Vol. 48, No. 2, Spring 1994, pp. 226-49; George Joff, "Low-Level Violence and Terrorism", in Roberto Aliboni, et. al. eds, Security Challenges in the Mediterranean Region, (London: Frank Cass, 1996), pp. 139-60.

55. Rodrigo de Rato, "Co-operation and Security in the Mediterranean", North Atlantic Assembly - Political Committee, (Brussels: North Atlantic Assembly, October 1995), pp. 1-16.

56. Werner Weidenfeld ed., Europe and the Middle East, (Gütersloh, Germany: Bertelsmann Foundation, 1995).

57. The Barcelona Declaration, (Barcelona: Conferencia EuroMediterranea, 1995).

58. In early 1996 the European Parliament had approved the admission of Turkey to the European Customs Union, and by November 1996 the EU had reached new "partnership pacts" with several Mediterranean countries, including Israel, Morocco and Tunisia.

59. Middle East Economic Digest, 24 November 1995.

60. France's pressures on its EU partners to adopt a more active political role in the Middle East had already led to the appointment of an EU special envoy (Miguel Moratinos) for the Middle East in 1996, the Union's first such appointment.

61. The French foreign minister (Hervé de Charette) quoted in Shada Islam, "Europe a Go-between?", Middle East International, No. 537, 8 November 1996, p. 5.

62. Term used by Martin Dedman, op. cit., p. 128.

63. Ronald S. Asmus, F Stephen Larrabee, Ian O. Lesser, "Mediterranean Security: New Challenges, New Tasks", NATO Review, Vol. 44, No. 3, May 1996, p. 27.

64. Issues such as monetary union, a single European foreign and security policy, the extension of the EU eastwards, future role of NATO in Europe, are some of the obstacles in the way of creating a unified, single, federated, regional body that the EU has the potential to become.

65. See Hugh Corbet, op. cit., pp. 55-69.

66. J. A. R. Marriott wrote in 1921 that the "root of the ["Eastern Question"] is to be found in the presence, embedded in the living flesh of Europe, of an alien substance - the Ottoman Turk. Akin to the European family neither in creed, in race, in language, in social custom, nor in political aptitudes and traditions, the Ottomans have long presented to the European Powers a problem, now tragic, now comic, now bordering on burlesque, but always baffling and paradoxical. How to deal with this alien substance has been for five hundred years the essence and core of the problem of the Near East". Europe and Beyond: A Preliminary Survey of World-Politics in the Last Half-Century 1870-1920, (London: Methuen, 1921), p. 47.

67. Turkey, it should be remembered, has enjoyed advantages (active membership of the NATO alliance, control of vast tracts of continental European territory in the past and a long tradition of interaction with other European civilizations) which today's aspirants from the Mediterranean do not enjoy.

68. Quoted by Meltem Müftüler, "Turkey and the European Community: An Uneasy Relationship", Turkish Review Quarterly Digest, Vol. 7, No. 33, Autumn 1993, p. 39.

69. Stephen Kinzeer, "Kinkel Tells Turkey it's not Ready for EU", International Herald Tribune, 27 March 1997.

70. Lionel Barber, John Barham and Bruce Clark, "Turkey: Nato Enlargement Threat Over EU", Financial Times, 20 January 1997.

71. Sarah Helm, "EU Smoothes the Path to Membership", Independent, 17 March 1997. In response to the European view, US State Department spokesman, Nicholas Burns, stated that "We strongly believe the European Union should allow for the possibility of Turkish membership... Turkey's future, we believe, ought to be grounded in Europe". Reuter, 11 March 1997.

72. The establishment of an European Economic Area, which arose from an agreement between the EC and the European Free Trade Association in May 1992 is another testimony to the EU's strategy. The EEA is the world's largest and most integrated economic zone.

73. "Trade Liberalization under GATT and by the EC: Implications for Israel", in Ephraim Ahiram and Alfred Tovias eds, Whither EU-Israeli Relations? Common and Divergent Interests, (Frankfurt am Main: Peter Lang, 1995), p. 66.

Chapter 10

Patterns of Reorientation in the Foreign Policies of Japan and China Toward the Middle East in the Post-Cold War Diplomacy: A Reflection on the Regional Determinants

Touraj Noroozi

Introduction

The era of post Cold War diplomacy alludes to the precarious geopolitical situations within which states undertake to reorient their foreign policies. In fact, the modalities through which a state's pattern of external relations change entail two important trends. These trends denote either an ordinary foreign policy change or a substantial intent to recast the role of a state within the global arena. Of course, in this era one cannot ignore how rapidly states do reorient their foreign policies. Events of this nature abound in our present memory. Russia's vacillations between ideological reassertions and tactical retrenchments in the international arena, old foes coming to terms in the Middle East leaving their signatures hastily on the peace accords, America's turnabouts in pursuing her Bosnian policy, all demonstrate the rapidity with which foreign policy reorientations have taken place since the end of the cold war.

Yet, there is a context in which these reorientations occur. This context embodies a complex combination of domestic, regional, and systemic factors that policy makers take into consideration in case of a foreign policy change. Although the systemic influences on a state's foreign policy change dictate certain external pressures, the internal workings of foreign policy accentuate the immediate strategic concerns of a regional character. Indeed, the regional determinants of foreign policy reorientation allude to a "regional context" wherein the systemic and the internal determinants intermingle. This context represents a normative environment that embodies the rules and norms that influence the calculations and goals of a particular state ranging from matters of prestige and nationalism to those of international trade.[1]

This study draws upon the "regional context " through which the foreign policy reorientations of China and Japan toward the Middle East are explained in terms of the regional determinants of the Middle East in post Cold War diplomacy. In the post Cold War era, the strategic dynamics of the Middle East region can be emphasized in three different arenas: the Gulf War of 1991, the Arab-Israeli conflict, and the revolutionary Islamism of Iran. The reason for this kind of emphasis lies in the strategic value each arena embodies regionally and globally.

Above all, the geostrategic dynamics of the region entail the security of world energy resources by safeguarding the free movement of oil from the Gulf countries, which necessitates a solid balance of power in the region. This balance has been threatened in the post Cold War era by three major events: the Iranian revolution of 1979, the Gulf War of 1991, and the political militancy of the Palestinian uprising since 1987, and the consequent Arab-Israeli peace process. In addition to their geostrategic components, these conflicts are also driven by rival ideologies that have caused international friction. Accordingly, such rival ideologies as the Ba'thist Arab nationalism of Iraq and the revolutionary Islamism of Iran have been competing in establishing their hegemony in the region. Other conflicts of the region are imbued with similar ethnonationalist and religious overtones that are disquieting to the regional balance of power.

The Middle East region is particularly important to the global strategies of China and Japan in terms of their commitments to the international power structure in the post Cold War era. Japan remains more or less committed to the power structure of North-Atlanticism reflected in her special relationship with the United States in the post

Patterns of Reorientation in the Foreign Policies of Japan   273
and China Toward the Middle East in the Post-Cold War
Diplomacy: A Reflection on the Regional Determinants

Cold War era. China endeavors to maintain its image as a maverick world power by committing herself to the workings of interdependence, utilizing her leverage at the United Nations.

In this case, regionally motivated foreign policy restructuring is germane to the situational expediency and to the role both North-Atlanticist Japan and interdependent China assume when a regional crisis occur. The regional determinants of Chinese and Japanese foreign policies in the Middle East seem significant, since they reflect not only the perplexing interconnectedness between the states of the Middle East region but also the intensity of "interaction" between them as regional diplomacy interplays with the global power relationships. The Gulf War of 1991 bears witness both to the intensity of interaction among the regional states and to the interplay between those states and the systemic power structure   of which China and Japan are true embodiments.[2]

Japan's Middle Eastern Policy: Reorientation within North-Atlanticism

Historically the Middle East has been a vital supplier of energy resources for Japan despite the lack of strategic encounters between the Middle East and Japan prior to the energy crisis of 1973. When the Arab producers cut their oil production by 25 percent in November 1973, Japan panicked since they categorized her as a non-friendly country. In reaction to the disruption of energy supply in the Middle East, Japan decided to dissociate herself from the United States. By the end of November, Japan's sudden pro-Arab shift had resulted in an increased diplomatic presence in the Arab states. The United States failed to provide Japan with a clear cut and concrete assurance about the future security of energy supply. Japan viewed this stance of her ally as a calculated response in her objective assessment of the energy situation.[3] Throughout the seventies, Japan continued to manifest a growing interest in playing a more active role in the conflicts of the region by extending her North-Atlanticist diplomatic arm.

During the 1979-81 American embassy hostage crisis in Iran, Japan cooperated with her West European allies to cope with the crisis diplomatically. The eruption of war between Iran and Iraq in 1980 was another moment of panic for Japan since the tanker routes in and around the Straits of Hormuz were jeopardized. To secure freedom of navigation in the Persian Gulf, Japan's foreign minister, Shintaro Abe, visited both countries in August 1983, and succeeded in preventing further escalation of the conflict by reassuring both sides of Japan's continued neutrality in the war. Furthermore, in 1984, Japan rebuffed an Arab League appeal to reduce her economic ties with Iran.[4] Indeed, Japan was the only global economic power able to talk to both sides, since she had reasserted her strategic alliance with North-Atlanticism in 1982. In response to the changes in the international environment since the Soviet invasion of Afghanistan and the military takeover in Poland, Prime Minister Zenko stated that Japan would ally itself more closely with the United States and the European allies.[5]

However, between 1986-88 Japan was pushed into a corner by her North-Atlanticist allies when the latter sent their fleet to the Gulf, internationalizing the regional conflict. Understanding the substance of her North-Atlanticist commitments, Japan focused on the implementation of legal restraints in defense issues.

Post Cold-War Diplomacy of Japan in the Middle East

In the historic downfall of the socialist regimes throughout 1989-1990, Japan recognized an opportunity to bolster her image as a more independent and emerging North-Atlanticist power. Japan's impetus to seek a role as a world power with international prestige was certainly deducted from specific strategic calculations: (a) diminished Soviet threat, (b) reduced American pressure on Japan's diplomacy, and (c) the consolidation of Japan's role as an economic hegemon in post Cold War diplomacy.

Reacting to the over-excitement resulting from the rapidity of events which brought an end to the Cold War, Prime Minister Kaifu Toshiki declared Japan's "motivated" diplomacy as the proper means to cope with the emerging post Cold War international situation. According to Toshiki, in the post Cold War era "the role of military might in the balance of power is diminishing and the importance of dialogue and cooperation is growing."[6] This foreign policy reorientation was short-lived, since the Iraqi invasion of Kuwait on August 1990 "punctured this ascending balloon and brought it swiftly back to earth."[7]

The Gulf crisis of 1990-91 shattered Japan's hope for a transitory period in the post Cold War diplomacy in which Japan could adopt a more independent foreign policy rather than merely reacting to the North-Atlanticist security impositions. Yet, this was not the first time

Patterns of Reorientation in the Foreign Policies of Japan 275
and China Toward the Middle East in the Post-Cold War
Diplomacy: A Reflection on the Regional Determinants

when the political crisis in the Middle East region had affected Japan's diplomatic deliberations.

The nature of Japan's response to the Gulf crisis was, however, induced by two major determinants of the post bipolar structure of the international system. First, Japan herself faced a puzzling situation of strategic uncertainty, for the removal of the East-West schism had created misgivings about the future power structure of the globe. Second, Japan had reservations about the course the United States would take in light of the overwhelming rigidities of its fiscal and energy policies. Furthermore, Japan was also worried about the complexities of her strategic relationship with the United States, particularly in regard to the disputed issue of manufacturing, competitiveness and the increasing US pressure on Japan. In fact, corporate power has emerged as a crucial key factor in Japan's foreign policy. In dealing with American impositions and pressures, the Japanese decision makers' debates over the adoption of proactive or reactive diplomacy have always been overshadowed by the exigencies laid down by the corporate power within Japan.

Japan and the Gulf War

Soon after the eruption of the Gulf War, Japan acted consistently in supporting the passage of a series of security council resolutions demanding Iraq's unconditional withdrawal. Even before the ratification of U.N. resolutions, Japan had decided voluntarily to impose economic sanctions against Iraq.

While the Japanese business community in Baghdad took action to protect the American hostages in Kuwait, the Japanese government, as an important contributor to Iraq's industrialization, exhausted all diplomatic leverages to persuade Iraq to end the aggression. However, Prime Minister Kaifu's meeting with Iraqi first deputy premier, Taha Yassin Ramadan, in Amman in October 1990 may have convinced the Japanese leaders to abandon further diplomatic initiatives in finding a peaceful solution.

The opposition of the majority of states in the Middle East region to the Iraqi invasion of Kuwait and the global isolation of Iraq at the time, seemed to Japan as credible assurances not to worry about the disruption of oil in the region. In fact, Prime Minister Kaifu's personal message to the Iraqi president, Saddam Hussein, in December 1990 contained a harsh tone since it dissuaded Mr. Hussein from "going down the same tragic path as Imperial Japan in the early 1940's."[8]

Therefore, after the United States and the other North-Atlanticist allies attacked Iraq militarily in January 1991, Japan's diplomatic response toward the Gulf War was limited to support of the U.N. resolutions isolating Iraq. Furthermore, Japan allocated eleven billion dollars for non-military, logistic support for the coalition forces, as well as an additional two billion in aid to the neighboring states in the Persian Gulf.[9]

The Gulf War drew Japan into a post Cold War strategic situation in which, due to her North-Atlanticist commitments of a non-military nature, she had to assume political and security responsibilities conforming to her economic prowess. Crucial to this conformity was the strategic issue of the free movement of oil in the Persian Gulf that motivaed Japan to contain Iraq so willingly.

The Arab-Israeli Conflict in Japan's Post Cold-War Diplomacy

In November 1973, immediately after its active diplomatic involvement in the Middle East, Japan called for a comprehensive peace to be concluded between the Arab states and Israel within the framework of the implementation of U.N. Security Council Resolution 242, stipulating Israeli withdrawal from Arab territories. This was a direct consequence of Japan's foreign policy reorientation toward the Middle East induced by the energy crisis that alerted Japan to the potential dangers of prolonged disruption in the oil flow from that region. This was more or less Japan's declared policy regarding the Arab-Israeli conflict until February 1977 when Japan allowed the Palestine Liberation Organization (PLO) to open a liaison office in Tokyo.

This decision was motivated by the American involvement in brokering a peace treaty between Egypt and Israel that culminated in the Camp David summit between the leaders of the United States, Egypt, and Israel. The Camp David Accords on the Palestinian question and the Egyptian-Israeli peace were signed in September 1978. In the same period Japanese Premier Taeko Fukuda's trip to Saudi Arabia produced a communique calling for the Israeli withdrawal from the Arab territories, including the Arab sector of Jerusalem.

Patterns of Reorientation in the Foreign Policies of Japan   277
and China Toward the Middle East in the Post-Cold War
Diplomacy: A Reflection on the Regional Determinants

During the early eighties, Japan exercised a policy of evenhandedness in relations with both sides. In 1981, PLO chairman, Yasser Arafat, visited Japan. In 1985, Foreign Minister Abe met with Arafat at a time when Tokyo was persuading Israel's Premier Shamir to accept a plan for a Middle East peace conference that would include the United States and the former Soviet Union.

Three years later, the PLO's shift in renouncing terrorism and in accepting Israel's right to exist precipitated Foreign Minister Uno's trip to Jordan, Israel, Egypt, and Syria. In this trip, he enunciated Japan's policy as one of "Contributing to a better world", entailing the facilitation of the peace process between the Arabs and Israelis.[10] In October 1989, an official invitation was extended to chairman Arafat. This gesture was counterbalanced when Israeli Defense Minister Moshe Arens was invited to Japan in the November of the same year, at a time when Israeli-Japanese trade had suddenly increased by more than fifty percent from 1986.

As a result, in June 1991 Japan's foreign Minister Taro Nakayana made a trip to Israel in response to the latter's official request to Japan to ensure that Japanese commercial firms would ignore the Arab boycott of Israel. Japan raised the issue with her other North-Atlanticist allies at the London summit of industrial democracies in July 1991. Consequently, the summit decided that the boycott was undesirable.[11]

Indeed, many regional affairs of the 1980s such as the Iran-Iraq war, the post-1973 oil glut, the Gulf War, and the PLO's acceptance of Israel's right to exist, had reduced the likelihood of triggering an Arab backlash against Japan. In 1990 Japan relied on the Middle East for seventy percent of its oil-based energy supply. Realizing all these regional exigencies, Japan still had a great concern for stability in the Middle East and the free follow of oil. In light of this, when she was invited by the United States and Russia to attend the peace conference, Japan played an active role in the Madrid Peace Conference in October 1991, pledging to disburse two hundred million dollars to assist the Palestinians.

Japan's support for Palestinian self-determination in the aftermath of the Gulf War conformed to the American policy of bringing Israel to the peace table at a time when the PLO's vacillation on the Kuwait crisis had diminished its credibility with many Arab governments in the region. In fact, America's active role in promoting the peace Accords strengthened the moderate Arab states such as Egypt and Jordan, who were actively involved in the peace process. The US involvement had also the blessing and the support of the oil producing Gulf states that would ultimately secure the oil supply lines for Japan.[12]

Japan and the Gulf Oil

In the decade following the Iranian Revolution, Japan's oil imports declined by 37%, but gradually moved back to record levels.[13] This, like the events of 1973, convinced Japan that she had little alternative but to rely on the Middle East region as her major source of energy. Therefore, Japan's relations with Saudi Arabia became a matter of paramount importance, or as the Saudi oil minister, Hisham Nazer, once put it, "Japan's policy is based on reciprocal security."[14] Japan's interest in downstream distribution of oil products in Saudi Arabia denotes the fact that any disruption in supplies by the Saudis would affect the latter's investments in the downstream activities.

Since 1994, Saudi Arabia has acquired a major stake in three Japanese refineries that will be enhanced by the possible construction of a new joint venture petrochemical complex in Saudi Arabia. Furthermore, a Japanese owned company named the Arabian Oil Company (A.O.C.), has gained the concession until the year 2000 for Saudi cooperation in the divided zone (formerly neutral zone) at the Saudi-Kuwait border. The company is engaged in producing Saudi crude output totaling 200,000 b/d with the prospect of more investments in the six countries of the Gulf Cooperation Council (G.C.C.). Overall, Japan wants to ensure supply security even in times of crisis by increasing her investments in these countries.[15]

Japan has also shown great interest in natural gas investments in the Gulf area since Abu Dhabi began supplying Japan with 2.5 million tons of liquefied natural gas each year. This figure was doubled after April 1994 following the completion of an expansion project on Abu Dhabi's Das Island. Yet, Japan desires to invest heavily in Iran's liquefied natural gas once Iran resolves its conflict with other North-Atlanticist powers. Clearly, US-Iran impasse imposes some constraints on Japan's commercial interests in Iran.[16]

Iran in Japan's post-cold war diplomacy

Understanding the vicissitudes of Japanese-Iranian relations in the post cold war diplomacy necessitates a clear examination of the

Patterns of Reorientation in the Foreign Policies of Japan   279
and China Toward the Middle East in the Post-Cold War
Diplomacy: A Reflection on the Regional Determinants

intricacies of US-Japan strategic entanglements within their North-Atlanticist alignment. Those intricacies may be pronounced in terms of weaknesses and intensity, depending on the nature of US-Iranian relations. In fact, the current triangular relationship between the United States, Japan, and Iran has often complicated the consistency of Japan's foreign policy toward Iran. In this relationship, Japan needs to address her North-Atlanticist commitments against the backdrop of inimical US-Iranian relations.

For strategically ordained regional reasons, Japan does not wish to see Iran isolated. Persian Gulf crude is vital to Japan's economic well-being. Almost 80 percent of Japan's oil supply comes from the Persian Gulf, only 10 percent of which is from Iran. Nevertheless, in the Japanese perception, Iran is not only regarded as an oil-based power, but one which plays an important role in maintaining the stability of the region. This may constitute an important pawn in Japan's strategic reasoning with the United States in their mutual goal of securing stability and the supply of oil. Thus, it is extremely important to view the degree of Japan's level of compliance with the American line of policy toward Iran. First, it was during the American embassy hostage crisis in Iran (1979-81) that Japan started to cope with Iran's militancy along with her other North-Atlanticist allies. About the same time, the Tokyo based conglomerate Mitsui ended its 4.5 billion dollar project that entailed the construction of thirteen petrochemical plants at Bandar Khomeini in the vicinity of the Persian Gulf.[17]

In spite of this, during the eighties, Japan remained a major trading partner of Iran, trying to serve as a mediator in the troubled US-Iranian relationship. As Japan's ubiquitous tendency to moderate Iran's political militancy never diminished during the Iran-Iraq war, Japan was the only economic power who could talk to both sides in bringing an end to the war. But a fruitful pursuance of Japan's diplomacy in ending the war was substantially overshadowed by the militarization of the war by her North-Atlanticist allies (the United States and the European Community), as they sent their fleet to the Gulf region, where tanker routes had been placed in jeopardy in and around the Straits of Hormuz.

Examining the impact of legal restraints on defense issues, Japan proposed a high precision navigational guidance system to G.C.C. at Japan's expense, making Gulf navigation safer. Japan also contributed 10 million dollars to finance the U.N. Iran-Iraq military observer group founded in August 1988 when the war had finally ended. With the end of the Iran-Iraq War, Japanese-Iranian relations entered a new phase as the post-Khomeini era coincided with that of post Cold War diplomacy. Under the presidency of Akbar Hashimi Rafsanjani Iran focused on reconstruction of its economic-industrial base, following a more pragmatic foreign policy.

During 1990-92, Japan became Iran's second largest trading partner after Germany. In November 1992, Japan resumed aid loans to Iran amounting to 280 million dollars for a hydroelectric project, thus defending Iran's right to high technology against American apprehensions about the expansion of relations between Tokyo and Tehran.[18]

Even in the case of the Salman Rushdie affair, although Japan defended freedom of speech, she also maintained that the customs of other states should be respected. Yet, Iran-Japan relations must be considered within the triangular relationship of Japan, Iran, and the United States. During the Bush administration Iran and the United States were responding to each other's strategic concerns. Iran's help for the release of American hostages in Lebanon and her neutrality in the Gulf war positively affected Japan's expansion of relations with Iran. However, improvements in US-Iranian relations had failed to materialize by the end of Bush presidency.

With the advent of the Clinton administration Japan found herself in an embarrassing situation over her Iran policy. Japan was Pressured by the United States to contain Iran due to the latter's alleged support of international terrorism and its secret plans to build a nuclear bomb. American intelligence supposedly had provided Japan with "evidence" in support of its charges.[19]

During 1993-94 however, Japan remained reluctant to support American containment of Iran despite the fact that the oil glut in the market had convinced her that the Iranian crude was not totally indispensable to Japan. In the thinking of Japan's foreign policy makers, this reluctance was due to Iran's strategic importance in maintaining stability in the Persian Gulf region.

Nevertheless, given Japan's historically motivated sensitivities toward nuclear proliferation and bombing, the United States used its intelligence to convince Japan to join the American policy of containing Iran despite the Japanese policy makers' prudent doubt of the veracity of the American intelligence information and analysis. This doubt ultimately affected Japan's intention of extending a 1.8 billion dollar loan to Iran in four parts by 1994. Reacting to American pressures, Japan delayed the second installment of the loan. Since then

Patterns of Reorientation in the Foreign Policies of Japan   281
and China Toward the Middle East in the Post-Cold War
Diplomacy: A Reflection on the Regional Determinants

the Khuzestan dam project has been frozen despite Iran's objections. In 1995, Japan's premier Murayama indicated that his country would ignore American objections and go through with the delayed second installment which was necessary to support the moderates in Iran.[20]

Soon after Murayama's statement Washington began to supply Tokyo with sensitive intelligence about Iran's activities. This was later followed by Clinton's executive order banning economic transactions with Iran that caused great controversy between the United States and her North-Atlanticist allies. But Japan remains reluctant to jeopardize her economic stake in Iran and that country's strategic significance in maintaining the security of the region. Although Washington has asked for the outright cancellation of the loan, Japan has chosen to freeze the project instead, at a time when the United States prefers to pressure Iran to change its behavior by creating economic pains for that country. Japan feels that it is dangerous to totally cut relations with Iran as she "is caught between the United States and Iran when an enemy of your friend is a friend".[21] In other words, Japan finds it very difficult to reconcile her North-Atlanticist commitments with her vital dependence on Persian Gulf oil and Iran's strategic role in securing the stability of the region. It denotes a role conflict in Japan's Middle Eastern policy within the context of the current triangular relationship between the United States, Japan and Iran, wherein lies a great deal of tensions as well as interactions.

China and The Middle East

Chinese foreign policy toward the Middle East in the post Cold War era has favored neither isolation nor a thorough commitment to the North-Atlanticist powers. Rather, it has revolved around an interdependence in economic and security arenas of realignment on a global scale.

Since 1949, Chinese anti-capitalism and anti-North-Atlanticist communist ideology has been a major source of inspiration for many Third World revolutionary and nationalist movements of which the Middle East is no exception.[22] Furthermore, the ideological assertion of China against both superpowers during 1949-1972 was personified in the cult of its leader Mao Zedung who had become an embodiment of anti-imperialism for Middle Eastern popular uprisings. Yet, China's self portrayal as the champion of the Third World causes had to be tested against the actual regional conflicts that would also precipitate rivalry within a bipolar context of international relations. One of these conflicts, the six day Arab-Israeli War of 1967, erupted in the midst of the Chinese cultural revolution when the Sino-Soviet ideological wrangles had reached their climax over global issues. As China lambasted the Soviets for their betrayal of the Arabs, massive pro-Arab demonstrations took place in the streets of Beijing fomenting extraordinary sympathy for the Palestinian cause.[23]

This event, in the eyes of the Chinese, was an expression of how oppressed nations suffer from the complicity of American imperialism and the Soviet revisionism, whereas the bourgeois Arab leadership remained incapable of rallying the cause of Palestine for the rest of the decade. Nevertheless, it was in 1970 that the Soviet decision to supply arms to the PLO reduced the Chinese influence among the Palestinians. Yet, when the champion of Arab nationalism, President Nasser of Egypt, died on 28 September 1970, China mourned the loss of a great Third World leader. This took place despite the fact that Egypt was angered by the Chinese belief that the pro-Soviet Nasser had betrayed the Palestinians. This ideological reassertion against the Soviet Union, which was also intensified by China's irredentist conflict over lost territories with the Soviets, facilitated a rapproachment with the United States. In fact, this was in response to the Nixon-Kissinger strategic initiative of warming up to China and containing the Soviets.

The result of this rapproachment in 1971-72 constituted a major reorientation in China's foreign policy from isolationist "self-reliance to diversification" as Holsti once observed. Meanwhile, as a new development in the region of the Middle East, Egypt's expulsion of the Soviet military advisers in July 1973 paved the way for a breakthrough in Sino-Egyptian relations. China declared her readiness to supply Egypt with arms if the latter was prepared to carry out a people's war against Israel on the Vietnam pattern.

Egypt's partial victory in the October 1973 war brought her the economic assistance of China. Thus, in 1976, when Egypt unilaterally abrogated the Egyptian-Soviet friendship treaty, Beijing promptly provided Egypt with free parts of the Soviet MIGs and other military equipment. China aimed at using ties to Egypt to consolidate a Third World coalition against the bipolar domination of the globe.[24]

For this reason, Egypt's rift with the rest of the Arab world induced by its signing of the Camp David peace Accords annoyed the Chinese but not to the extent of breaking off relations with Egypt, whose trade with China had reached $134 million in 1978.

Patterns of Reorientation in the Foreign Policies of Japan   283
and China Toward the Middle East in the Post-Cold War
Diplomacy: A Reflection on the Regional Determinants

China and the Middle East in post-cold war diplomacy: reorientation within "interdependence"

In 1982, Chinese foreign policy entered a new phase of reorientation when Deng Xiao Ping proclaimed an interdependent open door policy in which an assertive nationalism overshadowed Marxist-Maoist aspects of Chinese ideology in international affairs. Moreover, this reorientation was conditioned by China's economic modernization aspirations that had aimed to reach into the global environment for economic, technological, and human resources. However, the Middle Eastern determinants of Chinese foreign policy reorientation confronted China with a number of complexities in maintaining better relations with North-Atlanticist powers, as far as interdependence allowed. These regional complexities entailed two major features: (1) bilateral economic relations, arms sales, and transfer of nuclear technology to a number of Middle East countries; and (2)maintenance of its symbolic Third Worldist presence in the regional politics of the Middle East.[25]

In addressing the complexities of the region, throughout the eighties, China supported the idea of creating a Palestinian state while negating peace plans proposed by Brezhnev and Reagan. Only in 1987 did China supported the idea of a U.N. sponsored peace conference, and communicated its approval to Arafat when he made his seventh trip to China in 1989.

China and the Arab-Israeli conflict

In 1989 China announced her five-step peace proposal with which Israel disagreed as long as Sino-Israeli relations had not been established. The proposal designated the following:
1. Political settlement with no use of force
2. A U.N. sponsored Middle East peace conference
3. Direct talks between PLO and Israel
4. Israeli withdrawal from occupied territories
5. Establishment of a Palestinian state as a prerequisite for Chinese participation. [26]

This line of policy continued until March 1991 when Foreign Minister Qian reiterated that an international conference on the Palestine question was an inevitable consequence of the Gulf war. Even though China showed enthusiasm for the opening of the Madrid conference, she was not given a major role in the peace conference.

The impediment to active Chinese participation had been laid down by Israel which had demanded the establishment of Chinese-Israeli relations.

Furthermore, American clashes with China over the latter's arms sales policy, copyright violations, and human rights record further rebuffed China's initial enthusiasm to take a major part in the peace talks. Notwithstanding this, China had realized how the end of the Gulf War was going to impact China's Middle East policy by making China a peace broker along with the other powers in the region under the auspicious of the U.N.

The U.N. voted to rescind a resolution equating Zionism with racism by the end of 1991. China abstained, though she had voted for it earlier in 1975. Abstaining in this context of international behavior was the means China chose to alleviate the regional complexities of her Middle Eastern policy. On 24 January 1992, China established diplomatic relations with Israel which had recognized The Peoples Republic of China as "the sole legal government representing the whole of China of which Taiwan is an inalienable part". Arab reaction to China's establishment of relations with Israel, although critical in tone, was understanding in substance since Arab-Israeli relations had taken a less belligerent turn by the role the PLO and other moderate Arab regimes had played in the post Gulf War peace process.[27]

Nevertheless, it was during 1994-95 that Chinese-Israeli relations entered a new phase of cooperation when Israeli engineers started helping China adapt Lavi technology for a new fighter aircraft. This military cooperation, which enabled Israel to incorporate American technology from its defunct Lavi aircraft project into China's combat aircraft, fomented a mild confrontation between the United States and Israel. Meanwhile, in the spring of 1995, in order to safeguard its painfully crafted diplomatic ties with Beijing, Israel canceled its aircraft export deal to Taiwan.[28] Furthermore, Israel declined the Taiwanese president's request for a private pilgrimage to Christian holy sites when Israel and China started collaboration on military aviation worth $1bn.

China and the Gulf war

It was in the second half of 1990 that China endeavored to break its isolation by involving herself in diplomatic engagements and international trade relations in the aftermath of Tiananmen square

Patterns of Reorientation in the Foreign Policies of Japan   285
and China Toward the Middle East in the Post-Cold War
Diplomacy: A Reflection on the Regional Determinants

events. The pace of this foreign policy reorientation was somewhat gradual since China had to approach as many states as possible. The massacre of dissidents at Tiananmen square in June 1989 had jeopardized China's credible international standing.[29]

The Persian Gulf crisis of 1990-91 proved to be an event that unraveled the conflict China had encountered between her Third Worldism and the interdependent globalism she had favored after the Tiananmen events. China had maintained relatively favorable ties with most Middle Eastern countries despite the fact that she had also warmed up to the Israelis. Nevertheless, the crisis shattered China's Third Worldist image at a time that the latter was demonstrating an enthusiasm for involvement in global high politics.

Before the Iraqi invasion, Kuwait had functioned as a financial benefactor for China. Because of the destruction and dislocation caused by the war, China suffered a loss of two billion dollars in contracts and remittances. Furthermore, the activities of sixty Chinese companies in Iraq and Kuwait were terminated, resulting in a halt of remittances of nine thousand Chinese workers. China's swift responsiveness in condemning Iraq was accompanied by her active involvement in drafting and voting for ten successive U.N. security council resolutions aimed at pressuring Iraq into compliance. [30]

The regional complexities of Iraq's invasion of Kuwait and the controversies it had created around Islamic sentiments and Arab nationalism paved the way for China to override those complexities by resorting to the procedural rules of the security council and the non-aggression principles of the United nations. The Middle Eastern regimes were not alone in rewarding China for its responsible position during the Gulf War. Western nations were much quicker to reward China for its cooperative stances in the Unite Nations. The Bush administration, for its part, resumed high level contacts with China and did not oppose the World Bank's "non-basic human needs loan" to China.[31]

Meanwhile, China's persistence in exploring regional channels of diplomacy to bring a peaceful solution was evidenced in her extending an invitation to Iraq's first deputy prime minister, Taha Yassin Ramadan to visit Beijing in September 1990. He was told that the future of Iraq and a potential Arab retrenchment against American hegemony was at stake. This warning however, was to no avail.

The Iraqi regime's status as a pariah state made China move closer to Iran, Iraq's arch rival in the region. However, both Iran and China showed their concern for the Iraqi people by sending food and medicine to Iraq despite the U.N. sanctions. To show its displeasure with Saddam's policies, China barred Iraq from participation in the Beijing Asian Games held in September 1990. Yet, China's diplomatic relations with Iraq never ceased. In mid February 1991, Saddam Hussein's special envoy, Sadun Hammadi, called on the Chinese officials. He was informed of the Chinese position which insisited on an unconditional Iraqi withdrawal from Kuwait, opposition to the use of military force against Iraq, and preference for a peaceful Arab solution. Chinese foreign minister Qian made clear his country's policy line on the Gulf crisis as

> China does not have nor wishes to seek any self-serving interest in the Middle East region and its only concern is to maintain peace and stability of the region.[32]

By resorting to this rhetoric, China contrived to gain maximum concessions from the allied powers while rendering only minimal support to the U.N. resolutions that supported the use of military force against Iraq. In a way, China was probably thinking of her Third Worldist image in a region that by Chinese economists was considered as a "Super Bazaar", signifying the Middle East as a viable market for Chinese goods, transfer of technology and arms sales. The method by which China attempted to resolve her role conflict between pursuing global high politics and maintaining her Third Worldist prestige was epitomized in her abstention in the vote taken on U.N. Resolution 678 asking approval of the use of force against Iraq. China sided neither with Iraq and the Palestinians who had demanded a Chinese veto nor with the United States and her regional Arab allies who had expected China's positive vote in passing the resolution.[33] Accordingly, Foreign Minister Qian made an interesting justification for China's abstention on Resolution 678 by drawing upon a historical understanding of such behavior in Chinese foreign policy. As he put it, "Chinese people still clearly remember that the Korean war was launched in the name of the United Nations."[34]

No matter how the Chinese leadership now vies for a prominent place in global issues within the interdependent global environment of economic and technological development, the episode of the Gulf War suggests how that leadership desires to assert its activism in regional/global conflicts independent of the North Atlanticist powers in the post Cold War diplomacy. Whether that assertion is regarded as a

Patterns of Reorientation in the Foreign Policies of Japan   287
and China Toward the Middle East in the Post-Cold War
Diplomacy: A Reflection on the Regional Determinants

reactive positioning in global high politics rather than a well thought
out foreign policy reorientation, it still demonstrates China's self-image
of being a global power.

China and Iran

Due to the asymmetry that existed between China's geostrategic
anti-hegemonism in the region and her vast economic interests, the
outbreak of war between Iran and Iraq troubled China's foreign policy
in the Middle East . Not only had China supplied arms to both sides,
but her transfer of ballistic missiles to Saudi Arabia had created a
complex Chinese diplomacy in the region throughout the eighties.[35] In
this complex diplomacy, however, economic modernization and the
boosting of global trade predominantly defined the basis of Chinese
foreign policy reorientation in the post-Mao era, especially as the
Middle East had been viewed as a major component in China's
economic considerations. Yet, regional conflicts such as the Iran-Iraq
War unraveled the Chinese foreign policy which, often rhetorical and
expedient, never aimed at a substantial effort to resolve the conflict,
claiming outright neutrality throughout the war. Perhaps despite its
anti-hegemonist rhetoric which could have accommodated anti-
American Iranian sentiments, China remained skeptical about the
global agenda of the Islamic regime in Iran.[36]

Furthermore, China had decided to balance off Soviet influence in
both Iran and Iraq by selling arms to both warring parties. The sales
had amounted to twelve billion dollars by the end of the war in 1988.
Even as lucrative arms sales to both countries benefited China
enormously, the end of hostilities heralded new economic opportunities
for China in the post-war reconstruction eras in both Iran and Iraq.

Notwithstanding this, in 1991 Sino-Iranian relations entered a new
phase since China's assistance in Iran's post war reconstruction also
included the transfer of nuclear weapons technology. By this time, the
emerging arrangements in the post-Cold War diplomacy, as it had been
envisaged by the Bush administration under the rubric of a new world
order, was affecting Chinese foreign policy toward the United States.
The ramifications of this apparently American dominated new world
order created certain regional consequences for the Chinese-Iranian
relations in the post Cold War era.[37]

During 1991-92 two competing trends in Chinese foreign policy
became involved in a controversial debate as confrontation over the

human rights issue was regarded as an impediment toward China's opening to promote capitalism. By the end of 1992, Deng Xiao Ping's sweeping statements on Chinese-American relations carried the day for his pragmatic trend of foreign policy over the hard-liners in the armed forces and Chinese communist party.

Deng asserted that although China and the United States were different in political ideologies, no conflict existed between their fundamental interests. In fact, Deng denied that peaceful evolution was a serious threat as long as economic reform advanced material interests for most of the Chinese people. The complexities of Deng's statements actually denoted the multivalanced nature of the Chinese foreign policy for the years to ensue. [38]

Nevertheless, China was adamant about buttressing her strategic position in the Persian Gulf region as part and parcel of a grander scheme to contrive a regional alliance between China, Pakistan, and Iran. Such an alliance could stave off China's regional archenemy India, and to some extent, challenge the enhanced American position in the Gulf. Iran was quick to exploit China's Third Worldist anti-Western rhetoric by emphasizing the common stance in the Chinese-Iranian relations against the American hegemonic presence in the region. President Yang Shangkin's October 1991 visit to Pakistan and Iran ended with his public admission of nuclear cooperation with Iran, which became a point of irritation in the Sino-American relations for the rest of the decade.[39]

China's trade with Iran stood at $730 million during 1993-94. China expressed, an interest in atomic cooperation with Iran, and actually engaged in talks with the latter for the construction of two nuclear power plants under the rubric of "peaceful purposes" after International Atomic Energy Agency reports had confirmed that Iran lacked the capability to manufacture nuclear arms. Sino-Iranian cooperation had also included non-ferrous metals production and the establishment of petrochemical plants in Orumiyeh and Tehran. Yet, by the end of 1994, the United States had started to criticize Sino-Iranian atomic cooperation harshly, provoking a reactive response by Iranian President Rafsanjani that defended the peaceful nature of China's efforts in the reconstruction of the semi-completed nuclear power plant in Bushehr.[40]

Despite both government's occasional rejection of any interference from Washington in Sino-Iranian atomic cooperation, in May 1995 three points of disagreement emerged in their negotiations. First, China expressed uncertainty over her ability to provide all the technology Iran

Patterns of Reorientation in the Foreign Policies of Japan   289
and China Toward the Middle East in the Post-Cold War
Diplomacy: A Reflection on the Regional Determinants

Required since she partially depended on Germany, the Czech Republic, and the Netherlands in making other parts of nuclear technology. Second, the Chinese government failed to provide Iran with detailed plans and training of Iranian technicians. Finally, the Iranian side in Beijing failed to come up with solid financial arrangements.

As a result, by summer of 1995 neither side was in a hurry to overcome their disagreements, especially at a time when China prudently watched Iran's direct collision with the United States as a result of the latter's "containment" of Iran.[41] As a matter of fact, China's confused foreign policy on nuclear sales to Iran denotes how the new Chinese foreign policy reorientation toward activism since the Gulf War of 1991, is conditioned by the events in the Middle East where regional determinants of foreign policy and global power politics intermingle. As far as the geostrategics of global power politics is concerned, the Clinton administration has often pressured China not to transfer to Iran imports needed for the latter's nuclear programs and missile-related technology as part of Washington's "dual containment" of Iran and Iraq.

In doing so, the United States has attempted to use its leverage to threaten to press the Chinese on their human rights records, the Taiwan issue, and copyright violations resulting from China's illgal reproduction of American products. At the regional level, Iran's faltering economy has impaired the image of that country as an attractive commercial partner. Moreover, the American regional policy of dual containment in the Gulf, conflicts with China's strategy in building up an Asian alliance between China, Pakistan, and Iran. This informal alliance is based on a geostrategic cooperation in the context of the post-Cold War balance of power. Above all, Iran, Pakistan, and China have been strategically isolated in the post-Cold War era, though to different degrees.

The downfall of the Soviet Union relegated the geostrategic significance of Pakistan and China to the United States. Although this cannot be categorized with the antagonistic US-Iranian relations since 1979, it has given Iran a strong incentive to pursue her defense policy of strategic retrenchment and rearmament in the post-Cold War era.

Regionally, what brings these three states into this informal strategic alliance revolves around a common objective to contain the military power of India in southwest Asia. China has had a long history of rivalry with India over establishing hegemony in this region. Iran and Pakistan, on the other hand, have a mutual interest in containing India due to the abuse of the Muslim population in Kashmir, despite their own different interpretation of Islam.

Regardless of certain asymmetries in this informal regional alliance, the three states have based their collaboration on addressing each other's defense needs through arms trade, technological exchange, and economic cooperation.[42] In October 1995, China was apparently playing games with both Iran and the United States by saying she had "suspended" reactor sales to Iran whereas the United States viewed the latter as a "termination" in the atomic cooperation between the two countries. In November, Bruce Reidel, the American deputy assistant secretary of defense for Near East and South Asia, maintained that China "has cooperated to some extent with the US in blocking chemical related shipments to Iran".[43] In January 1996, China's reactor deal with Iran came to a standstill when China's deputy foreign minister, in a visit to Tehran, alluded to the fact that "they might continue the cooperation but it would not include the construction of two planned 300-mega power plants."[44]

Iran publicly confirmed the Chinese stance that the power plant project had been frozen.[45] In February, Iran test fired the Chinese made C-802 missiles, delivered a year earlier, in the vicinity of the American Fifth fleet in the Gulf. The Pentagon recommended retaliation against the Chinese since the military significance of such an act was that it was fired from a ship denoting mobility in naval warfare.[46] Yet Washington also feared that further punishment of China would prompt the latter to go forward with the power plant sale due to the previous Chinese "mish-mash" policy on nuclear sales to Iran.[47] It seems that China is buying time to balance off the regional determinants of foreign policy against the global ones by drawing upon the imperatives of economic interdependence.

Furthermore, renewed Islamic unrest in Xinjang province in 1990 had fomented China's condemnation of the political uses of religion that Tehran advocates. In other words, Iran and China remain ideological adversaries even though in some pragmatic arenas of Third Worldism they may concur on the same course of action. At the present, China's foreign policy towards Iran is neither revolutionary Third Worldist nor one characterized by the norms of North-Atlantic cooperation. It is a product of situational expediency conditioned by the geopolitical determinants of the Persian Gulf region.

Patterns of Reorientation in the Foreign Policies of Japan   291
and China Toward the Middle East in the Post-Cold War
Diplomacy: A Reflection on the Regional Determinants

Concluding Remarks

The Middle Eastern determinants of foreign policy reorientation of Japan and China entail two significant leitmotifs: the immediate strategic dynamics of the events and the intensity of interaction between the regional actors and the major global powers.

In addressing those leitmotifs, Japan and China have reoriented their foreign policies toward the Middle East in different ways. Since 1982, Japan's foreign policy towards the Middle East has aimed at patterns of reorientation within North-Atlanticism that constitute the evolving relationships among the United States, Western Europe, and Japan. Although for a short period of time in the post Cold War era Japan tried to reduce its full commitments to North-Atlanticism, events such as the Iraqi invasion of Kuwait rapidly moved Japan into a more comprehensive pattern of realignment with the US and European powers. Yet, in dealing with the American containment of Iran, Japan has somehow reluctantly accommodated her ally's expectation while emphasizing the regional role Iran can play in the dynamics of balance of power in the Persian Gulf.

Chinese foreign policy toward the Middle East in the post Cold War era has not favored either isolation or a thorough commitment to the North-Atlanticist powers. Rather, China's foreign policy has revolved around an interdependence in economic and security areas of reorientation in the post Cold War global context. This reorientation has been partly conditioned by China's economic modernization aspirations that have aimed at reaching into the global environment for economic, technological, and human resources to gain more equitable rewards than in noninterdependent systems.

The Middle Eastern determinants of Chinese foreign policy reorientation have presented China with a great deal of complexity in maintaining better relations with North-Atlanticist powers as far as interdependence allows, on one hand, and also continuing her symbolic Third Worldist presence in the Middle East, on the other. This role conflict in China's foreign policy was temporarily resolved in the Gulf crisis of 1990-91 when China resorted to the procedural rules of the Security Council, whereas in dealing with the other political dynamics of the region China has merely acted out of situational expediency rather than a Third Worldist revolutionarism.

Notes

1. K.j. Holsti, Why Nations Realign: Foreign Policy Restructuring in the Post War World, (London: George Allen& Unwin, 1982), pp. 11-20. See also George J. Demko and William B.Wood, Reordering the World: Geopolitical Perspectives on the 21st Century, (Boulder: Westview Press, 1994), pp. 3-12.

2. See Ibid. See also Efraim Karsh, The Gulf Conflict 1990-91: Diplomacy and War in the New World Order, (Princeton, N.J.: Princeton University Press,1993), pp. 4-18.

3. Kunio Katakura and Motoko Katakura, Japan and the Middle East, (Tokyo:The Middle East Institute of Japan,1991), pp. 68-72.

4. Ibid., p. 74. See also, Valarie Yorke, Oil, the Middle East and Japan's Search for Economic Security, ed. N. Akao (London:RIIA,1983), pp. 53-55.

5. Robert Gilpin," Where does Japan Fit in the International Relations?", in The International Relations of Japan, ed. Kathleen Newland (London:Macmillan, 1990), pp. 15-17.

6. Katakura, Japan and the Middle East, p. 32.

7. Ibid.

8. Yasumasa Kuroda, "Japan: an Economic Superpower in Search of its Proper Political Role in the Post-Cold War Era" in The Gulf War and the New World Order, ed. Tareq Ismael & Jacqueline Ismael (Gainesville, Fla.: University Press of Florida, 1994) pp. 132-33.

9. Ibid., p. 134.

10. Katakura, Japan and the Middle East, p. 134.

11. Ibid., p. 89.

12. Steven Spiegel and David Previn, Practical Peacemaking in the Middle East, (New York: Galand Publishing, 1995), p. 225.

13. Katakura, Japan and the Middle East, p. 69.

Patterns of Reorientation in the Foreign Policies of Japan   293
and China Toward the Middle East in the Post-Cold War
Diplomacy: A Reflection on the Regional Determinants

14. Ibid.

15. See Middle East Economic Digest (MEED),15 December 1995, pp. 29-32.

16. Ibid.

17. Michael M. Yoshitsu, Caught in the Middle East: Japan's Diplomacy in Transition, (Lexington: Lexington Books, 1984), pp. 86-101.

18. See MEED, 15 December 1995, p. 30.

19. Kazuo Takahashi, "When an enemy of your friend is a friend: A Japanese view of the American-Iranian relationship" in Middle East Insight, Vol. 11 No.36, p 37.

20. Ibid.

21. Ibid.

22. George McTurman Kahin, The Asian-African Conference: Bandung, Indonesia, April 1955, (Ithaca,N.Y.:Cornell University Press, 1956), pp. 11-16.

23. Lillian Craig Harris: China Considers the Middle East, (London: I.B.Tauris, 1993), 121. See also Mohammad Heikal, The Cairo Documents, (London: Mentor Paperback, 1973), pp. 20-23.

24. Harris, China Considers the Middle East, p. 148.

25. John Calabrese, China's Changing Relations with the Middle East, (London: Virago press, 1984), pp. 11-12.

26. Ibid., p. 90.

27. Harris, China Considers the Middle East, pp. 262-263.

28.See P.R. Kumaraswamy, "Israel and China: Military Cooperation" in Middle East International, No.510 (10 June 1995), pp. 18-19.

29. Harris, China Considers the Middle East, p. 248.

30. Ibid., pp. 246-247.

31. Ibid., pp. 248-249.

32. Qian Qichen, "Adhering to Independent Foreign Policy" in Beijing Review, (30 December 1991-5 January 92), pp. 5-7.

33. Harris, China Considers the Middle East, p. 250.

34. Qichen, op. cit.

35. See Lillian Craig Harris, "Myth and Reality in China's Relation with the Middle East" in Chinese Foreign Policy: Theory and Practice, ed. Thomas Robinson and David Shambaugh (Oxford: Clarendon Press, 1994), p. 339.

36. Harris, China Considers the Middle East, pp. 202-204.

37. Safa Haeri, "Iran and China: Nuclear Cooperation" in Middle East International, 8 (November 1991): p. 14.

38. See Beijing Review, No. 37 (May 2-8 1994), pp. 18-19.

39. John Calabrese, Revolutionary Horizons: Regional Foreign Policy in Post Khomeini Iran, (New York: St. Martin's Press,1994), pp. 34-35.

40. Kaveh Afrasiabi, After Khomeini: New Directions in Iran's Foreign Policy, (Boulder,Colo.: Westview, 1994), pp. 177-183.

41. See China Quarterly, 142 (June 1995): p. 11.

42.Calabrese, Revolutionary Horizons, pp. 38-40.

43. See "Chinese Now Says Reactor Deal with Tehran is dead" Iran Times, 12 January 1996, p. 12.

44. Ibid.

45. Ibid.

Patterns of Reorientation in the Foreign Policies of Japan   295
and China Toward the Middle East in the Post-Cold War
Diplomacy: A Reflection on the Regional Determinants

46. "China Deplores US Plan Against Iran" <u>Kayhan Havai</u>, 17 January 1996, p. 24.

47. Ibid.

Index

-A-

Abdallah, Crown Prince of Saudi Arabia, 198
Abe, Shintaro, 273
Adorno, Theodor, 92
Afghanis, 64
Afghanistan, 4-5, 12, 18
Afro-Asian majority (world's population), 138
Ahmadis, 61, 76, as minority in Pakistan, 62
Alawis, as minority in Syria, 62
Alawites, as religious minority, 61. *See also* Nusaris
Albright, Madeline, 39, 44
Alevis, as religious minority, 61
Algeria, 2, 3, 18, 24, 25, 26, 28, 29, 30, 53, 54, 55, 58, 59, 60, 61, 70-71, 75, 76, 89; family code, 152; feminist groups, 52; militant Islamist movement, 151; women's movement, 65-167
Animists, as minority, 62
Arab Co-operation Council, 243
Arab Maghreb Council, 243
Arab Jerusalem, 66
Arab nationalism, 95, 97, 98; as founding ideology of Iraqi Ba'th, 187
Arab unity, and Iraqi invasion of Kuwait, 242
Arab Women's Solidarity Association, 152
Arab Women's Tribunal, 150
Arab-Israeli Peace Process, 2, 6, 11, 12, 13, 22, 38
Arafat, Yasir, 98, 118, 121, 125
Arab-Israeli Peace Process, 2, 6, 11, 12, 13, 22, 32, 38, 243, 250, 251, 256,
Arabs, as minority in Iran and Israel, 62
Argentina, 111
Armenians, as minority, 61

Arms sales to "friendly Arab regimes", U.S., 89
Asia Pacific Economic Cooperation, 255
Al-Assad, Hafez, 16, 27, 101, 103, 111, 177-178, 180-181, 189
Al-Assad, Rif'at, 101
Association of Southeast Asian Nations (ASEAN), 1, 41
Ataturk (Mustafa Kemal), 28
Azerbaijan, 186
Azerbaijanis, 66; as minority in Iran, 62
Aziz, Tariq, 34

-B-

"Backlash states," 32, 35
Baghdad, 21, as "strategic reserve" to Syria and Jordan, 178
Baghdad-Damascus highway, 179
Bahai'is, as minority in Iran, 61, 62, 76
Bahrain, 35, 42-43, 53, 54, 58, 60, 76, 102, 243
Baker, James, 17
Bakthiaris, as minority in Iran, Pakistan, 62
Baluchis, as minority in Iran, 62
Barzani, Massoud, 182, 183, 189 *See also* Kurdish Democratic Party Al-Bashir, General Omar Hassan Ahamad (Sudan), 55
Ba'th, 98, 100, 184
Ba'thist (secular nationalist), 3
Bedowin, 59
Begin, Menachem, 117
Beirut, 123, 150
Ben-Gurion, David, 109, 126
Berbers, as minority in Algeria and Morocco, 61, 62, 77
Bethlehem, 119
Bosnia, 25, 28, 271
Brzezinski, Zbigniew, 38, 39, 92
Bush, George, 16, 22, 32

-C-
Camp David, 75, 116, 179, 184
Canada, 37
Carter, Jimmy, 38
Caspian Sea, 3, 7, 18
Caucasus, 3, 18, 19, 244
Central Intelligence Agency (CIA), 32;
  restored shah to power, built up
  SAVAK, 197
Chechnya, 25, 28; impact on Russian
  Middle East foreign policy, 221
China, 2, 5, 7, 9, 12-13, 17, 37, 38, 42,
  113; anti-capitalism, anti-North
  Atlanticist communist ideology, 281;
  image as maverick world power, 273;
  reorientation toward Middle East, 272-
  295; women's conference, 150-151
Circassians, as ethnic minority, 61
Civil-political rights, 52
"Clash of Civilization" worldview, 68
Clinton Administration, 4, 9, 11, 16, 17,
  22, 31-40, 119, 121, 129, 280 Dual
  containment,173-210; Cold War
  origins of,174; as regional re-fighting
  of Cold War 203
"Cold Peace" (Arab states and Israel),
  136
Cold War containment paradigm, 7, 11,
  204
Collectif 95 Maghreb Egalité, 150
Communism, 27, 32, 68, 86, 88, 134
Conference on Security and Co-
  operation in the Middle East, 242
Constitutionalism, 74
Convention Against Torture and other
  Crimes, Inhuman and Degrading
  Treatment or Punishment, 53, 54
Coptic Christians, as minority in Egypt,
  61, 62
Cuba, 18
Czechoslovakia, 32

-D-
Dar al-Harb (abode of war), 94

Dar al-Islam (abode of Islam), 94
Dar as-Sulh (abode of concord), 94
Deideologization, 17, 85
Democratization, 8, 27, 28, 29, 30, 31,
  69-70, 74-77, 109, 147-148; U.S.
  "enlargement" policy, 173; in Yemen,
  201; 203; 157, 158
Détente, 40
Desert Storm, 34
Diahnine, Nabila, 166
Domino theory, 185
Druze, 61; as religious minority in
  Lebanon, 62
Dual containment policy, 4, 5, 32, 35,
  43-44, 45, 173, 176, 203; east-west
  paradigm, 174; artificial duality and
  downfall, 180
Dubai, 38
Duvalier, Jean-Claude, 111

-E-
East Asian Newly Industrializing
  Countries (NICs), 239
Eastern Orthodox Christians, as
  minority, 61
Easternization of the workplace, 240
Economic, social, and cultural rights, 52
Egypt, 2, 3, 17, 18, 20, 21, 22, 23, 24, 25,
  26, 27, 28, 29, 30, 35, 39, 42, 53, 54,
  58, 59, 60, 61, 73, 75, 100, 103, 113,
  116, 134, 152, 180, 187, 198
El Salvador, 111, 130, 139
Erbakan, Necmettin, 164
Ethiopia, 111
Eurasia, 12
Euro-Mediterranean Dialogue, 237
Euro-Mediterranean Partnership, 251
"Euro-scepticism," 247
European-Middle East relations, fission
  analogy, 236
European Union (EU), 1, 4, 5, 6, 9, 12,
  41-42; Mediterranean policies, 236;
EU-MENA (Middle East and North
  Africa region) relations, 239
Export-Import Bank, 127

"Extremism," 174, 185, 188, 200

-F-
Fahd, King of Saudi Arabia, 103
Fahd Plan, 116
Family law, 149, 151
Fascism, 86
Fa'th movement, 92, 100
Feminism, 148, 155, 164
Feminist transnational networks, 154-155
Figh (Islamic jurisprudence), 57
Fitnah (sedition), 102
Food for Peace, 127
France, 126, 180
Frankfurt School ("culture industry"), 90
Freedom House, 195
Front for Islamic Salvation (FIS), 24, 25

-G-
Gaza, 65, 113, 117, 119, 120, 122, 123, 129, 137
Gemayal, Amin, 123
Gender Empowerment Measure (GEM), 58-59
Georgians, as ethnic minority, 61
Germany, 16, 38
Globalization, 236; and autonomy and "soul" of a state, 237
Golan region, 122, 136
Gorbachev, Mikhail, 17, 18
Great Britain, 126, 131
Great Satan phenomenon, 184
Grenada, 16
Gross National Product (GNP), 113, 128
Gulf Cooperation Council, 7, 17, 20, 21, 22, 35, 36, 40, 44, 104, 134, 174, 175; marginalization to passive protectorate, 176; 193, 243, 244
Guatemala, 111, 130

-H-
Hadith, 95, 96
Haiti, 111

HAMAS, 25, 28, 38, 118
Hasan, King, 103
Hebron, 119
Hezbollah, 25, 28, 123-125, 135, 177, 178, 181, 186
Hindus, as religious minority in Pakistan, 62, 67
Hobbesian worldview (Israel), 108
Holocaust, 108, 114
Human Development Index (HDI), 55, 56, 76
Human rights, 8, 10, 29, 51-84, 148, 150
Hungary, 32
Hussein bin Talal, King of Jordan, 103, 121
Hussein, Saddam, 3, 4, 16, 17, 18, 20, 33, 34, 36, 40, 44, 66, 91, 95, 99, 103, 180, 188-189

-I-
India, 2, 7, 165
Indonesia, 28, 133
Indyk, Martin, 32, 173, 180
Integrism, 166
Inter-Arab trade relations, 246
International Action Center, 35
International Covenant on Civil and Political Rights (ICCPR), 53, 54
International Covenant on Economic, Social, and Cultural Rights (ICESCR), 53, 54
International Human Rights Conventions, 54
International Monetary Fund (IMF), 28, 147
Intifadah, 72, 112
Iran, 2, 3, 4, 7, 11, 12, 17, 18, 19, 20, 21, 23, 25, 27, 28, 32, 33, 34, 35, 37, 38, 39, 40, 42, 43, 44, 54, 55, 58, 59, 60, 61, 62, 64, 72, 77, 111, 112, 130, 135, 174, 191, 192, 193, 195, 197
Iran-Iraqi War, 12, 13, 20, 179, 244
Iraq, 2, 4, 7, 11, 12, 16, 17, 18, 19, 20, 21, 23, 25, 27, 28, 32, 33, 34, 35, 37, 38, 39, 40, 42, 43, 44, 54, 55, 58, 59,

60, 61, 62, 64, 66, 70, 71, 77, 102, 112, 134, 136, 151, 174, 177, 178, 181, 191, 184
Iraqi Shi'a Muslims, as refugees in Iran and Saudi Arabia, 64
Islam, 2, 24, 88, 93-94
Islamic confrontationalist paradigm, 202
Islamic "culture industry," 96
Islamic determinants of foreign policy, myth of, 94
Islamic fundamentalism, 3, 23, 25, 26, 96-97
Islamic Revival, 19, 24, 33, 51, 67-69
"Islamic threat," 15, 24
Islamic Summit, 27, 39
Islamization, 11, 19, 70-71
Islamophobia, 88
Israel, 2, 3, 5, 11, 16, 17, 18, 22, 23, 27, 32, 34, 36, 37, 38, 44, 53, 54, 55, 58, 59, 62, 63, 65, 91, 99, 100, 104, 107-146; supplying arms to Nicaraguan Contras, 111; advisors assisting Contras, 130; and Third World, 138
Israel Occupied Territories (O.T.), 62-63
Israeli Arabs, 114
Israeli-Syrian track, discussion of resurrection, 253

-J-
Jadid, Salah, 95
Jama'at Islamiyyia (Islamic group), 25
Japan, 2, 5, 7, 9, 12, 13, 16, 35, 37, 41, 113; commitment to North Atlantic power structure and U.S., 272-273; energy crisis of 1973, 273; reorientation toward Middle East, 271-295, response to Persian Gulf Crisis, 274-276;
Jerusalem, 66, 137
Jewish Diaspora, 130
Jews, as minority in Morocco, 61, 62
Jordan, 2, 3, 6, 19, 24, 25, 26, 27, 29, 30, 53, 54, 55, 58, 59, 62, 64, 65, 71, 72, 77, 89, 91, 99, 100, 101, 1;03, 113,

116, 117, 121, 130 149, 151, 176, 178, 180, 183, 187
Jordanian-Israeli Peace Treaty, 250
Jordanian-Palestinian Peace Treaty, 6
Jordanian Women's League, 150
Judaism, fundamentalist revival of, 88

-K-
Kazakhistan 7, 186
Khader, Asma (Jordan), 150
Khatami, Muhammad (Iran), 27-28, 36-37, 39, 40, 42
Khartoum, 71
Khomeini, Ayatollah Ruhollah 19, 29, 196
Kissinger, Henry 116, 132
Knesset, 121
Kurdish Democratic Party (KDP), 182-183, 189
Kurdistan, 66
Kurdistan Workers Party (PKK), 63, 65
Kurds, 5, 6, 61, 62, 63, 64, 66-67, 76, 180, 183, 189; as ethnic minority in Iraq, Iran, Turkey, 62-63; as refugees, 64, 66-67
Kuwait, 4, 6, 12, 16, 17, 18, 20, 21, 23, 27, 29, 37, 39, 53, 58, 59, 60, 65, 95, 98, 102, 180, 190, 193, 242
Kyrgyzstan, 186

-L-
Labor Alignment (Israel), 114
Labor Party (Israel), 107, 118, 122, 126
Labor Zionist leadership (Israel), 114, 115, 138
Lake, Anthony, 34, 35, 173 (See also Clinton Administration, dual containment)
Laz, as ethnic minority, 61
Lebanese National Movement, 123
Lebanon, 25, 38, 58, 59, 62, 64, 65, 89, 90, 91, 102, 103, 112, 113, 123-125, 130, 135, 136, 137, 151, 177, 178, 187
Levant, 123

Liberalization, 147-148, 185
"Liberation theology," 67-68
Libya, 18, 19, 23, 25, 27, 30, 53, 54, 55, 58, 151, 194
Likud Party, 63, 107, 114, 115, 118, 120, 123, 126, 129

-M-

Maastricht Treaty, 12, 242, 247, 248, 249
Madrid negotiations, 22, 117, 244
Maghreb, 99, 181
al Mahdi, Sadiq (Sudan), 55
Mao Zedung, as embodiment of anti-imperialism for Middle Eastern popular uprisings, 1949-1972, 281
Maronite Christians, as religious minority in Lebanon, 62
Marxist parties, 89
Mashreq (Fertile Crescent) 99, 174, 176, 181, 186
Militant Islam, 24-25
Maslahat ad-dawlah (interest of the state), 93
Mecca, 21, 40
Media, 25, 26
Meir, Golda, 109
MENA (Middle East and North Africa), foreign direct investments in, 241; subregionalization, 7; 154, 235-261; economic Balkanization threat from EU, 239; instability and weak economic base, 241
MENACA (Middle East, North Africa, and Central Asia), 240
Messianism, ideological, 87, 165
Middle Eastern State system, geometric metaphor, 200
Morocco, 27, 53, 58, 59, 60, 61, 71, 90, 113, 133, 152
Mubarak, Hosni, 21, 22, 23, 43, 99, 187
Muhammad, 94
Multinational corporations, 1
Muslim republics of former Soviet Union, 18

Muslim Women's Parliament, 150
Muslims, seen as monolithic bloc, 88; diversity of, 92
Mutual reinforcibility, 191

-N-

Nablus (Palestine), 119
Al-Nahda (Tunisia), 25
NAFTA (North American Free Trade Agreement), 41
Nasir, 89, 95, 97
Nasser, Jamal Abdul, 19, 24, 28, 89, 184
Nasserist movement, 98
Nationalization (of petroleum industry), 6
Nativistic approaches to human dignity and equality, 53
NATO North Atlantic Treaty Organisation, 28
NATO-Mediterranean dialogue, 245
Natural gas, 6-7
Nazism, 86
Netanyahu, Benjamin, 36, 38 , 109, 119, 126, 194
Non-governmental organizations (NGOs), 148, 149, 153-154, 56, 158-159, 161, 163-165, 168
North Africa, 12, 51, 70, 77, 147, 152
North American Free Trade Agreement (NAFTA), 41
North Atlantic Treaty Organization (NATO), 28
"Northern Tier" states, 12
Nuclear Non-Proliferation Treaty (NPT) of 1995, 193
Nuclear weapons, 18
Nusayris, as religious minority, *See* Alawites, 61

-O-

Oman, 2, 29, 35, 53, 58, 76
OPEC, 4, 17, 44
Organisation for Security and Cooperation in Europe (OSCE), 245

Oslo Accords, 114, 118, 119, 120, 129, 137
Oslo Agreement, 63
Oslo II, 63
Ottoman Empire, 97

-P-

Pakistan, 25, 53, 57, 58, 59, 60, 61, 198
Palestine, 10, 17, 34, 112, 116, 119, 121, 130, 137, 151, 187
Palestinian Territories, 115
Palestinian Council, 63
Palestinian Covenant, 63
Palestinian diaspora, 117, 137
Palestinians, 6, 34, 61; as minority in Israel Occupied Territories, 62-63; 64-66, 76, 99, 100, 101, 107, 109, 114, 120, 131, 139
Palestinian-Israeli Peace Accord, 6, 17, 22, 250
Palestinian Liberation Organization (PLO), 4, 16, 18, 19, 23, 65, 100, 116, 117, 118, 121, 123, 136
Palestinian National Authority, 126, 129, 196, 251
Panama, 16
Pan-Arabism, 20, 186, 188
Pan-Islamic, 19, 23
Pashtuns, as minority in Pakistan, 62
Patriotic Union of Kurdistan (PUK), 189
Pax Americana, 6, 26, 42, 43, 107-146
Peace integration paradigm, 202
Peres, Shimon, 32, 109, 120, 194
Persian Gulf, 7, 23, 34
Persian Gulf Crisis, 237
Persian Gulf War of 199, 2, 4, 7, 13, 16, 18, 22, 26, 34, 44, 42, 66, 134, 175
Persian Gulf monarchies, 4, 7, 175
Petro-dollar, 6, 29, 43, 147
Political Islam, reconstruction of, 51
Populist Islam, 2, 20, 21, 24, 29, 74
PPP dollars, 58
Primakov, Yevgeniy, 221
Private voluntary organizations (PVOs), 148

Protestants, as religious minority, 61
Protocol relating to the Status of Refugees, 53
Ptolemaic view of political universe, 190

-Q-

Al-Qaddafi, Muammar, 27, 28, 987, 103
Qatar, 21, 35, 43, 53, 54, 55, 58, 101
Qur'an, 93, 95, 96

-R-

Rabin, Yitzhak, 32, 109, 120, 176
Rafah party, 29
Rafsanjani, Akhbar Hashimi, 40, 191
Reagan Administration, 116, 117, 175
Realpolitik, and Israeli foreign relations, 109
Refugees, 64-67
Refugee Working Group, 65
Regime types, 9
Regionalization, as response to globalization, 236
Rogers Plan, 116
Roma, as ethnic minority in Turkey, 62
Rome Platform, 70
Roman Catholics, as minority, 61
Russia, 7, 9, 11-12, 15, 17, 18, 19, 28, 38, 180
Russian Federation, 238
Russian and Soviet foreign policies toward Middle East, 211-222
Ryiadth, 40

-S-

El-Saadawi, Nawal, 152
Sadat, Anwar, 21, 75, 93, 103, 116
Saharawis, as minority in Morocco, 62
Saudi Arabia, 5, 7, 10, 16, 17, 18, 19, 21, 22, 23, 26, 27, 35, 39, 40, 42, 44, 53, 54, 55, 57, 58, 59, 60, 62, 64, 76, 95, 98, 100; myth of nonalignment, 101; 180, 183, 198
Scowcroft, Brent, 39
Secours Populaire Libanais, 150

Sephardic Jews, 114; as majority in
    Israel, 138
Serbia, 28
Sese Seko, Mobutu, 111
Shamir, Yitzhak, 18, 32
Shari'a (Islamic law), 57, 75
Al-Shaykh, Sharm, 25
Sheikhdoms, 16, 42
Shi'is, as minority in Lebanon, Saudi
    Arabia, 61, 62
Shi'ites, 21, as minority in Iraq, 62; as
    native to Lebanese farming villages,
    124
Siege mentality, 25
Sinai Peninsula, 116
Sindhis, as minority in Pakistan, 62
Soccer, Iran-U.S. World Cup match, 39
"Solidarity rights" ("third generation" of
    rights), 52
Somalia, 28, 41
South Africa, 130
Structural adjustment policies, 153
Subregionalization, 242, 245
Sudan, 23, 24, 25, 53, 54, 55, 58, 59, 60,
    77
Sudan People's Liberation Army
    (SPLA), 62
Sudanese Human Rights Organization,
    71
Sunni Arabs, as minority in Iraq, 62; in
    Egypt, 187
Syria, 4, 6, 18, 19, 20, 23, 29, 36, 38, 44,
    54, 55, 58, 59, 60, 62, 65, 95, 109,
    111, 113, 121, 122, 124, 130, 133,
    134, 137, 151, 176, at crossroads
    between dual containment, 177; 178,
    179, 182

-T-
Tajikistan, 186
Talaban, Jalal, 182, 189
Technological revolution, 1
Tehran, 21, 27
Tehran-Damascus axis, and dual
    containment, 177

Al Thani, Hamid bin Khalifa (Crown
    Prince of Qatar), 43
Theologocentrism, 89
Transnational organizations, 1
Truman Doctrine (containment), 43
Tunisia, 2, 24, 29, 30, 53, 58, 59, 60, 152
Turkmenistan, 186
Turkmens, 61; as minority in Iran, 62
Turkey, 3, 5, 12, 18, 19, 24, 29, 30, 37,
    39, 53, 54, 55, 57, 58, 59, 60, 62, 63,
    64, 66, 67, 72, 73, 77, 133

-U-
USSR (Union of Soviet Socialist
    Republics), 12, 16, 17, 18, 19, 20, 32,
    85, 88, 95; collapse of, 111, 174, 236
United Arab Emirates (UAE), 7, 29, 37,
    53, 54, 58, 59, 60
United Arab Republic (UAR), 98
United Kingdom, 10
United Nations, 33, 34, 55, 56
UNICEF (United Nations Children's
    Fund), 35
United Nations Convention on the
    Elimination of All Forms of
    Discrimination Against Women, 149-
    150
United Nations Decade for Women, 154
United Nations Development
    Programme (UNDP), 55, 56
United Nations Relief and Works
    Agency for Palestinian Refugees
    (UNRWA), 65
United Nations Resolution 688, 66 See
    also Kurds
United Nations Security Council, and
    Israel's settlement drive, 110
United States, 7, 9, 10, 15, 17, 19, 21, 22,
    23, 24, 25, 26, 27, 31-40
Universal Declaration of Human Rights
    (UDHR), 52
Uzbekistan, 37

-V-
Vietnam, 16, 100, 139

-W-
Warsaw Pact, 244
Weber, Max, 15, 44
Welfare Party, 25
West Bank, 25, 65
Western European Union, 237
Women's organizations, 11
World Bank, 28
World War II, 32

-Y-
Yazidis, as religious minority, 61
Yemen, 19, 26, 27, 53, 58
Yugoslavia, 41

-Z-
Zaire, as ally of Israel, 111

About the Editor and the Contributors

Manochehr Dorraj is an Associate Professor of political science at Texas Christian University. He is the author of From Zrathustra to Khomeni: Poulism and Dissent in Iran (Boulder and London: Lynne Reinner publishers, 1990). His publications on Middle East have appeared in *The Oxford Encyclopedia of Islam, Central Asian Survey,The Muslim World, Arab Studies Quarterly, The Journal of Third World studies, The Journal of Developing Societies, The Review of Politics, The Digest of Middle Eastern Studies, Peace Review, and Social Compass.*

Mahmood Monshipouri is Associate Professor of political science and the Chair of the Department at Quinnipiac College. He is the Author of Islamism, Secularism and Human Rights in the Middle East (Boulder and London: Lynne Rienner Publishers, 1998). His publication on Middle East have appeared in *The Muslim World, Middle East policy, The Journal of Third World Studies , The Journal of Third World Spectrum, and Ethics and International Affairs.*

As'ad Abukhalil is Associate Professor of political science at California State University in Stanislaus and Research fellow at the Center for Middle Eastern studies at University of California at Berkley. He is the author of Historical Dictionary of Lebanon (Lanham, MD: Scarecrow press, Forthcoming). His publication on Middle East have appeared in *The Oxford Encyclopedia of Islam, The Encyclopedia of Modern Middle East, Middle East journal, Middle Eastern Studies, The Muslim World, Arab Studies Quarterly, Arab studies Journal and The Harvard International Review.*

Stephen Zunes is an Assistant professor of political science at the University of San Francisco.He is Currently finishing two books on U.S. Foreign Policy in the Middle East. He is a frequent contributor to such Journals as *Middle East Policy, The Current History, Peace Review, Arab Studies Quarterly and The Third World Quarterly.*

Valentine Moghadam is an Associate Professor of Sociology and the Director of Women's Studies Program at Illinois State University. She is the author of Gendering Economic reform: Women and

Structural Change in Middle East and North Africa (Boulder and London: Lynne Reinner Publishers,1997). She is a frequent contributor to such Journals as *Gender and Society, Development and Change,Gender and History, World development, Critical Sociology, Social Compass, International sociology, Arab Studies Quarterly, and International Journal of Middle Eastern Studies.*

Laura Drake is an Assistant professor with specialization in International relation of Middle East at American University. Her publications have appeared in *The Journal of Palestinian Studies, Middle East Affairs, Middle East Insight, Middle East International, Middle East Policy and Arab Studies Quarterly.*

Mark Katz is professor of Government and politics at George Mason University. He is the author of Russia and Arabia : Soviet Foreign Policy toward the Arabian Peninsula (Baltimore: John Hopkins University Press, 1986). His numerous Publications have appeared in *International Security, Current History, Orbis, washington Quartely, The New York Times, The Wall Street Journal, The Washington Post and the Los Angeles Times.*

Anoushiravan Ehteshami is readear in International Relations and Director of Postgraduate Studies at the Center for Middle Eastern and Islamic Studies, University of Durham, UK. He is the Co-author of Syria and Iran: Middle Powers in a Penetrated Regional System (London: Routledge Publishers, 1997). His numerous articles have appeared in *Third World Quarterly, Middle East Strategic Studies Quarterly, International Relations, Political Studies, European Affairs and Scandanavian Journal of Development Alternatives.*

Touraj Noroozi is a Teaching Fellow at Middle East Center, University of Utah. He is the author of Forthcoming book Islamic Utopianism and International Relations: Reflections on the Symbolics of Khomeni's Neither East Nor West International Doctrine.

About the Book

The present volume provides a comprehensive account of the post-Cold War Middle East and analyzes the foreign policy challenges that they pose. The book is divided into two parts. The first part comprises five chapters covering some of the regional developments in the post Cold-War era. The second part deals with the foreign policies of the United States, Russia, the European Union, China, and Japan toward the region. The contributions in this book present a critical and nuanced analysis that is sensitive to the regional complexities as well as to the context of foreign policy responses of the great powers. The contributors have attempted to link theoretical and historical considerations to the current realities. The essays contained in this volume demonstrate that the Middle East contrary to Samuel Huntington's contention, is not out of step with history, but rather very much a part of it, shaped by it as well as molding it. These new realities have created a new political dynamic and have charted new political configurations. These regional realities in turn have impacted the relations among the Middle Eastern countries, the global politics in general and the policies of the great powers toward the region in particular. The emerging portrayal of the region sketched in this volume portends a future that is unpredictable and complex. This complexity demands a new foreign policy response that is more sensitive to the regional realities as well as the aspirations of Middle Eastern people.